FUNDAMENTALS OF MATHEMATICS

Fifth Edition

Betty L. Pratt
Seneca College

Maria Sairoglou
Seneca College

ISBN: 978-1-927737-48-4

Fundamentals of Mathematics, Fifth Edition

Printed and Bound in Canada

Authors: Betty L. Pratt and Maria Sairoglou

Developmental Editor: Arbana Miftari
Art Director: Aleksandar Vozarevic
Copy Editor: Aarti Motala
Assistant Editors: Erika DeVega, Svitlana Berezova

Interactive Learning Resources: Charles Anifowose
Online Assessments & Test Bank: Ali Alavi, Howard Wu
Technology & Data Solutions: Zach Williams, Ryan Schwarz

Marketing Director: Harsha Varlani

Online Resources: IntroMath

This book is dedicated to my loved and adored late parents who encouraged me to pursue love and the open doors that it presented; it still brings meaning to my heart.
Betty Pratt

This book is dedicated to my father Lazarus, who instilled in me the passion to be a life-long learner, to my husband Adam, whose love and support made it possible for me to complete this labour of love, and to my daughter Penelope, who is the driving force behind everything I do.
Maria Sairoglou

PREFACE

The passion and driver for creating this textbook was to provide the learners with a tool that would fully support their learning process. Achieving success in the fundamentals of mathematics helps to build a foundation for future studies and supports future success in business and personal endeavors. This resource provides options to meet a variety of learning styles and guides the learners as they work through the chapters and exercises. The purpose is to create confidence in our students and foster a love and understanding of mathematics and its importance in our day-to-day lives. Enjoy the journey!

Betty and Maria

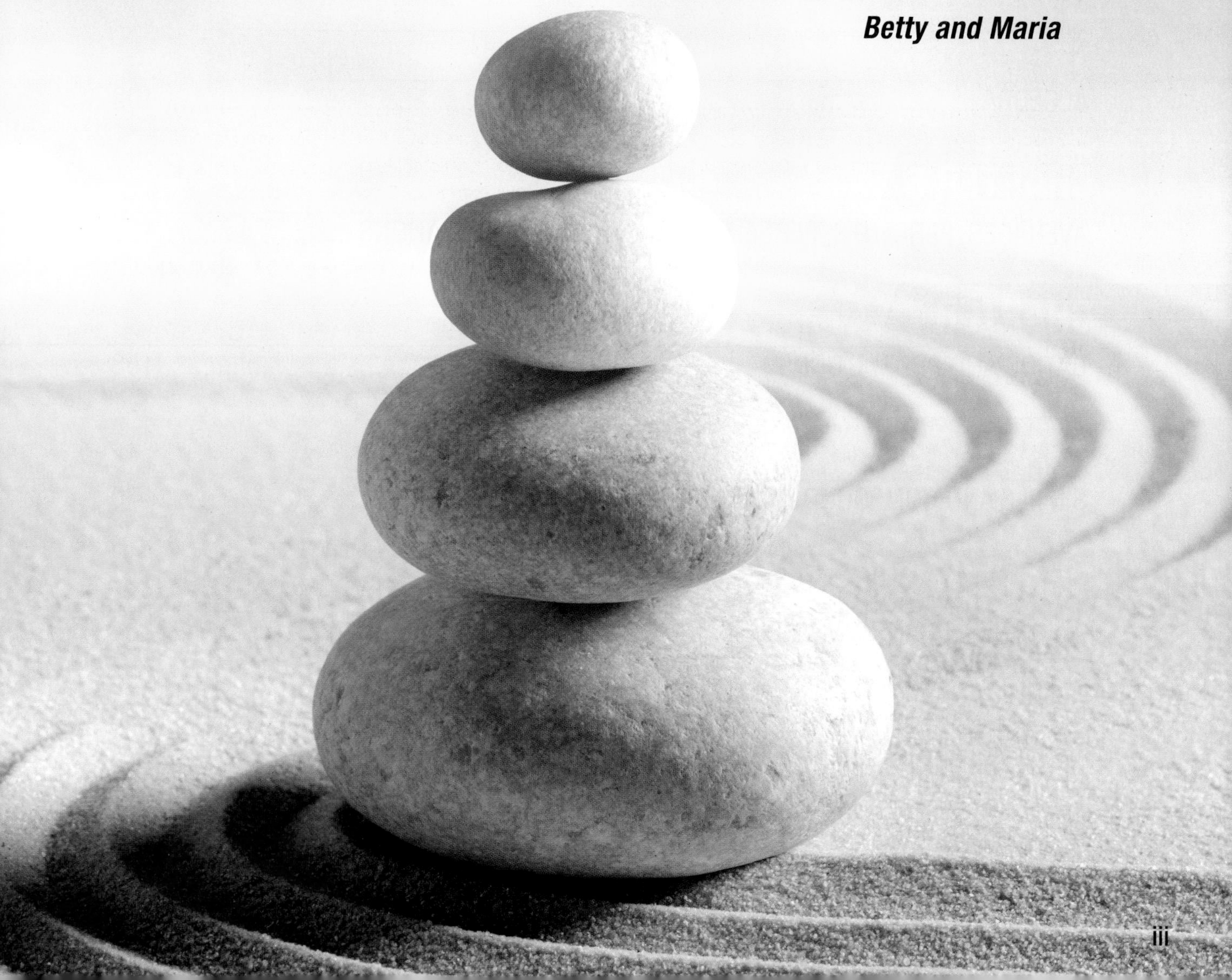

BRIEF CONTENTS

CONTENTS

ACKNOWLEDGMENTS

The authors and Vretta would like to thank the following professors for their detailed feedback, which helped us update the Fifth Edition of the Fundamentals of Mathematics textbook and its accompanying online resources:

Adam Farag, Fanshawe College
Adam Lorentz, Algonquin College
Hannah Sweet, Seneca College
Michael LePine, St. Clair College AA & T
Michelle Ripley, St. Clair College
Sandra Efu, Keyano College

FUNDAMENTALS OF MATHEMATICS

Fifth Edition

Betty L. Pratt
Seneca College

Maria Sairoglou
Seneca College

CHAPTER 1

WHOLE NUMBERS

LEARNING OBJECTIVES

Studying this chapter will provide you with the knowledge needed to:

- Read and write whole numbers in standard, expanded, and word form.
- Identify the place value of whole numbers and apply it to round numbers to the required place values.
- Perform arithmetic operations with whole numbers.
- Fill in a blank cheque using whole numbers.
- Estimate reasonable answers using whole numbers.

TOPICS

1.1 Place Value of Whole Numbers

1.2 Reading and Writing Whole Numbers

1.3 Rounding Whole Numbers

1.4 Addition of Whole Numbers

1.5 Subtraction of Whole Numbers

1.6 Multiplication of Whole Numbers

1.7 Division of Whole Numbers

1.1 PLACE VALUE OF WHOLE NUMBERS

Whole numbers are arranged in groups of three 'places' that represent the ones, tens, and hundreds digits. This pattern does not change as numbers grow larger; what changes is the value of each group. The value groups begin with units, and increase to thousands, millions, billions, trillions, and so on.

Let's look at the whole number **743,021,466,285** and consider the positional value and unit of each digit. The place values of this number, starting from the right, are: ones, tens, hundreds, thousands, ten thousands, hundred thousands, millions, ten millions, hundred millions, billions, ten billions, and hundred billions.

Exhibit 1.1: Place Values of a Twelve-Digit Whole Number

EXPANDED FORM OF A WHOLE NUMBER

In Exhibit 1.1, we see that every digit of the number 743,021,466,285 has a specific place value. If we break down a number into its place values, we have the **expanded form** of the number. In Example 1.1(A), the number has been broken down into the number of specific place values of each digit. The result, as shown, gives the **expanded form** of a 10 digit number.

EXAMPLE 1.1: Identifying Place Values of a Ten-Digit Whole Number

Break down the number **1,324,576,809** into its place values.

Solution:

9 ones	9 × 1	9
0 tens	0 × 10	0
8 hundreds	8 × 100	800
6 thousands	6 × 1,000	6,000
7 ten thousands	7 × 10,000	70,000
5 hundred thousands	5 × 100,000	500,000
4 millions	4 × 1,000,000	4,000,000
2 ten millions	2 × 10,000,000	20,000,000
3 hundred millions	3 × 100,000,000	300,000,000
1 billion	1 × 1,000,000,000	1,000,000,000

The above example represents the expanded form of the ten digit number 1,324,576,809.

Did You Know?

A septillion is
1,000,000,000,000,000,000,000,000

1.1 EXERCISES

Answers to the odd numbered exercises are available at the end of the textbook.

For Exercises 1 and 2, express the given numbers in their expanded form.

1. a. 23,748 b. 605,301 c. 12,453,889 d. 5,029,684,173,270
2. a. 95,254 b. 826,785 c. 65,371,746 d. 8,100,425,235,842

3. In the number 3,084,169,752, what is the place value of each of the numbers indicated below?

   a. 0 b. 1 c. 2 d. 3 e. 4
   f. 5 g. 6 h. 7 i. 8 j. 9

4. In the number 4,960,357,821, what is the place value of each of the numbers indicated below?

   a. 8 b. 1 c. 9 d. 5 e. 4
   f. 2 g. 3 h. 0 i. 6 j. 7

5. What number in $398,675,093,188 is represented by each of the following place values?

   a. Thousands b. Hundreds c. Ten Billions d. Hundred Thousands e. Millions
   f. Ones g. Ten Thousands h. Hundred Millions i. Tens j. Hundred Billions

6. What number in $47,902,518,407 is represented by each of the following place values?

   a. Ones b. Ten Thousands c. Hundred Millions d. Tens e. Ten Millions
   f. Thousands g. Hundreds h. Ten Billions i. Hundred Thousands j. Millions

1.2 READING AND WRITING WHOLE NUMBERS

When reading or writing numbers, it is important that we understand the correct practices involved. The proper way to read or write numbers is often overlooked, but it is a key factor in ensuring correct and thorough communication.

Did You Know?

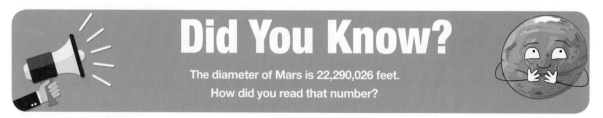

The diameter of Mars is 22,290,026 feet.
How did you read that number?

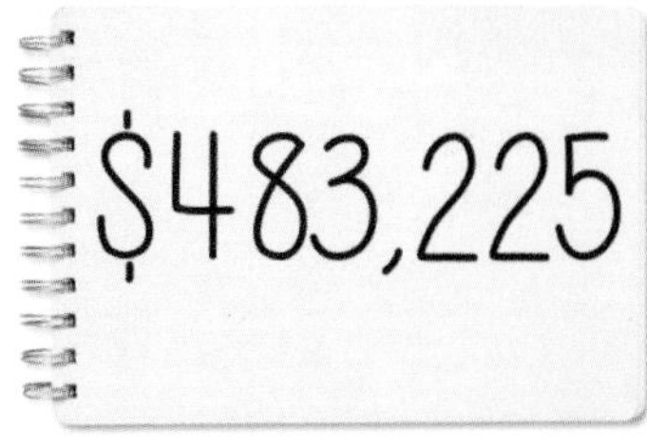

If asked to read the number shown on the left, we might read it as:

Four hundred ***and*** *eighty-three thousand, two hundred* ***and*** *twenty-five dollars*

Strictly speaking, we should read it as:

Four hundred eighty-three thousand, two hundred twenty-five dollars

Notice the difference? In a casual conversation, it is unlikely that anyone will point out that the first way of reading the number is in fact incorrect. The reason why this way of reading or saying this number is incorrect is because you do not say **'and'** when reading whole numbers. The only time we say '**and**' is when reading decimal numbers, where the decimal point is read as **'and'**. We will talk more about that in Chapter 2.

By the end of this section, you will be able to properly read and write whole numbers. We can think of it as if we were learning a new language. In any language, it is important to have standard rules of grammar and meaning, so that everyone that reads a sentence understands it more or less the same way.

NUMBER FORMS

Numbers can be expressed in standard form or word form.

Table 1.2: Standard and Word Form of Whole Numbers

Standard Form	Word Form
5,800	Five thousand, eight hundred
32,987	Thirty-two thousand, nine hundred eighty-seven
5,625,234	Five million, six hundred twenty-five thousand, two hundred thirty-four

Important points to remember while reading and writing whole numbers:

- Always start from the left side and continue to the right.
- Do not use the word **'and'**.
- If a number is larger than 999, place a comma between every three digits of the number, starting from the right to left. When writing these numbers in word form, ensure that you include a comma in the same place that is indicated in the standard form of the number.

  For example: 8,209 would be written as *eight thousand, two hundred nine*.

- When writing numbers in word form, ensure you include 'dollar(s)' at the end of the number if the standard form contains a '$' sign. When a number has a dollar sign, read the dollar sign after the number.

  For example: $93 is read as *ninety-three dollars.*

- Numbers between 21 and 99 should be written with a hyphen between the digits.

  For example: 26 is written as *twenty-six*.

EXAMPLE 1.2 (A): Converting Whole Numbers from Standard to Word Form

Express the following whole numbers in their word form:

i	214	ii	456
iii	1,790	iv	33,965
v	$7,344,971	vi	$322,875,030

Solution:

i **214**
Two hundred fourteen

ii **456**
Four hundred fifty-six

iii **1,790**
One thousand, seven hundred ninety

iv **33,965**
Thirty-three thousand, nine hundred sixty-five

v **$7,344,971**
Seven million, three hundred forty-four thousand, nine hundred seventy-one dollars

vi **$322,875,030**
Three hundred twenty-two million, eight hundred seventy-five thousand, thirty dollars

EXAMPLE 1.2 (B): Converting Whole Numbers from Word to Standard Form

Express the following numbers in their standard form:

i Seven hundred ninety-seven
ii Sixteen thousand, four hundred thirty-five
iii Fourteen million, three hundred seventy-five thousand, sixty-two
iv Fifty-six million, three hundred thousand, eighty-four dollars
v Eight billion, seven hundred fifty-two million, nine thousand, one hundred twenty-three dollars

Solution:

i **Seven hundred ninety-seven**
797

ii **Sixteen thousand, four hundred thirty-five**
16,435

iii **Fourteen million, three hundred seventy-five thousand, sixty-two**
14,375,062

iv **Fifty-six million, three hundred thousand, eighty-four dollars**
$56,300,084

v **Eight billion, seven hundred fifty-two million, nine thousand, one hundred twenty-three dollars**
$8,752,009,123

Illustration 1.2: Writing a Cheque

Writing numbers correctly in standard and expanded form is very important when it comes to writing cheques. Suppose we are writing a cheque for $578.

Step 1: Fill in the date in the top right corner.

Date 04-04-2019
DD-MM-YYYY

Step 2: Write the name of the person or company the money is payable to on the "Pay to the order of" line.

Pay to the order of Oliver King

Step 3: Write the **amount of money numerically** in the box at the end of the "Pay to the order of" line.

$ 578.00

Step 4: Write the **amount of money in words** below the "Pay to the order of" line.

The sum of Five hundred seventy-eight

Step 5: On the bottom left, describe what the cheque is for.

Memo 3 concert tickets

Step 6: Complete with signature on bottom right.

Authorized signature Georgie Powers

Mr. Georgie Powers
#9, 1215 Lake Sylvan Ave.
Toronto, ON
Tel: (011)555-4545
№
Date 04-04-2019
DD-MM-YYYY
Pay to the order of Oliver King
$ 578.00
The sum of Five hundred seventy-eight
Dollars
Memo 3 concert tickets
Authorized signature Georgie Powers
123894593 123893 38923467843

For a cheque with a stub like below, do the same as above and then fill in the stub on the left side of the cheque. The stub is kept as a record of the payment.

DATE ____ 001001

TO ____

FOR ____

PST AMOUNT	BALANCE FORWARD		
GST AMOUNT	THIS CHEQUE		
	DEPOSIT		
GST NO.	DEPOSIT		
	OTHER		
	BALANCE		

Bank name №

Date ____

Pay to the order of ____ $ ____

The sum of ____ Dollars

Memo ____ Authorized signature ____

123894593 123893 38923467843

1.2 EXERCISES

Answers to the odd numbered exercises are available at the end of the textbook.

For Exercises 1 to 4, express the given numbers in their word form.

1.	a. $956	b. $1,239	c. 34,221	d. 75,884	e. $818,034	f. $3,999,065,100
2.	a. $728	b. $6,889	c. 91,308	d. $579,003	e. 233,067,155	f. 43,500,699,002
3.	a. 1,234	b. 23,345	c. 298,442	d. $4,675,987	e. 98,345,224	f. $567,448,982
4.	a. 99,999	b. 102,456	c. 1,003,123	d. $78,448,999	e. 9,999,999	f. $123,948,442

For Exercises 5 to 8, express the numbers in their standard form.

5. a. Three hundred eighty-four dollars
   b. Twelve thousand, nine hundred thirty-two
   c. Thirty-two million, five hundred thousand, twenty-three dollars
   d. Sixteen billion, two hundred ninety-five million, one thousand, six hundred fifty-four dollars
   e. Seventeen million, four hundred twenty-seven thousand, forty-five

6. a. Fifteen thousand, thirty-one dollars
   b. Thirteen thousand, five hundred ninety-six
   c. One hundred fifteen million, seven hundred six thousand, seven dollars
   d. Eleven billion, six hundred thirty-one million, ten thousand, two hundred twenty-two dollars
   e. Nineteen million, eight hundred fifty-six thousand, seventy-two

7. a. Three thousand, four hundred twenty-five dollars
   b. Nineteen thousand, eighty-four
   c. One million, two thousand, two hundred twenty-two dollars
   d. Two hundred thirty thousand, forty-three
   e. Five billion, one hundred thirty-one million, eighty-nine dollars

8. a. Five thousand, eight hundred eighty-three
   b. Fourteen thousand, sixty-six dollars
   c. Nine million, nine hundred ninety-nine thousand, ninety-nine dollars
   d. Fourteen billion, forty-five million, seventy-two thousand, three dollars
   e. Thirty-four million, four hundred ninety-nine thousand, one

1.3 ROUNDING WHOLE NUMBERS

Rounding is the process through which we express numbers to an approximate value. For example, according to a census in 2017, the population of Canada was 36,708,083. However, that number is constantly changing. For most purposes, it would be acceptable if we were to say that the population of Canada in 2017 was 37,000,000, or thirty-seven million. By doing this, we have rounded 36,708,083 to the nearest million.

Illustration 1.3 (A): Rounding Whole Numbers

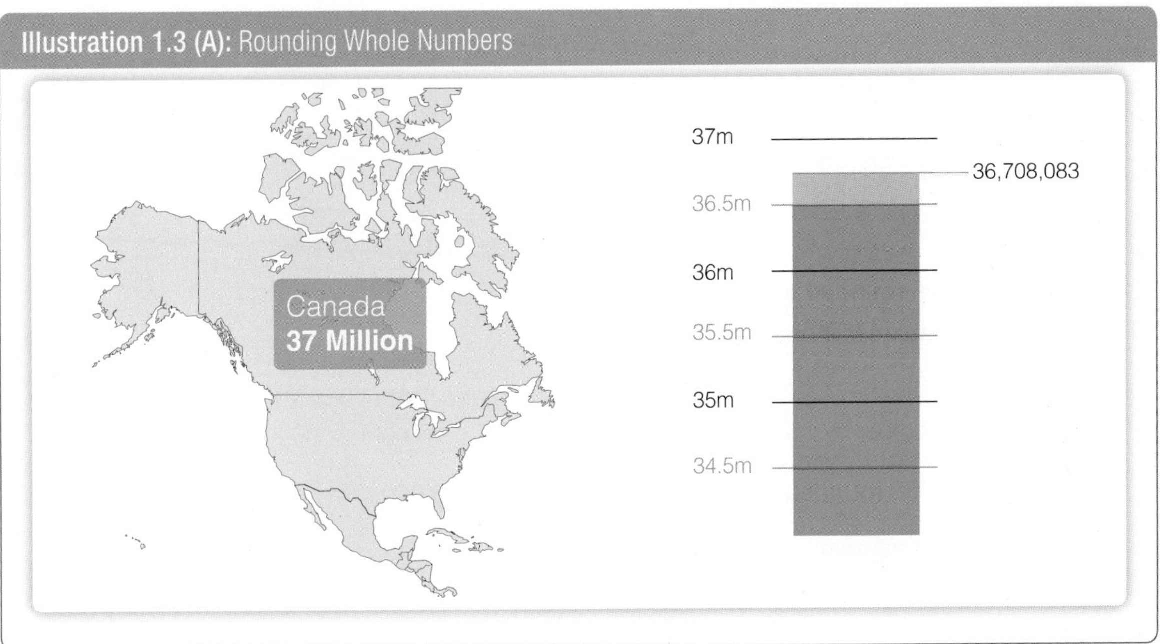

The process of rounding follows some simple rules. The rules of rounding whole numbers are explained in Illustration 1.3 (B).

Illustration 1.3 (B): Rounding Whole Numbers

Let's round two numbers to the nearest thousand.

Rule	Round Down	Round Up
Identify the number you are to round.	53,267	53,824
Look at the number directly to the right of the number you are to round.	53,267	53,824
If that number is **less than 5**, then the number you are rounding remains the same; if that number is **5 or greater**, then the number you are rounding increases by 1.	<5 53,267	>5 53,824
Change all the numbers **after** the one you have rounded to zeroes.	53,000	54,000

EXAMPLE 1.3: Rounding Whole Numbers

Round the following whole numbers to the indicated place values.

i 126 to the nearest ten

ii 9,558 to the nearest thousand

iii $54,142 to the nearest $100

iv 654,328 to the nearest ten thousand

v 4,681,356 to the nearest million

Solution:

i **126 to the nearest ten**

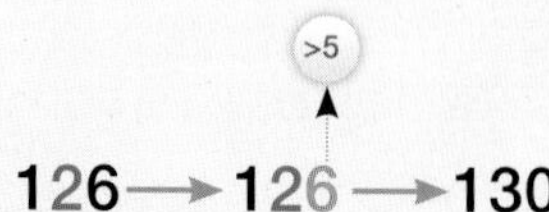

Therefore, 126 rounded to the nearest ten is 130.

ii **9,558 to the nearest thousand**

The number in the thousands place is 9. The number to the right of 9 is 5; therefore, we increase the rounding number by 1, and we change the numbers to the right of the rounding number to 0.

Therefore, 9,558 rounded to the nearest thousand is 10,000.

iii **$54,142 to the nearest $100**

<5

54,142 → 54,142 → 54,100

Therefore, $54,142 rounded to the nearest $100 is $54,100.

iv **654,328 to the nearest ten thousand**

The number in the ten thousands place is 5. The number to the right of 5 is less than 5; therefore, the rounding number remains the same, and we change the numbers to the right of the rounding number to 0.

Therefore, 654,328 rounded to the nearest ten thousand is 650,000.

v **4,681,356 to the nearest million**

The number in the millions place is 4. The number to the right of 4 is greater than 5; therefore, we increase the rounding number by 1, and we change the numbers to the right of the rounding number to 0.

Therefore, 4,681,356 rounded to the nearest million is 5,000,000.

DISCUSSION

Do the following three statements have the same meaning?

- Round to the nearest dollar.
- Round to the nearest whole number.
- Round to the nearest one.

ESTIMATING WHOLE NUMBERS

Estimating can be thought of as the process of finding an approximate value. This is done in situations where the exact answers are not required.

We can estimate values by rounding numbers to the tens, hundreds, thousands, etc.

For example, estimate the following costs of flights to different parts of the world by rounding them to the closest ten:

$452, $579, $674, and $1094.

Answer: $452 can be estimated to $450

$579 can be estimated to $580

$674 can be estimated to $670

$1094 can be estimated to $1090

Another option would be to estimate the numbers to the closest hundred in which case, $452 becomes $500, $579 becomes $600, $674 becomes $700, and $1094 becomes $1100.

1.3 EXERCISES

Answers to the odd numbered exercises are available at the end of the textbook.

1. Round the following numbers to the indicated place value:

   a. 824 to the nearest ten

   b. 7,992 to the nearest thousand

   c. 43,647 to the nearest hundred

   d. 19,269,300 to the nearest million

2. Round the following numbers to the indicated place value:

   a. 90,459 to the nearest hundred

   b. 3,891,135 to the nearest million

   c. 65,389 to the nearest ten thousand

   d. 190,284 to the nearest hundred thousand

3. Round the number $23,608,544 to each of the place values indicated below:

   a. Nearest ten

   b. Nearest thousand

   c. Nearest million

   d. Nearest hundred

   e. Nearest ten thousand

   f. Nearest ten million

   g. Nearest hundred thousand

4. Round the number $732,895,174 to each of the place values indicated below:

   a. Nearest ten thousand
   b. Nearest thousand
   c. Nearest ten million
   d. Nearest hundred thousand
   e. Nearest ten
   f. Nearest hundred million
   g. Nearest million
   h. Nearest hundred

5. Round the following numbers to the indicated place value:

   a. $32,654 to the nearest $100
   b. $9,273 to the nearest $10
   c. $128,344 to the nearest $100,000
   d. $7,839,022 to the nearest $10,000
   e. $4,359,921 to the nearest $1,000
   f. $633 to the nearest $10

6. Round the following numbers to the indicated place value:

   a. $7,295 to the nearest $10
   b. $472,008 to the nearest $10,000
   c. $21,747 to the nearest $1,000
   d. $549 to the nearest $100
   e. $192,850 to the nearest $10,000
   f. $647,196 to the nearest $1,000

7. The populations of Ontario and British Columbia in 2017 were 14,193,384 and 4,817,160, respectively. Express each of these numbers rounded to the nearest million.

8. Andrew's website business made a profit of $22,457 last year. Express his profit rounded to the nearest thousand dollars.

9. Eddie and his wife traveled 3,586 km on their new bikes. Express the distance traveled rounded to the nearest hundred kilometres.

10. The average distance between the Earth and the Moon is 384,410 km. Express this distance rounded to the nearest hundred thousand km.

1.4 ADDITION OF WHOLE NUMBERS

Addition, as we know, is the operation that determines the total number of objects within a collection, or from different groups. Basic addition has its roots in counting.

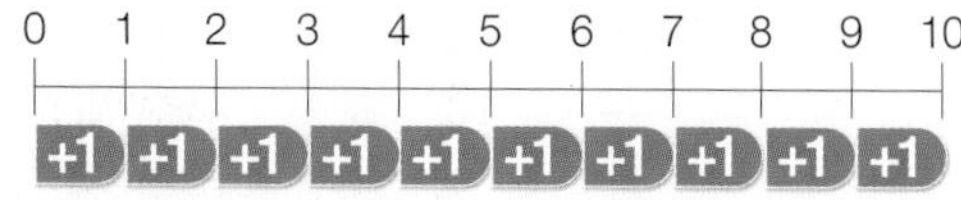

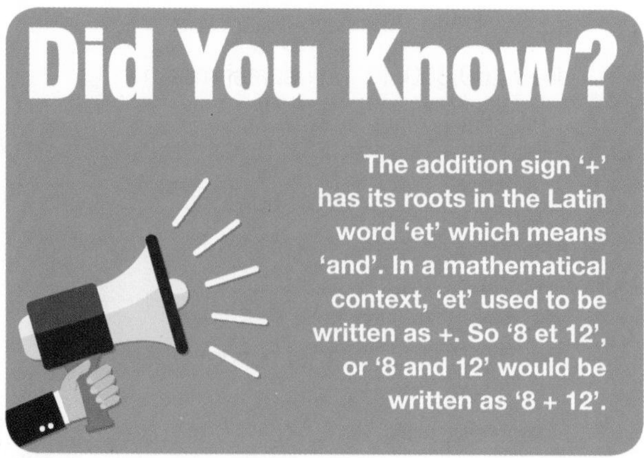

Did You Know?
The addition sign '+' has its roots in the Latin word 'et' which means 'and'. In a mathematical context, 'et' used to be written as +. So '8 et 12', or '8 and 12' would be written as '8 + 12'.

When adding larger, more complex numbers as well as bigger groups of numbers, it is useful to have simple algorithms to perform addition. One of these algorithms is **columnar addition**. In columnar addition, digits of numbers are aligned vertically by their place values and added one at a time from the lowest to highest place values. If the sum exceeds the place value of the column, part of the number is **carried-over** to the column with the next higher place value.

EXAMPLE 1.4: Adding Whole Numbers

Add the following numbers:

i 2 + 5

ii 12 + 42

iii 6 + 15 + 38

iv 45 + 328 + 7 + 843 + 91

Solution:

i 2 + 5

Visual addition:

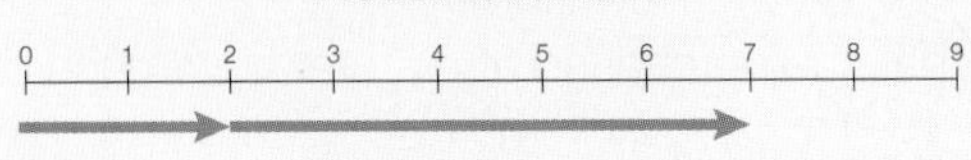

Columnar addition:

2	
+ 5	2 + 5 = 7
7	

ii 12 + 42

Visual addition:

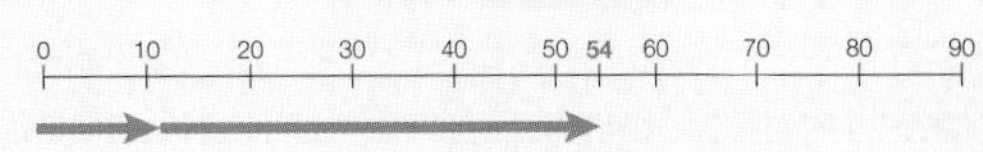

Columnar addition:

12	2 + 2 = 4
+ 42	1 + 4 = 5
54	

iii 6 + 15 + 38

Visual addition:

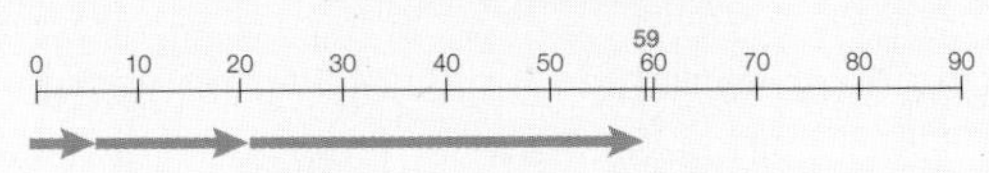

Columnar addition:

1 (carry) 6	
15	6 + 5 + 8 = 19
+ 38	1 + 1 + 3 = 5
59	

iv 75 + 358 + 7 + 883 + 91

Visual addition:

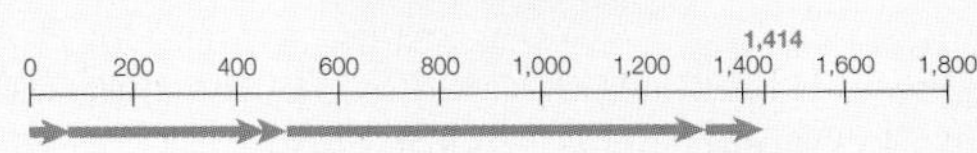

Columnar addition:

2 (carry)	
75	
3 (carry)	
358	5 + 8 + 7 + 3 + 1 = 24
7	2 + 7 + 5 + 8 + 9 = 31
883	3 + 3 + 8 = 14
+ 91	
1414	

Did You Know?

In 1973, Oakland A's relief pitcher Rollie Fingers received an extra $300 for growing the longest mustache on the team and an additional $100 to pay for his mustache wax. What amount of total extra money did he receive?

1.4 EXERCISES

Answers to the odd numbered exercises are available at the end of the textbook.

1. Add the following numbers:

   a. 623 + 35 + 12 b. 7,691 + 99 + 213 c. 992 + 45 + 90 d. 6,721 + 341 + 81

   e. 561 + 88 f. 8,991 + 221 + 6 g. 450 + 771 + 91 h. 10 + 891 + 214

2. Add the following numbers:

   a. 1,121 + 2,516 b. 349 + 891 + 88 c. 28,375 + 714 + 14 d. 17,050 + 9,875 + 212

   e. 43,515 + 239 + 675 f. 876 + 151 + 25 g. 12 + 2,183 + 4,145 h. 1,278 + 891 + 10

3. If Sylvia paid $129, $39, $135, and $2 for four items that she purchased at a store, how much did she spend in total at the store?

4. Tao spent $225, $245, $213, and $250 on car maintenance over the past four months. How much did he spend in total over these months on car maintenance?

5. Michelle had $1,000 in the bank and then made deposits of $55, $300, and $56. How much did she have in the bank after these deposits (ignore the interest earned over the period)?

6. Sebastian had $884 in his savings account. Over the following five weeks, he saved an additional $25, $124, $184, $112, and $30, each week, respectively. What was the total amount in his savings account after the five weeks (ignore the interest earned over the period)?

7. The Griggs family decided to go strawberry picking together. They filled up 4 baskets of strawberries. They counted each basket separately and had 45, 31, 36, and 29 strawberries in each basket respectively. How many strawberries did they collect in total?

8. Penelope decided to go on a road trip with some friends. They drove approximately 500 km from Toronto to Montreal, 165 km from Montreal to Ottawa, and finally 520 km from Ottawa to Hamilton. At the end of their trip, they had to drive 65 km back to Toronto. How many kilometres did they drive in total?

9. Raj had some money he wanted to invest and decided to buy shares of various companies. If he bought 212 shares from Company X, 176 shares from Company Y, and 303 shares from Company Z, how many shares did he buy in total?

10. Ahmed is in charge of organizing a conference and needs to print agendas for all of the attendees. The people attending are employees from 4 different companies. The 4 companies have 94, 211, 168, and 173 employees attending, respectively. How many agendas does Ahmed need to print in total?

1.5 SUBTRACTION OF WHOLE NUMBERS

Subtraction is the reverse operation of addition. It can be thought of as removing objects from a group. If addition is like counting, then subtraction is like counting backwards.

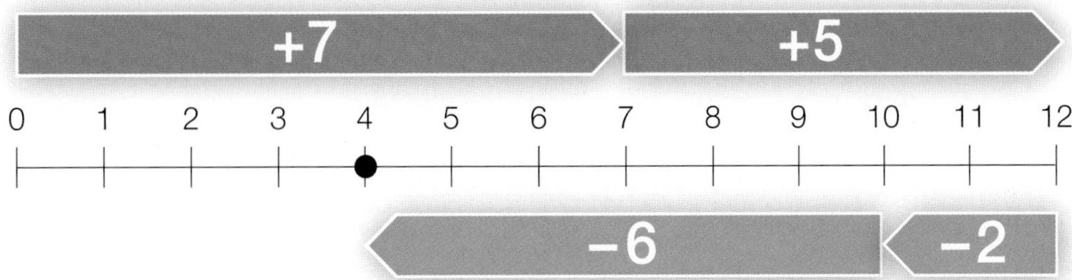

Columnar subtraction is similar to columnar addition. For subtraction, instead of **carry-overs**, we have the concept of **borrowing**. To subtract numbers, we begin by aligning numbers by place values, and then subtracting the number at the bottom from the number at the top, at each place value starting from the right. If the number on the top is greater than the number on the bottom, you do not need to borrow. However, if the number on the top is smaller than the number on the bottom, we borrow a digit from the next highest non-zero place value. Note that this increases the borrowing place value by the order of the next highest place value not just by 1.

Did You Know?

Under Captain Kirk's command, there were 430 crew members on the Enterprise. Under Captain Jean-Luc Picard's command, there were 1,012. How many more crew members did Captain Jean-Luc Picard have?

EXAMPLE 1.5 (A): Subtracting Whole Numbers

Subtract the following numbers:

i	54 – 28	ii	758 – 463
iii	1,530 – 823	iv	42,851 – 25,689
v	6,000 – 314	vi	3,000 – 125

Solution:

i **54 – 28**

$$\begin{array}{r} {\scriptstyle 4\ 14} \\ \not{5}\ \not{4} \\ -\ 2\ 8 \\ \hline 2\ 6 \end{array}$$

4 < 8; we need to *borrow* from the tens place value. The 4 becomes a 14 and the 5 reduces to a 4.

14 – 8 = 6

4 – 2 = 2

EXAMPLE 1.5 (A): Subtracting Whole Numbers *continued*

Solution:

ii 758 – 463

$$\begin{array}{rrrr} & {\scriptstyle 6} & {\scriptstyle 15} & \\ & \not{7} & \not{5} & 8 \\ - & 4 & 6 & 3 \\ \hline & 2 & 9 & 5 \end{array}$$

8 – 3 = 5
5 < 6; we need to *borrow* from the hundreds place value. The 5 becomes 15 and the 7 becomes a 6.
15 – 6 = 9
6 – 4 = 2

iii 1,530 – 823

$$\begin{array}{rrrrr} & & {\scriptstyle 15} & {\scriptstyle 2} & {\scriptstyle 10} \\ & \not{1} & \not{5} & \not{3} & \not{0} \\ - & & 8 & 2 & 3 \\ \hline & & 7 & 0 & 7 \end{array}$$

0 < 3; we need to *borrow* from the tens place value. The 0 becomes a 10 and the 3 becomes a 2.
10 – 3 = 7
2 – 2 = 0
5 < 8; we need to *borrow* from the thousands place value. The 5 becomes a 15 and the 1 becomes a 0.
15 – 8 = 7

iv 42,851 – 25,689

$$\begin{array}{rrrrrr} & & & & {\scriptstyle 14} & \\ & {\scriptstyle 3} & {\scriptstyle 12} & {\scriptstyle 7} & \not{\scriptstyle 4} & {\scriptstyle 11} \\ & \not{4} & \not{2} & \not{8} & \not{5} & \not{1} \\ - & 2 & 5 & 6 & 8 & 9 \\ \hline & 1 & 7 & 1 & 6 & 2 \end{array}$$

1 < 9; we need to *borrow* from the tens place value. The 1 becomes an 11 and the 5 becomes a 4.
11 – 9 = 2
4 < 8; we need to *borrow* from the hundreds place value. The 4 becomes a 14 and the 8 becomes a 7.
14 – 8 = 6
7 – 6 = 1
2 < 5; we need to *borrow* from the ten thousands place value. The 2 becomes a 12 and the 4 becomes a 3.
12 – 5 = 7
3 – 2 = 1

v 6,000 – 314

$$\begin{array}{rrrrr} & {\scriptstyle 5} & {\scriptstyle 9} & {\scriptstyle 9} & {\scriptstyle 10} \\ & \not{6} & \not{0} & \not{0} & \not{0} \\ - & & 3 & 1 & 4 \\ \hline & 5 & 6 & 8 & 6 \end{array}$$

0 < 4; we need to *borrow* from the tens place value BUT we cannot borrow from there, since there is a 0 in the tens place. So, we continue until we find a number we CAN borrow from; that is 600.

600 – 1 = 599; the zero in the ones column now becomes a 10

10 – 4 = 6
9 – 1 = 8
9 – 3 = 6
5 – 0 = 5

vi 3,000 – 125

$$\begin{array}{rrrrr} & {\scriptstyle 2} & {\scriptstyle 9} & {\scriptstyle 9} & {\scriptstyle 10} \\ & \not{3} & \not{0} & \not{0} & \not{0} \\ - & & 1 & 2 & 5 \\ \hline & 2 & 8 & 7 & 5 \end{array}$$

0 < 5; we need to *borrow* from the tens place value BUT we cannot borrow from there, since there is a 0 in the tens place. So, we continue until we find a number we CAN borrow from; that is 300.

300 – 1 = 299; the zero in the ones column now becomes a 10

10 – 5 = 5
9 – 2 = 7
9 – 1 = 8
2 – 0 = 2

EXAMPLE 1.5 (B): Subtracting Multiple Numbers One by One

Juan decided to go on a cruise so he took out $10,000 USD from his bank account. From that, he spent $6,000 USD on his flight and stateroom (including tax). He bought clothes in Miami before boarding the cruise ship. They cost $1,675 USD (including tax). He spent $856 USD at a hotel for two nights including food and entertainment (including tax). How much money did he have left?

Solution:

$$\begin{array}{r} {}^{10} \\ \not{1}\,\not{0}\,0\,0\,0 \\ -\quad 6\,0\,0\,0 \\ \hline 4\,0\,0\,0 \end{array}$$

We start by subtracting his first expense of $6,000 from the $10,000 he started with. This gives us a balance of $4,000.

Next, we subtract the $1,675 he spent on clothing from the $4,000 balance.

$$\begin{array}{r} {}^{3\ \ 9\ \ 9\ \ 10} \\ \not{4}\,\not{0}\,\not{0}\,\not{0} \\ -\quad 1\,6\,7\,5 \\ \hline 2\,3\,2\,5 \end{array}$$

0 < 5; we need to borrow from the tens place value BUT we cannot borrow from there, since there is a 0 in the tens place. So, we continue until we find a number we CAN borrow from; that is 400.

400 – 1 = 399; the zero in the ones column now becomes a 10

10 – 5 = 5

9 – 7 = 2

9 – 6 = 3

3 – 1 = 2

Now, from the $2,325 we subtract $856 for the cost of the hotel.

$$\begin{array}{r} {}^{1\ \ 15} \\ 2\,3\,\not{2}\,\not{5} \\ -\quad 8\,5\,6 \\ \hline 9 \end{array}$$

5 < 6; we need to borrow from the tens place, so we take 1 from 2, leaving us with 1 in the tens place.

15 – 6 = 9

$$\begin{array}{r} {}^{2\ \ 11\ \ 15} \\ 2\,\not{3}\,\not{2}\,\not{5} \\ -\quad 8\,5\,6 \\ \hline 6\,9 \end{array}$$

1 < 5; we need to borrow from the 3 in the hundreds place. The 3 becomes a 2 and the 1 in the tens place becomes 11.

11 – 5 = 6

$$\begin{array}{r} {}^{1\ \ 12\ \ 11\ \ 15} \\ \not{2}\,\not{3}\,\not{2}\,\not{5} \\ -\quad 8\,5\,6 \\ \hline 1\,4\,6\,9 \end{array}$$

2 < 8; we need to borrow from the 2 in the thousands place. The 2 becomes a 1 and the 2 in the tens place becomes 12.

12 – 8 = 4

1 – 0 = 1

Therefore, Juan is left with $1,469.

EXAMPLE 1.5 (C): Subtracting Multiple Numbers Using Addition First

Nasrin and Bianca were planning an engagement party for their friends. Their budget was $3000. They spent $900 on a venue for the group, $1510 for decorations, food, and drinks. Did they go over their budget? If so, by how much? If not, how much did they have left (tax is included in the prices)?

Solution:

The budget for Nasrin and Bianca was $3,000. The expenses were $900 plus $1,510. First we will add all of the expenses together.

$$\begin{array}{r} {}^{1} \\ 1\,5\,1\,0 \\ +\quad 9\,0\,0 \\ \hline 2\,4\,1\,0 \end{array}$$

0 + 0 = 0
1 + 0 = 1
5 + 9 = 14
1 + 1 = 2

So the total spent was $2,410. Now we subtract the total expense from the total budget.

$$\begin{array}{r} {}^{2\;9\;10} \\ \not{3}\,\not{0}\,\not{0}\,0 \\ -\quad 2\,4\,1\,0 \\ \hline 5\,9\,0 \end{array}$$

Starting from the right column, 0 - 0 = 0

Moving to the next digit, 0 < 1; we need to borrow from the hundreds place value BUT we cannot borrow from there, since there is a 0 in the hundreds place. So, we continue until we find a number we CAN borrow from; that is 30.

30 – 1 = 29; the zero in the tens column now becomes a 10

10 – 1 = 9

9 – 4 = 5

2 – 2 = 0

Therefore, Nasrin and Bianca have $590 left over. We would have gotten the same answer if we subtracted each expense step by step like in Example 1.5 (B), but adding the expenses first is easier. This method is very useful when there are multiple numbers that need to be subtracted.

1.5 EXERCISES

Answers to the odd numbered exercises are available at the end of the textbook.

1. Subtract the following numbers:

   a. 132 – 54 b. 2,453 – 457 c. 3,659 – 1,118 d. 10,725 – 245

   e. 991 – 481 f. 5,981 – 121 g. 27,183 – 5,061 h. 1,375 – 891

2. Subtract the following numbers:

   a. 555 – 312 b. 1,375 – 278 c. 50,491 – 3,781 d. 5,193 – 659

   e. 781 – 345 f. 998 – 671 g. 2,390 – 884 h. 3,009 – 1,357

3. Salima borrowed $200 from her mother to buy a bike. If she spent $192 on the bike, how much did she have left?

4. Mary had 500 metres of fabric in her store. If she sold 145 metres of this fabric, how much did she have left?

5. Last year, Kareem planned 800 fashion shows. Later, 323 were cancelled. How many shows did Kareem actually have?

6. Zhang received $2,000 from her father at the beginning of the month. During the month she spent $750 on rent, $286 on transportation, $445 on food, and $112 on telephone charges. What balance did she have at the end of the month?

7. William had $1,000 in the bank and used his debit card to spend $289 and $35. How much did he have left in the bank?

8. Angelo had $400 in his bank account. During the month, he spent $46, $36, and $12 from the account. What was his balance in this account at the end of the month?

1.6 MULTIPLICATION OF WHOLE NUMBERS

Multiplication of whole numbers can be thought of as repeated addition. For example, if we were to add 2 + 2 + 2 + 2 + 2 + 2 + 2, we would get 14. Another way to look at this problem is as 7 sets of 2.

In multiplication problems, each of the numbers being multiplied is called a **factor** and the answer is called the **product**.

Factors

$7 \times 2 = 14$

Product

Illustration 1.6 (A): Multiplication of Whole Numbers

$7 \times 2 = 2 + 2 + 2 + 2 + 2 + 2 + 2$

Adding separately, we would count a total of 14 objects. One soon realizes that this can also be represented by 7 × 2, which also gives us 14. It is much easier to use multiplication than repetitive counting. When multiplying, it helps to know the multiplication table. The multiplication table for numbers up to 12 is provided in Table 1.6. You can use it as an aid for memorizing the multiplication of two numbers. You may need to refer to the table at first, but with practice, you will become more confident in multiplying numbers without using the table.

Did You Know?
A bumblebee flaps its wings at 160 beats per second.
How many beats per minute is this?

Just like columnar addition and subtraction, there is also an algorithm for solving multiplication problems when the numbers get larger. Let's look at examples of **columnar multiplication**. Remember that the process is simpler if we place the larger number at the top and the smaller number at the bottom.

Illustration 1.6 (B): Multiplying Whole Numbers

Calculate 89 × 13 by following these steps for multiplying whole numbers:

Step 1: Start with the bottom number furthest to the right (3) and multiply it by each of the numbers across the top.

$$\begin{array}{rrr} & \overset{2}{8} & 9 \\ \times & 1 & 3 \\ \hline & & 7 \end{array}$$

Q: What is 3 × 9? A: 27
Q: Where do we put the 7? A: Under the 3
Q: How much do we carry? A: 2

$$\begin{array}{rrr} & \overset{2}{8} & 9 \\ \times & 1 & 3 \\ \hline 2 & 6 & 7 \end{array}$$

Q: What is 3 × 8? A: 24
Q: What is the answer after adding the carry over (2)? A: 24 + 2 = 26
Q: Where do we put the 26? A: to the left of the 7

Step 2: Continue the same procedure with the next digit in the bottom number (1).

$$\begin{array}{rrr} & \overset{2}{8} & 9 \\ \times & 1 & 3 \\ \hline 2 & 6 & 7 \\ & 9 & 0 \end{array}$$

Q: What is 1 × 9? A: 9
Q: Where do we put the 9? A: Before placing the 9, we place a 0 directly beneath the 7. The 9 is then placed to the left of the 0.
Q: Is there anything to carry over? A: No

$$\begin{array}{rrr} & \overset{2}{8} & 9 \\ \times & 1 & 3 \\ \hline 2 & 6 & 7 \\ 8 & 9 & 0 \end{array}$$

Q: What is 1 × 8? A: 8
Q: Where do we put the 8? A: to the left of the 9

Step 3: Add the results from Step 1 and 2. This is your final product.

$$\begin{array}{rrrr} & & \overset{2}{8} & 9 \\ & \times & 1 & 3 \\ \hline & 2 & 6 & 7 \\ + & 8 & 9 & 0 \\ \hline 1 & 1 & 5 & 7 \end{array}$$

Q: What is 267 + 890? A: Add each column and place the sum under the column
→ 7 + 0 = 7
→ 6 + 9 = 15 (carry the 1)
→ 1 + 2 + 8 = 11

Use zeros to make sure the columns are aligned properly. The first row doesn't need extra zeros for alignment. However, the second row should move one place to the left. Putting a zero there instead of a blank space helps to keep the solution aligned properly. The third row should move to the left one more place (two in total). If there is a fourth row, there should be three zeros. This continues and keeps order and alignment. Example 1.6 shows how to do this.

EXAMPLE 1.6: Performing Columnar Multiplication

Multiply the following numbers using columnar multiplication.

i 25 × 5   ii 51 × 8

iii 31 × 14   iv 354 × 214

Solution:

i **25 × 5**

```
    2
    2 5
×     5
-------
  1 2 5
```

5 × 5 = 25

5 × 2 = 10 → 10 + 2 = 12

ii **51 × 8**

```
    5 1
×     8
-------
  4 0 8
```

8 × 1 = 8

8 × 5 = 40

iii **31 × 14**

```
      3 1
  ×   1 4
---------
    1 2 4
+   3 1 0
---------
    4 3 4
```

4 × 1 = 4

4 × 3 = 12

Place 0 beneath 4

1 × 1 = 1

1 × 3 = 3

124 + 310 = 434

iv **354 × 214**

```
          1
          2   1
          3   5   4
×         2   1   4
-------------------
      1   4   1   6
      3   5   4   0
+  7  0   8   0   0
-------------------
   7  5   7   5   6
```

4 × 4 = 16

4 × 5 = 20 → 20 + 1 = 21

4 × 3 = 12 → 12 + 2 = 14

Place 0 beneath 6

1 × 4 = 4

1 × 5 = 5

1 × 3 = 3

Place 0 beneath 0 and 4

2 × 4 = 8

2 × 5 = 10

2 × 3 = 6 → 6 + 1 = 7

1,416 + 3,540 + 70,800 = 75,756

Table 1.6: Multiplication Table

	0	1	2	3	4	5	6	7	8	9	10	11	12
0	0	0	0	0	0	0	0	0	0	0	0	0	0
1	0	1	2	3	4	5	6	7	8	9	10	11	12
2	0	2	4	6	8	10	12	14	16	18	20	22	24
3	0	3	6	9	12	15	18	21	24	27	30	33	36
4	0	4	8	12	16	20	24	28	32	36	40	44	48
5	0	5	10	15	20	25	30	35	40	45	50	55	60
6	0	6	12	18	24	30	36	42	48	54	60	66	72
7	0	7	14	21	28	35	42	49	56	63	70	77	84
8	0	8	16	24	32	40	48	56	64	72	80	88	96
9	0	9	18	27	36	45	54	63	72	81	90	99	108
10	0	10	20	30	40	50	60	70	80	90	100	110	120
11	0	11	22	33	44	55	66	77	88	99	110	121	132
12	0	12	24	36	48	60	72	84	96	108	120	132	144

1.6 EXERCISES

Answers to the odd numbered exercises are available at the end of the textbook.

1. Multiply the following numbers:

   a. 6 × 425 b. 276 × 7 c. 87 × 35 d. 90 × 8

   e. 1,483 × 32 f. 70 × 384 g. 215 × 64 h. 513 × 846

   i. 629 × 9 j. 813 × 99 k. 389 × 78 l. 1,267 × 7

2. Multiply the following numbers:

   a. 17 × 436 b. 8 × 4,602 c. 21 × 5,937 d. 304 × 827

   e. 56 × 193 f. 3 × 5,739 g. 48 × 29 h. 648 × 315

   i. 347 × 12 j. 1,872 × 3 k. 1,389 × 18 l. 982 × 8

3. An audio store purchased 6 stereo systems at a wholesale cost of $943 for each system with the intention of reselling them at a markup. How much did they pay in total for the stereo systems?

4. The Simpson family purchased 4 round-trip tickets to Australia. Each ticket cost $1,779. How much did they pay in total for the tickets?

5. A shipment contained 18 cartons of key chains. If there were 348 key chains in each carton, how many key chains were there in total?
6. Solomon worked 38 hours/week at his full-time job. He took 4 weeks of vacation throughout the year, leaving 48 weeks that he actually worked. How many hours did he work in total for the year?
7. A company wants to organize an all-employee team-building event. If there are 165 employees and the cost for each employee is $48, how much would the company have to pay in total?
8. Debbie is a teacher and had to buy classroom supplies for the beginning of the new school year. She bought 8 measuring kits at $12 each, 9 packs of markers at $7 each, and 25 rulers at $3 each. How much did she spend in total?

1.7 DIVISION OF WHOLE NUMBERS

Division is the opposite operation of multiplication. It can be thought of as splitting a number into equal parts, or finding out how many times a number is contained in another number. For example, when dividing the number 24 by the number 8, we are trying to find the number of times that 8 fits into 24.

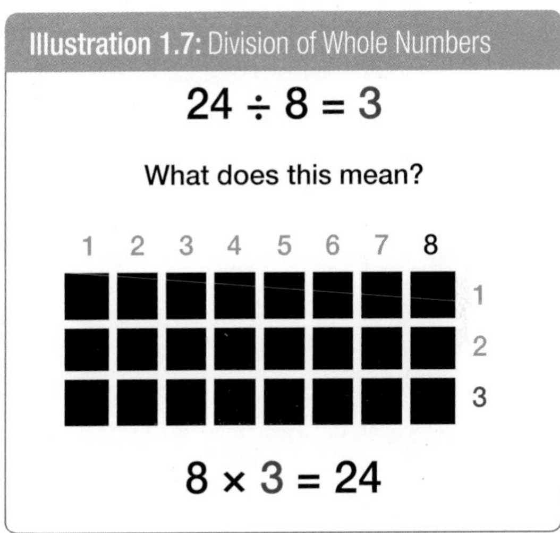

EXAMPLE 1.7 (A): Dividing Whole Numbers

Divide the following numbers: **18 ÷ 3**

Solution:

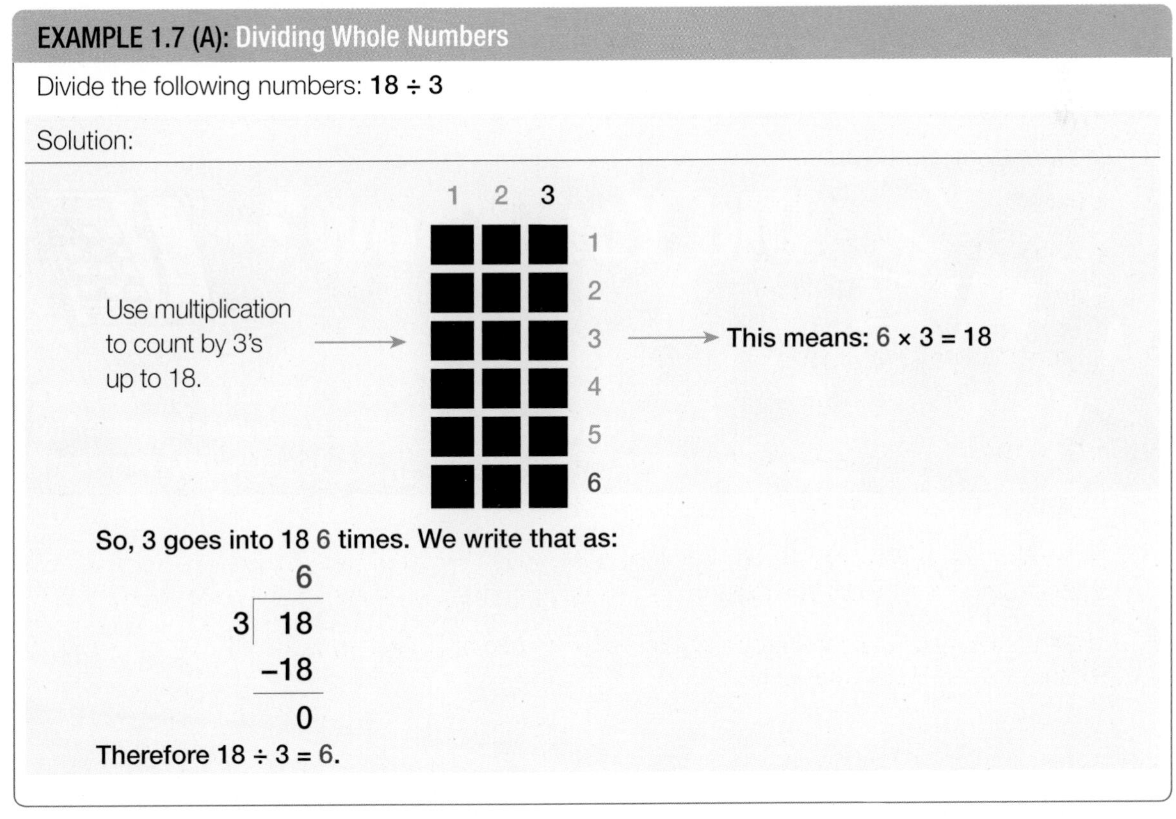

1 2 3
1
2
3
4
5
6
Use multiplication to count by 3's up to 18.
This means: 6 × 3 = 18
So, 3 goes into 18 6 times. We write that as:
6
3 | 18
−18
0
Therefore 18 ÷ 3 = 6.

When dividing numbers, the number that is being divided is called a **dividend**. The number by which the dividend is divided is called a **divisor**. The result of the division is called a **quotient**. When the numbers cannot be divided evenly, the number that is left is called a **remainder**.

```
                  3  ←— quotient
              ┌────
divisor ——→ 2 │  7  ←— dividend
                −6
              ─────
                 1  ←— remainder
```

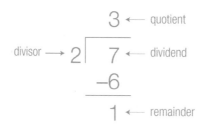

The algorithm used for performing more complicated divisions is called **long division**. Long division is like a series of questions and answers that continue until there is no remainder or until the desired number of decimal places is reached. Let's look at an example involving division with whole numbers.

EXAMPLE 1.7 (B): Dividing Whole Numbers Using Long Division

Divide the following whole numbers using long division: **127 ÷ 5**

Solution:

```
     25
   ┌────
 5 │ 127
    −10↓
    ────
     27
    −25
    ────
      2
```

Q: How many times does 5 go into 1?	A: 0	
Q: How many times does 5 go into 12?	A: 2	
Q: What is 5 x 2?	A: 10	Remainder: 2
Q: What number do we bring down?	A: 7	
Q: How many times does 5 go into 27?	A: 5	
Q: What is 5 x 5?	A: 25	Remainder: 2

Therefore, when dividing 127 by 5 we get a quotient of 25 and a remainder of 2.

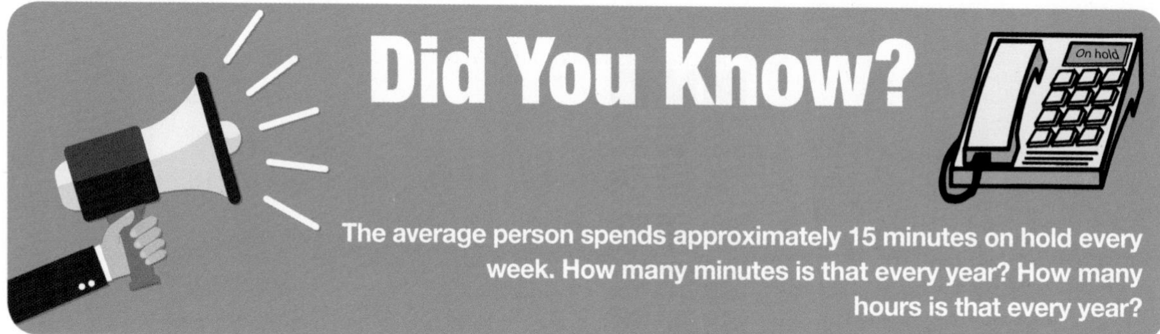

1.7 EXERCISES

Answers to the odd numbered exercises are available at the end of the textbook.

1. Divide the following numbers:

   a. 465 ÷ 5 b. 585 ÷ 9 c. 708 ÷ 6 d. 3,928 ÷ 4

   e. 9,066 ÷ 3 f. 19,250 ÷ 7 g. 23,086 ÷ 17 h. 17,664 ÷ 23

2. Divide the following numbers:

   a. 723 ÷ 3 b. 392 ÷ 7 c. 756 ÷ 9 d. 3,255 ÷ 5

   e. 6,624 ÷ 4 f. 17,080 ÷ 8 g. 36,803 ÷ 13 h. 23,495 ÷ 37

3. Divide the following numbers, giving the quotient and the remainder:

   a. 38 ÷ 3 b. 110 ÷ 7 c. 85 ÷ 15 d. 143 ÷ 17

4. Divide the following numbers, giving the quotient and the remainder:

   a. 26 ÷ 5 b. 115 ÷ 9 c. 146 ÷ 12 d. 174 ÷ 24

5. Darren, Nina, and Alek rented a building to run their business. The monthly rent was $4,389. They decided to split the rent equally. How much rent will each of them have to pay?

6. A bowling team decided to go out for dinner to celebrate their win. There are 5 members on the team and they split the final bill equally amongst themselves. If the final bill was $240, how much did each team member pay?

7. A company had 378 employees. The employees worked in 9 different departments. How many employees worked in each department if each department had the same number of employees?

8. During summer camp, all of the children attending had to be separated into 8 different groups. If there were 192 children in total, how many were in each group?

9. A box of 6 financial calculators was purchased for $162. How much did each calculator cost?

10. Four friends decide to start a company together and need to invest $14,900 in total. If they agree that each of them will invest the same amount, how much will each of them have to invest?

REVIEW EXERCISES

Answers to the odd numbered exercises are available at the end of the textbook.

1. Write $61,057,689,409 in word form.

2. Write $675,021,754,769 in word form.

3. Write *two million, three hundred thirty-two thousand, seven hundred nine* in standard form.

4. Write *three million, two hundred thousand, six hundred seven* in standard form.

5. Express $3,897,100,453 in its expanded form.

6. Express $5,027,136,498 in its expanded form.

7. Identify the digit in the number in Exercise 1 that has each of the following place values:

   a. thousands b. tens c. millions d. hundred thousands e. hundreds

8. Identify the digit in the number in Exercise 2 that has each of the following place values:

   a. thousands b. tens c. millions d. hundred thousands e. hundreds

9. What is the place value of the following digits of the number in Exercise 1? There may be more than one, or none.

   a. 6 b. 3 c. 5 d. 0 e. 1

   f. 4 g. 7 h. 8 i. 2 j. 9

10. What is the place value of the following digits of the number in Exercise 2? There may be more than one, or none.

   a. 6 b. 3 c. 5 d. 0 e. 1

   f. 4 g. 7 h. 8 i. 2 j. 9

11. Round the following numbers to the indicated place values:

   a. 307 to the nearest ten

   b. $56,827 to the nearest thousand

12. Round the following numbers to the indicated place values:

   a. 407 to the nearest hundred

   b. $78,827 to the nearest thousand

13. Calculate the answers in the following situations:

   a. Jodi had $2,500 in the bank and then spent $86, $200, and $1,500 on three different purchases. How much did she have in the bank after these expenses?

   b. If there were 680 boxes of staples for 200 students, how many boxes could each student have?

   c. Abdul had $3,000 in the bank and took out $579 for text books and another $267 for other school supplies. How much did he have left in the bank?

   d. Suppose Fed Ex delivers approximately 1,900 large cartons per week. Each carton has at least 500 parcels. At least how many parcels per week does Fed Ex deliver?

   e. Carlos borrowed $5,000 from his parents to go on a tour. When he returned home, he gave them back $36. How much does he still owe them?

14. Calculate the answers in the following situations:

   a. Carla was a first-year college student and had $3,500 in the bank to cover her expenses. She spent $1,100 on new text books, $700 on used text books, $75 on binders, paper, pens, markers, and pencils. She also had to allow $1,000 for travelling expenses to go home. How much did she have in the bank after these expenses were paid?

   b. If Carla bought an on-line access card for $50 to submit the homework for one of her classes, how much did she have left after that purchase?

   c. Desmond, Carla's brother, had $4,000 in the bank and stayed in residence (paid by his grandmother) and therefore didn't have to allow for travelling expenses. However, he had to allot $1,800 for food. Also, he took out $1,579 for new and used text books and another $207 for other school supplies. How much did he have left in the bank?

   d. At the end of the first semester, who had the most money left over, Carla or Desmond? By how much?

   e. Carla and Desmond's parents gave them each $1,000 to go for a holiday after their first semester. They were able to combine this amount with what they had left over in their accounts. How much did they each have to spend?

15. On May 1, 2019 Jessica Mitchell wrote a cheque for $782 to Duka Property Management for her maintenance fees. Complete the cheque below as she would have, but without the signature.

Nº

Bank name

Date ____________

Pay to the order of ____________ $ [ ]

The sum of ____________

____________ Dollars

Memo ____________ Authorized signature ____________

123894593 123893 38923467843

16. On December 24, 2018 Avram Weinrib wrote a cheque for $300 as a donation for the Salvation Army. Fill out the cheque as he would have, but without the signature.

Nº

Bank name

Date ____________

Pay to the order of ____________ $ [ ]

The sum of ____________

____________ Dollars

Memo ____________ Authorized signature ____________

123894593 123893 38923467843

17. Estimate the total number of employees working in a Tim Horton's group of stores in Ontario based on the information below by rounding to the nearest ten.

    Store A: 34 employees

    Store B: 21 employees

    Store C: 9 employees

    Store D: 28 employees

    Store E: 19 employees

18. Estimate the amount (to the closest dollar) of the total cost of pens in an accountant's office. There are 5 red markers costing $3 each, 4 black markers costing $2 each, and 7 blue ball-point pens costing $1 each.

CHAPTER 2

DECIMAL NUMBERS

LEARNING OBJECTIVES

Studying this chapter will provide you with the knowledge needed to:

- Read and write decimal numbers in standard and expanded form.
- Identify the place value of decimal numbers and apply it to round numbers.
- Perform arithmetic operations with decimal numbers.
- Solve word problems involving decimal numbers.
- Estimate the sums, differences, products, and quotients of decimal numbers using rounding.
- Estimate solutions to different application problems involving decimal numbers.

TOPICS

2.1 INTRODUCTION TO DECIMAL NUMBERS

As discussed in Chapter 1, we often overlook the rules of correctly expressing numbers because our day-to-day conversations do not necessarily require us to follow the rules. However, there are situations when we are expected to express numbers with more precision. For instance, if we are to engage in conversations pertaining to investments or business relations, then it is important that we express ourselves in a correct, clear, and professional manner. This is where the use of decimal numbers is important. Decimal numbers are used in situations where we are required to express numbers with more accuracy. As discussed in Chapter 1, the numbers system looks at the position of a digit in relation to the decimal point. Digits located to the left of the decimal point represent values that are greater or equal to one, while numbers to the right of the decimal point represent values that are greater or equal to zero but less than one. In other words, the numbers to the right of the decimal point represent decimal numbers.

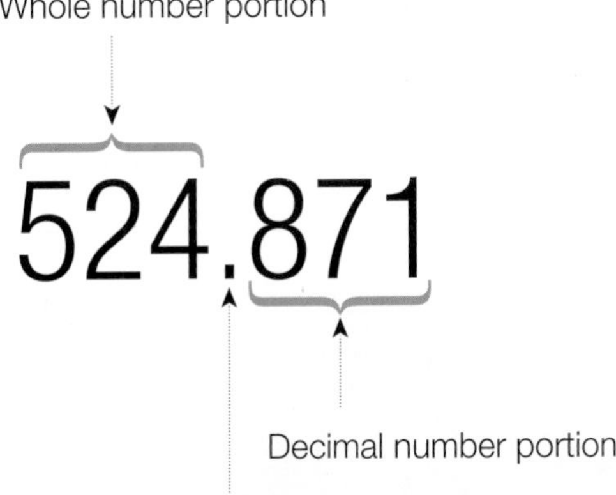

Decimal numbers are used to express money values, units of measurement, and more. An example of how decimals can be expressed in different ways is currency conversion. If you go to a bank or a currency exchange institution, you will notice that the values expressed have more than two decimal places. Often they are expressed with four or five decimal places to ensure accuracy.

CANADA CAD 0.9512 0.8883
CHINA CNY 7.3169 6.0910
EURO EUR 0.6644 0.6100
JAPAN JPY 109.00 102.00
SINGAPORE SGD 1.3712 1.2630
HONG KONG HKD 7.0043 6.4072
NEW ZEALAND NZD 1.1646 1.0675
2.7818

Figure 2.1: Foreign Currency Exchange Rates

DISCUSSION

Think of three different situations when using decimal numbers would be more appropriate than using whole numbers.

2.2 PLACE VALUE OF DECIMAL NUMBERS

In Chapter 1, we discussed the place value of whole numbers and how they are broken into groups of values such as units, thousands, millions, etc.

Decimals represent a portion of the ones position. They are not separated by values or patterns because they belong to the first whole number before the decimal and are a continuation of that number.

The place value of decimals begins with the tenths place value and is indicated by the 'th' at the end.

Exhibit 2.2: Place Value of a Seven-Digit Decimal Number

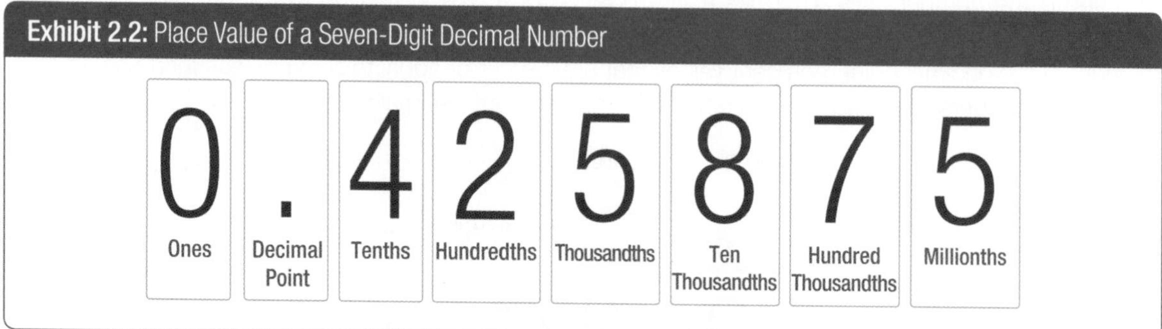

Did You Know?
When a person sees someone they like, their eyebrows raise for approximately two-tenths of a second.

EXPANDED FORM OF A DECIMAL NUMBER

In Exhibit 2.2, every digit has a specific place value. If we break down a number into its place values, we have an **expanded form** of the place values of the number. In Example 2.2 (A), the number has been broken down into specific place values of each digit. The result, as shown, gives the **expanded form of a six digit number**.

EXAMPLE 2.2: Place Value of a Six-Digit Decimal Number

Break down the number 0.73425 into its place values.

Solution:

The decimal number 0.73425 can be broken down into its place values as follows:

7 tenths	7×0.1	0.7
3 hundredths	3×0.01	0.03
4 thousandths	4×0.001	0.004
2 ten thousandths	2×0.0001	0.0002
5 hundred thousandths	5×0.00001	0.00005

The above numbers represent the expanded form of the decimal number 0.73425.

2.2 EXERCISES

Answers to the odd numbered exercises are available at the end of the textbook.

For Exercises 1 and 2, express the decimal numbers in their expanded form.

1. a. 53.83 b. 123.456 c. 245.9183 d. 7,821.01325

2. a. 912. 81 b. 78.981 c. 423.7123 d. 981.15691

3. In the number $74,820.53196, what is the place value of each of the numbers indicated below?
   a. 5 b. 6 c. 7 d. 8 e. 9
   f. 0 g. 1 h. 2 i. 3 j. 4

4. In the number $51,629.48073, what is the place value of each of the numbers indicated below?
   a. 2 b. 3 c. 0 d. 6 e. 7
   f. 8 g. 1 h. 9 i. 5 j. 4

5. What number in 936.052871 is represented by the following place values?
   a. Thousandths b. Hundreds c. Ones d. Hundred thousandths e. Millionths
   f. Tenths g. Tens h. Hundredths i. Ten thousandths

6. What number in 203.847159 is represented by the following place values?
   a. Millionths b. Ten thousandths c. Tens d. Hundredths e. Tenths
   f. Ones g. Thousandths h. Hundreds i. Hundred thousandths

2.3 READING AND WRITING DECIMAL NUMBERS

In Chapter 1, when we learned about reading and writing whole numbers, we emphasized the importance of the use of the word '**and**'. We explained that this word should not be said when expressing whole numbers. The only time we should say '**and**' when expressing numbers is when there is a decimal number present.

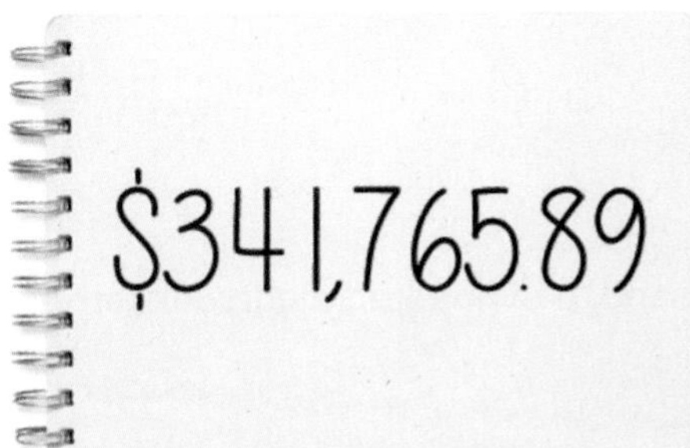

If asked to read the number shown on the left, we might say:

*Three hundred **and** forty-one thousand, seven hundred **and** sixty-five dollars **and** eighty-nine cents.*

Strictly speaking, we should say:

*Three hundred forty-one thousand, seven hundred sixty-five dollars **and** eighty-nine cents.*

The meaning would be understood in both instances, but there is a proper way to express this number using words.

As with whole numbers, decimal numbers can be expressed in standard form and word form.

Table 2.3: Standard and Word Form of Decimal Numbers

Standard Form	Word Form
25.21	Twenty-five **and** twenty-one hundredths
400.651	Four hundred **and** six hundred fifty-one thousandths
422.1523	Four hundred twenty-two **and** one thousand, five hundred twenty-three ten thousandths

When reading or writing decimal numbers, the same rules that we learned in Chapter 1 apply to the whole number portion. As you can see from the table above, we read and write the numbers to the left of the decimal point as a whole number, we write the decimal point as "and", and then we write the numbers to the right of the decimal point as a whole number, followed by the place value of the last digit.

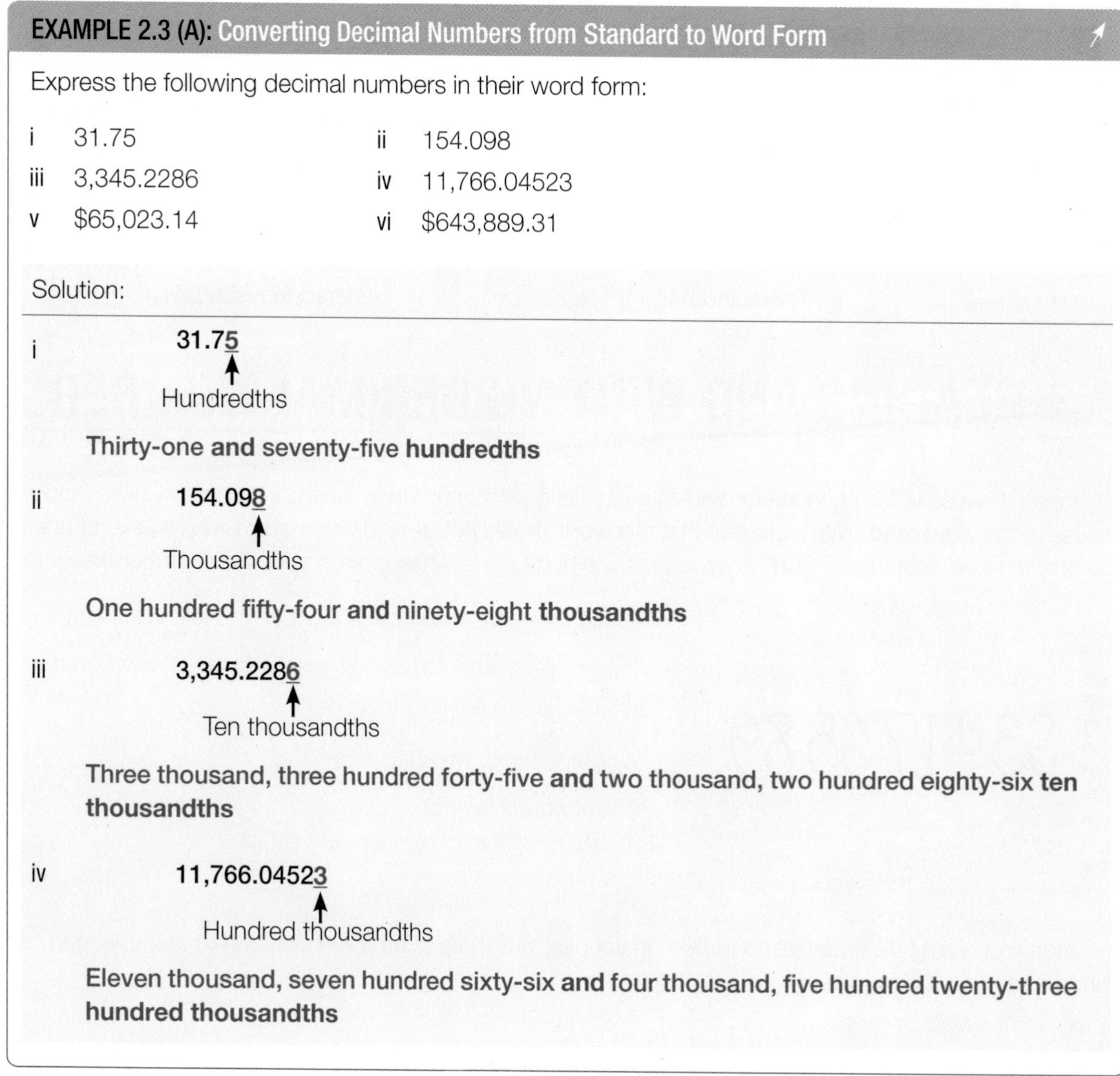

EXAMPLE 2.3 (A): Converting Decimal Numbers from Standard to Word Form

Express the following decimal numbers in their word form:

i 31.75 ii 154.098

iii 3,345.2286 iv 11,766.04523

v $65,023.14 vi $643,889.31

Solution:

i **31.75**

Hundredths

Thirty-one and seventy-five hundredths

ii **154.098**

Thousandths

One hundred fifty-four and ninety-eight thousandths

iii **3,345.2286**

Ten thousandths

Three thousand, three hundred forty-five and two thousand, two hundred eighty-six ten thousandths

iv **11,766.04523**

Hundred thousandths

Eleven thousand, seven hundred sixty-six and four thousand, five hundred twenty-three hundred thousandths

EXAMPLE 2.3 (A): Converting Decimal Numbers from Standard to Word Form *continued*

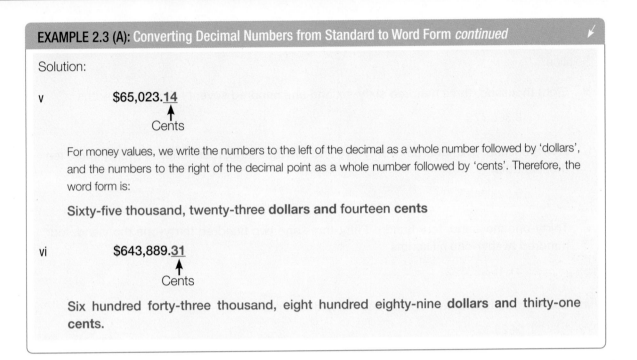

Solution:

v

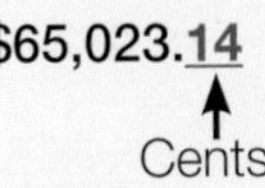

For money values, we write the numbers to the left of the decimal as a whole number followed by 'dollars', and the numbers to the right of the decimal point as a whole number followed by 'cents'. Therefore, the word form is:

Sixty-five thousand, twenty-three dollars and fourteen cents

vi

Six hundred forty-three thousand, eight hundred eighty-nine dollars and thirty-one cents.

To convert the numbers from word form to standard form, we follow similar rules. The place value of the last digit determines the number of decimal places to the right of the word 'and'. The word 'and' is replaced with a decimal point, and the numbers to the left of the word 'and' represent the whole number portion.

EXAMPLE 2.3 (B): Converting Decimal Numbers from Word to Standard Form

Express the following numbers in their standard form.

i Fifty-three and nine tenths

ii Four hundred forty-eight and forty-seven hundredths

iii Eight thousand, three hundred sixty-six and one hundred seventy-five thousandths

iv Five thousand, five hundred twenty-five and five thousand, four hundred twenty-three ten thousandths

v Thirty-one thousand, four hundred fifty-three and two hundred thirty-one thousand, four hundred twenty-one millionths

vi Six hundred twenty-five dollars and thirty-five cents

vii Seven thousand, nine hundred ninety-eight dollars and nineteen cents

viii Five and nine thousandths

ix One hundred forty-seven and fifty-nine thousandths

Solution:

i **Fifty-three and nine tenths**

53.9

ii **Four hundred forty-eight and forty-seven hundredths**

448.47

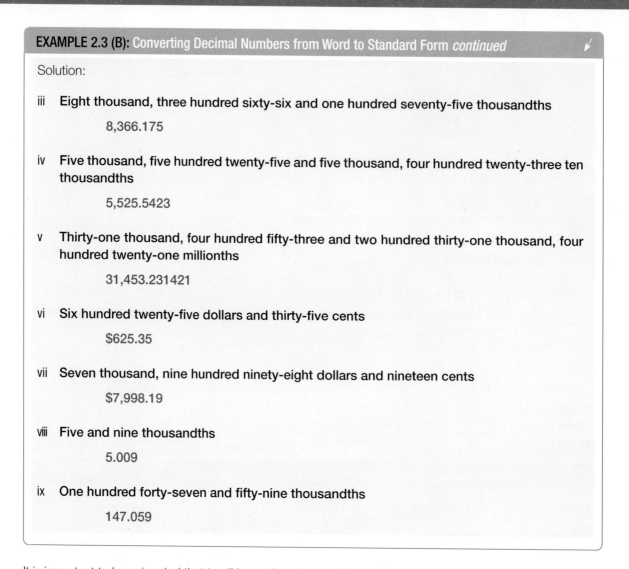

EXAMPLE 2.3 (B): Converting Decimal Numbers from Word to Standard Form *continued*

Solution:

iii **Eight thousand, three hundred sixty-six and one hundred seventy-five thousandths**

8,366.175

iv **Five thousand, five hundred twenty-five and five thousand, four hundred twenty-three ten thousandths**

5,525.5423

v **Thirty-one thousand, four hundred fifty-three and two hundred thirty-one thousand, four hundred twenty-one millionths**

31,453.231421

vi **Six hundred twenty-five dollars and thirty-five cents**

$625.35

vii **Seven thousand, nine hundred ninety-eight dollars and nineteen cents**

$7,998.19

viii **Five and nine thousandths**

5.009

ix **One hundred forty-seven and fifty-nine thousandths**

147.059

It is important to keep in mind that 'and' is not the only word that can be used to express a decimal point in a decimal number; it is, however, the most common, especially when expressing money values. An alternative way to communicate decimal numbers is to use the word 'point' to express the decimal point.

For example, if a piece of wood measures 152.65 cm in length, you can express it as:

One hundred fifty-two **point** sixty-five centimetres, or

One hundred fifty-two **point** six five centimetres.

You could express C$2.00 = €1.3563 in word form as:

Two Canadian dollars is equal to one **point** three five six three Euros.

Illustration 2.3: Writing a Cheque

Writing numbers correctly in standard and expanded form is very important when it comes to writing cheques. Let's write a cheque for $344.27.

Step 1: Fill in the date at the top right corner.

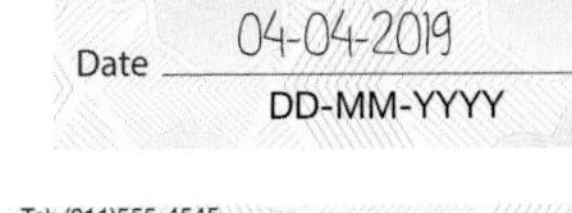

Step 2: Write the name of the person or company the money is payable to on the "Pay to the order of" line.

Step 3: Write the **amount of money numerically** in the white box at the end of the "Pay to the order of" line.

Step 4: Write the **amount of money in words** below the "Pay to the order of" line.

DD-MM-YYYY
Pay to the order of Asha Taylor $ $344.27
The sum of Three hundred forty-four dollars and twenty-seven cents

Step 5: On the bottom left, describe what the cheque is for.

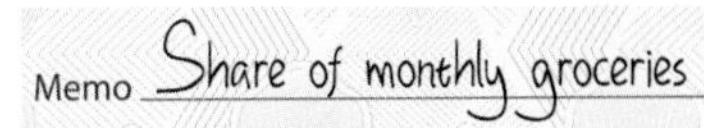

Step 6: Complete with signature on the bottom right.

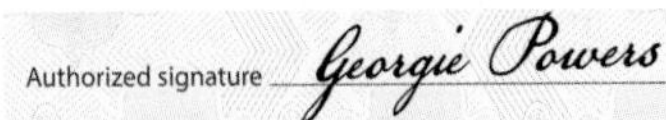

Mr. Georgie Powers
#9, 1215 Lake Sylvan Ave.
Toronto, ON
Tel: (011)555-4545
№
Date 04-04-2019
DD-MM-YYYY
Pay to the order of Asha Taylor $ $344.27
The sum of Three hundred forty-four dollars and twenty-seven cents
Dollars
Memo Share of monthly groceries Authorized signature Georgie Powers
123894593 123893 38923467843

2.3 EXERCISES

Answers to the odd numbered exercises are available at the end of the textbook.

For Exercises 1 and 2, express the decimal numbers in their word form.

1. a. 864,410.8 b. $32,985.02 c. $60,257.49 d. 32.958
   e. 410,664.872 f. 0.3855 g. 95,231.0476 h. 537,032.61941

2. a. 245.6 b. $735,200.64 c. $1,809,332.75 d. 0.284
   e. 18.328 f. 238.7501 g. 537,032.6194 h. 98,243.126734

3. Express the following numbers in their decimal form:
    a. Five hundred and sixty-nine hundredths
    b. Four point eight three six two
    c. Three hundred forty-five hundred thousandths
    d. Twenty-six thousand, five hundred ninety-seven point three zero five
    e. Sixty-eight thousand, nine hundred fifty-four dollars and thirty-six cents
    f. One billion, seventy million, nine hundred twenty-eight thousand, five dollars and three cents
4. Express the following numbers in their decimal form:
    a. Nine hundred eighty-six and nine tenths
    b. Twenty-three point twenty-five
    c. Four thousand, nine hundred forty-four and fifty-two hundred thousandths
    d. Twenty-two thousand, six hundred eighty point zero nine two
    e. Seven hundred eighty-two thousand, nine hundred eighty-three dollars and ninety-nine cents
    f. Eighty-four million, three hundred sixty-seven thousand, nine hundred two dollars and eighteen cents

2.4 ROUNDING DECIMAL NUMBERS

Rounding decimal numbers refers to the process of reducing the number of digits to the right of the decimal point to a specified place value.

Rounding decimal numbers is similar to rounding whole numbers, except that of all the digits after the rounded number are dropped instead of being turned into zeroes.

Illustration 2.4 (A): Comparison Between Rounding a Whole Number and a Decimal Number

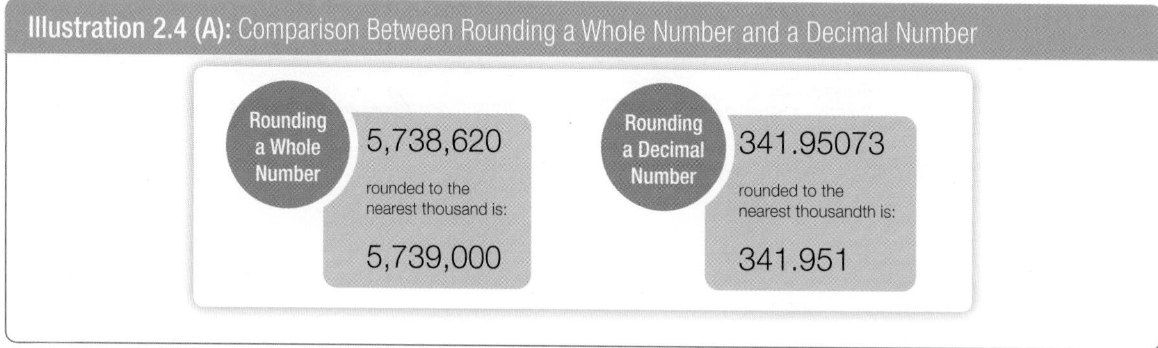

Rounding a Whole Number
5,738,620
rounded to the nearest thousand is:
5,739,000
Rounding a Decimal Number
341.95073
rounded to the nearest thousandth is:
341.951

Let's see how the rounding rules apply to decimal numbers by rounding two numbers to the nearest hundredth.

Illustration 2.4 (B): Rounding Decimal Numbers

Rule	Round Down	Round Up
Identify the number to be rounded.	2 5 . 2 3 3 6	2 5 . 2 3 6 2
Look at the number directly to the right of the number that is to be rounded.	2 5 . 2 3 3 6	2 5 . 2 3 6 2
If that number is **less than 5**, the number you are rounding remains the same; if that number is **5 or greater**, the number you are rounding increases by 1.	<5 2 5 . 2 3 3 6	>5 2 5 . 2 3 6 2
All the numbers after the rounded number can be dropped.	2 5 . 2 3	2 5 . 2 4
	Therefore, 25.2336 rounded to the nearest hundredth is 25.23.	Therefore, 25.2362 rounded to the nearest hundredth is 25.24.

EXAMPLE 2.4 (A): Rounding Decimal Numbers

Round the following decimal numbers to the indicated place values.

i 90.736 to the nearest tenth

ii 647.927 to the nearest hundredth

iii 234.45682 to the nearest thousandth

iv $32.9486 to the nearest cent

Solution:

i **90.736 to the nearest tenth**

The number in the tenths place is 7. The number to the right of 7 is less than 5; therefore, the rounding number remains the same, and we drop all of the numbers to the right of the rounding number.

Therefore, 90.736 rounded to the nearest tenth is 90.7.

ii **647.927 to the nearest hundredth**

The number in the hundredths place is 2. The number to the right of 2 is greater than 5; therefore, we increase the rounding number by 1, and we drop all of the numbers to the right of the rounding number.

Therefore, 647.927 rounded to the nearest hundredth is 647.93.

EXAMPLE 2.4 (A): Rounding Decimal Numbers *continued*

Solution:

iii **234.45682 to the nearest thousandth**

The number in the thousandth place is 6. The number to the right of 6 is greater than 5; therefore, we increase the rounding number by 1, and we drop all of the numbers to the right of the rounding number.

Therefore, 234.45682 rounded to the nearest thousandth is 234.457.

iv **$32.9486 to the nearest cent**

The number in the hundredths (cent) place is 4. The number to the right of 4 is greater than 5; therefore, we increase the rounding number by 1, and we drop all of the numbers to the right of the rounding number.

Therefore, $32.9486 rounded to the nearest cent is $32.95.

EXAMPLE 2.4 (B): Rounding to Two Decimal Places

Round the following numbers to **two decimal places**.

i 2.456
ii 67.678
iii 50.512
iv $56.786
v $67.225
vi $5.673

Solution:

Since we are rounding to two decimal places, we need to look at the third decimal place. If it is a **5 or more**, increase the second decimal by one. If the third decimal is **less than 5**, the second decimal remains the same.

i The third decimal is 6, which is greater than 5, so **2.456 becomes 2.46**.

ii The third decimal is 8, which is greater than 5 so **67.678 becomes 67.68**.

iii The third decimal is 2, which is less than 5 so **50.512 becomes 50.51**.

With currency, the same rule applies when rounding to two decimal places.

iv The third decimal is 6 which is greater than 5 so **$56.786 becomes $56.79**.

v The third decimal is 5 which is equal to 5 so **$67.225 becomes $67.23**.

vi The third decimal is 3 which is less than 5 so **$5.673 becomes $5.67**.

If there are several decimals after the second decimal, we still only look at the third decimal to change the second decimal.

For example, 6.672334 becomes 6.67 because the third decimal (2) is less than 5.

When there is a "9" to be rounded, it can be confusing because when rounded up it becomes 10. For example, rounding 1.199 to two decimal places becomes 1.20. The third decimal place is 9, which is greater than 5, so the second decimal place increases by 1. The second decimal place is 9 so increasing it by 1 makes 10. The 1 of the 10 is added to the existing first decimal, increasing it from a 1 to a 2.

EXAMPLE 2.4 (C): Rounding a "9"

Round the following to **two decimal places.**

i	4.591	ii	23.094
iii	8.096	iv	45.189
v	23.999	vi	2.009
vii	4.099	viii	$67.296
ix	$45.998	x	$3.349

Solution:

i The third decimal place is 1 (less than 5) so **4.591 becomes 4.59**.

ii The third decimal place is 4 (less than 5) so **23.094 becomes 23.09**.

iii The third decimal place is 6 (greater than 5). One is added to 9 which becomes 10 so **8.096 becomes 8.10**.

iv The third decimal place is 9 (greater than 5). One is added to the second decimal place 8 which becomes 9 so **45.189 becomes 45.19**.

v The third decimal place is 9 (greater than 5). One is added to the second decimal place so the 9 becomes 10 and the 1 is added to the first decimal place. The first decimal place is 9 so when 1 is added, it becomes 10. The 1 is added to the ones place which becomes 4. So **23.999 becomes 24.00**.

vi The third decimal place is 9 (greater than 5) so the second decimal place becomes 1 and **2.009 becomes 2.01**.

vii The third decimal place is 9 (greater than 5) so 1 is added to the second decimal place. So the 9 of the second decimal place becomes 10 and **4.099 becomes 4.10**.

viii *Currency rounds in the same manner as non-currency.*

The third decimal place is 6 (greater than 5) so 1 is added to the second decimal place, which changes the 9 to a 10. The second decimal place becomes a 0 and the first decimal place increased to a 3. So **$67.296 becomes $67.30**.

ix The third decimal place is 8 (greater than 5) so 1 is added to the second decimal place. The second decimal place becomes a 0 and 1 is added to the first decimal place. This causes the ones place to increase by 1 and **$45.998 becomes $46.00**. *It is important to keep the 00 after the decimal point since we are dealing with money.*

x The third decimal place is 9 (greater than 5) so the second decimal place becomes 5 and **$3.349 becomes $3.35**.

Suppose something costs $2.72. In Canada, if you pay with a debit card you would pay the full $2.72, but with cash you would only need to pay $2.70. Essentially, since the penny no longer exists, when we pay with cash we must round to the nearest nickel!

When rounding decimal numbers, you may see the requests expressed in different ways. Some of the most common are: "round to the nearest cent", "round to the nearest hundredth", "round to the nearest dollar", "round to the nearest whole number" etc. It is important to understand that often the same request can be expressed in different ways.

When we see a price tag with a value of $17.49, the 'cent' value is the 2nd decimal place, in this case the 9. Cent is the French word for 'hundred,' and therefore the cent place value is also the hundredths place value.

A common error that is made is to assume that the 'cent' value is the 'tenth' position (or the first decimal place), when in fact it is the 'hundredth' place value (the second decimal place). For example, when asked to round $23.7693 to the nearest cent, often times the number is wrongly rounded to $23.80 instead of $23.77.

DISCUSSION

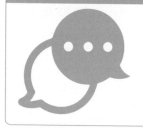

Do the following three statements have the same meaning?

- Round to the nearest cent.
- Round to the nearest hundredth.
- Round to two decimal places.

2.4 EXERCISES

Answers to the odd numbered exercises are available at the end of the textbook.

For Exercises 1 and 2, round the numbers to the nearest whole number (or dollar).

1. a. 14.7 b. 901.736 c. 6.2699 d. $10.81 e. $12.99

2. a. 0.5 b. 23.540 c. 547.3901 d. $42.74 e. $248.99

For Exercises 3 and 4, round the numbers to the nearest tenth.

3. a. 74.903 b. 6.7196 c. 985.4722 d. 0.9995 e. $58.373

4. a. 16.924 b. 19.0927 c. 304.7733 d. 4.9918 e. $7,554.641

For Exercises 5 and 6, round the numbers to the nearest hundredth (or cent).

5. a. 4.662 b. 76.3059 c. 65.73510 d. $948.0255 e. $14.999

6. a. 9.991 b. 50.2661 c. 120.33190 d. $0.99999 e. $18.006

For Exercises 7 and 8, round the numbers to the nearest thousandth.

7. a. 0.47118 b. 647.92746 c. $1.56466 d. $104.99999 e. $6,470.31850

8. a. 3.56137 b. 884.91335 c. $16.45555 d. $29.99999 e. $7,224.67770

9. Round 3,440,929.63492517 to each of the place values indicated below:
   - a. Nearest one
   - b. Nearest millionth
   - c. Nearest thousand
   - d. Nearest ten millionth
   - e. Nearest tenth
   - f. Nearest hundredth
   - g. Nearest hundred thousand
   - h. Nearest ten thousandth
   - i. Nearest million
   - j. Nearest thousandth
   - k. Nearest hundred
   - l. Nearest hundred thousandth

10. Round 2,864,032.40385769 to each of the place values indicated below:
   - a. Nearest tenth
   - b. Nearest ten millionth
   - c. Nearest thousand
   - d. Nearest ten thousandth
   - e. Nearest hundred
   - f. Nearest million
   - g. Nearest thousandth
   - h. Nearest hundred thousandth
   - i. Nearest millionth
   - j. Nearest hundredth
   - k. Nearest one
   - l. Nearest hundred thousand

2.5 ADDITION OF DECIMAL NUMBERS

As we learned in Chapter 1, addition is the process of determining the total amount or number of objects.

When adding numbers that include decimals, you must align the decimal points one on top of the other. The order in which the numbers are placed is not important, as the answer will be the same regardless, but the alignment of the decimal points can be the difference between a right and a wrong answer.

Illustration 2.5 (A): Aligning Decimal Numbers by Decimal Points

648.9 + 32.063 + 19.5 should be expressed as:

$$\begin{array}{r} 648.9 \\ 32.063 \\ +\ 19.5 \\ \hline \end{array}$$

It is often helpful to include zeroes in the blank spaces, as this assists in ensuring that the numbers are aligned. Using the above example, it would now look like this:

$$\begin{array}{r} 648.900 \\ 32.063 \\ +\ 19.500 \\ \hline \end{array}$$

When adding numbers that include whole numbers and decimals, it is important to remember that whole numbers still have a decimal point present, even though we do not write or say it. For example, the numbers 8 and 8.0 are the same, but we tend to drop the .0 as it is not necessary to include. It is important to remember that the .0 is still a part of the number because when we add decimal numbers, we need to be mindful of where we place whole numbers.

Illustration 2.5 (B): Aligning Whole Numbers and Decimal Numbers by Decimal Points

When asked to add **56.731 + 12 + 902.66**

it is common for the addition to be expressed as:

$$\begin{array}{r} 56.731 \\ 12 \\ +\ \ 902.66 \\ \hline \end{array}$$

when it should be expressed as:

$$\begin{array}{r@{.}l} 56&731 \\ 12& \\ +\ 902&66 \\ \hline \end{array} \qquad \text{OR} \qquad \begin{array}{r} 56.731 \\ 12.000 \\ +\ \ 902.660 \\ \hline \end{array}$$

DISCUSSION

You wrote a quiz that was out of 20 marks. You received it back with a mark of 16, but the instructor uploaded your mark online as 16.0. Was your grade uploaded correctly?

EXAMPLE 2.5: Adding Decimal Numbers

Add the following numbers:

i 14.267 + 25.15

ii 462.26 + 125.851

iii 138.061 + 4.6 + 80

Solution:

i **14.267 + 25.15**

The decimal point moves straight down into the answer.

$$\begin{array}{r} {}^{1} \\ 14.267 \\ +\ \ 25.150 \\ \hline 39.417 \end{array}$$

ii **462.26 + 125.851**

$$\begin{array}{r} {}^{1\,1} \\ 462.260 \\ +\ \ 125.851 \\ \hline 588.111 \end{array}$$

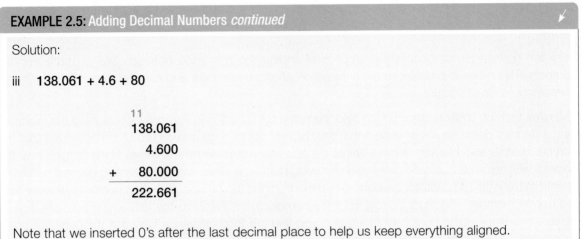

EXAMPLE 2.5: Adding Decimal Numbers *continued*

Solution:

iii **138.061 + 4.6 + 80**

$$\begin{array}{r} {\scriptstyle 11} \\ 138.061 \\ 4.600 \\ +\ \ 80.000 \\ \hline 222.661 \end{array}$$

Note that we inserted 0's after the last decimal place to help us keep everything aligned.

2.5 EXERCISES

Answers to the odd numbered exercises are available at the end of the textbook.

1. Add the following numbers:

   a. 87.54 + 36
   b. 31.8 + 64.553 + 1.002
   c. 539.6 + 3.071 + 99
   d. 62.401 + 9 + 4.59
   e. 74 + 1.2948 + 15
   f. 34.071 + 4.6 + 80
   g. 33.7 + 2.698 + 141.5
   h. 3.1 + 842 + 90.773

2. Add the following numbers:

   a. 43 + 84.27
   b. 9.7 + 16.857 + 63.201
   c. 5.487 + 325.6 + 85
   d. 671.412 + 93 + 41.28
   e. 85 + 4.14521 + 931
   f. 741.2 + 65 + 98.461
   g. 531.261 + 84.7 + 7.8
   h. 55.1 + 9,328 + 451.788

3. Brandon bought some new clothes for the winter from four different stores. He decided to add his receipts to see how much he spent in total. The four amounts he spent were: $36.74, $22.49, $74.06, and $108.44. How much did he spend in total?

4. Jillian worked at a restaurant four nights each week. She wanted to see how much she made in tips for the week she just finished. If she made $90.50, $64.35, $73.91, and $58.04, how much did she make in tips for the week?

5. Karen, Joe, and Abdul were meeting at a downtown location. Karen drove 21.4 km, Joe drove 14.83 km, and Abdul drove 9.64 km. What is the combined number of kilometres they drove?

6. A builder needed to buy hardwood flooring for three homes that were being built. The homes needed 746.98, 590.33, and 826.74 square feet of hardwood flooring, respectively. How many square feet of hardwood did the builder need to purchase in total?

7. Kamal had $1,658.43 in his account and received some cheques in the mail for his birthday. The cheques were for $55.50, $40.86, and $65.75. If he deposits these cheques into his account, how much will he have in total?

8. Elena is having a party for her daughter's birthday and wants to ensure that she stays within her $250 budget. If the items she has already bought cost $32.65, $44.87, $9.29, and $101.14, how much of her budget has she spent so far?

2.6 SUBTRACTION OF DECIMAL NUMBERS

Subtracting decimal numbers is the process of finding the difference between two or more decimal numbers. This process is similar to the subtraction of whole numbers and can also be referred to as the reverse operation of addition.

The rules that we apply to addition are also the same for subtraction in regards to aligning the numbers by the decimal point. You must ensure that the decimal points align one on top of the other and that the numbers before and after the decimal points are also aligned. Make sure to fill any blank spaces after the decimal with zeros so that each place value for every number is filled. When subtracting decimal numbers, start from the right and subtract the bottom number from the top number. If the top number is smaller than the bottom number, you must borrow from the number immediately to the left, where possible. Follow these same steps going from right to left until you find the total difference between the numbers being subtracted. Let's look at how these rules apply by performing some subtractions.

EXAMPLE 2.6: Subtracting Decimal Numbers

Subtract the following numbers:

i 60.54 – 16.12
ii 97.80 – 56.16
iii 781 – 65.99

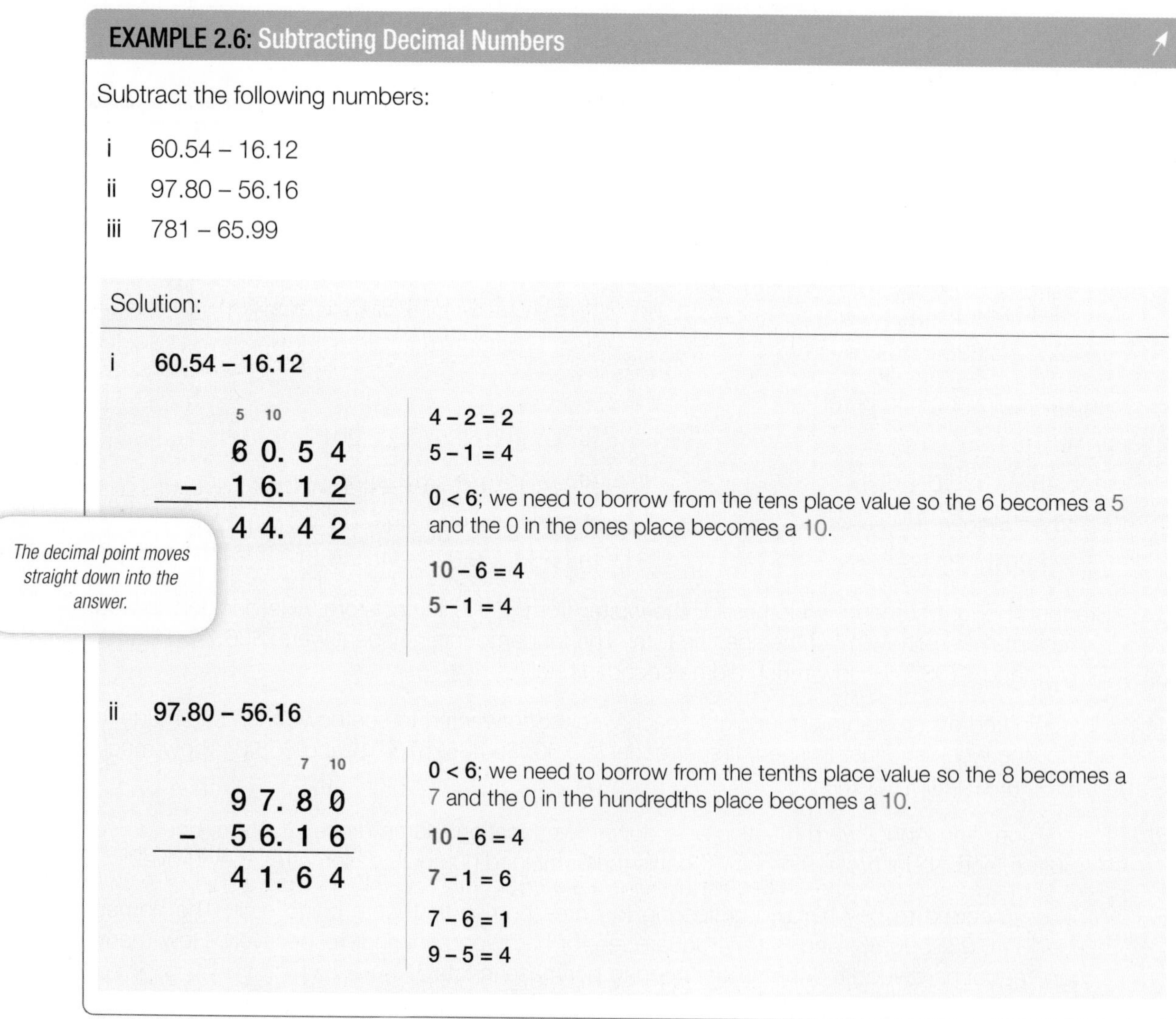

Solution:
i 60.54 – 16.12
5 10
6 0. 5 4
– 1 6. 1 2
4 4. 4 2
4 – 2 = 2
5 – 1 = 4
0 < 6; we need to borrow from the tens place value so the 6 becomes a 5 and the 0 in the ones place becomes a 10.
10 – 6 = 4
5 – 1 = 4
The decimal point moves straight down into the answer.
ii 97.80 – 56.16
7 10
9 7. 8 0
– 5 6. 1 6
4 1. 6 4
0 < 6; we need to borrow from the tenths place value so the 8 becomes a 7 and the 0 in the hundredths place becomes a 10.
10 – 6 = 4
7 – 1 = 6
7 – 6 = 1
9 – 5 = 4

EXAMPLE 2.6: Subtracting Decimal Numbers *continued*

Solution:

iii **781 – 65.99**

0 9 10 7 8 ~~1~~. ~~0~~ ~~0~~ – 6 5. 9 9 0 1	**0 < 9**; we need to borrow from the tenths place value BUT we cannot borrow from there either, since there is a 0 in the tenths place. So, we continue until we find a number we CAN borrow from; that is the 1 in the ones place. **10 – 1 = 9**; the zero in the hundredths column now becomes a 10 **10 – 9 = 1** **9 – 9 = 0**
7 10 9 10 7 ~~8~~ ~~1~~. ~~0~~ ~~0~~ – 6 5. 9 9 7 1 5. 0 1	**0 < 5**; we need to borrow from the tens place value. So the 8 becomes a 7 and the 0 in the ones column becomes a 10. **10 – 5 = 5** **7 – 6 = 1** **7 – 0 = 7**

2.6 EXERCISES

Answers to the odd numbered exercises are available at the end of the textbook.

1. Subtract the following numbers:
   a. 357.21 – 94.66
   b. 80.54 – 16.7
   c. 438.2 – 30.41
   d. 423 – 99.35
   e. 73.64 – 54
   f. 785.093 – 429.63
   g. 27.491 – 14.538
   h. 6.3902 – 4.865

2. Subtract the following numbers:
   a. 132.36 – 110.87
   b. 35.63 – 18.9
   c. 276.6 – 67.22
   d. 322 – 67.45
   e. 91.99 – 49
   f. 432.174 – 267.47
   g. 87.462 – 64.213
   h. 23.2713 – 19. 657

3. Dasha needed to withdraw some money from her savings account in order to purchase a new bike. She had $3,650 in her account and the bike cost $429.63. How much remains in her savings account after the withdrawal?

4. Vikram paid $1,465 for a trip to Cuba last year booked through his travel agent. This year he found a deal online at a price of $1,184.29. How much cheaper was the ticket this year?

5. If a piece of wood is 64.76 inches in length and 31.97 inches is cut from it, how long is the remaining piece of wood?

6. Aarav used to drive a total of 93.64 km to and from work each day. He recently moved and now drives a total of 57.86 km to and from work on a daily basis. How many km less does he drive now each day?

7. Akito created a budget of $345 for his back to school purchases. He bought a new backpack for $32.75, two textbooks for $83.50 each, and writing materials for $44.82. How much of his budget does he have left?

8. Shane made $2,450 each month after taxes. Each month, he paid $840.50 for rent, $275.25 for utilities, $130.87 for gas for his car, and $215.50 for food. How much of his pay is Shane left with after paying for his monthly expenses?

2.7 MULTIPLICATION OF DECIMAL NUMBERS

Multiplying decimal numbers is the same as multiplying whole numbers.

Multiplication does not require the decimal numbers to be aligned the way that addition and subtraction do. What is important to remember is to still align the numbers from right to left.

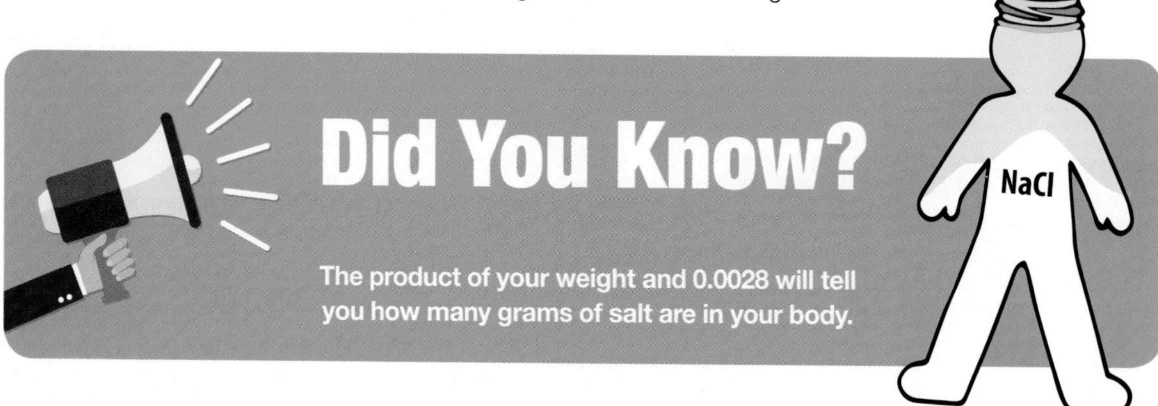

Illustration 2.7: Multiplying Decimal Numbers

Calculate 3.12 × 4.5 by following these steps:

Step 1: Before beginning, you have the option to remove the decimal points and add them later, or leave them as they are. Start with the bottom number furthest to the right (5) and multiply it by each of the numbers across the top.

	3. ¹1 2	Q: What is 5 × 2?	A: 10
×	4. 5	Q: Where do we put the 0?	A: Under the 5
	0	Q: How much do we carry?	A: 1

	3. ¹1 2	Q: What is 5 × 1?	A: 5
×	4. 5	Q: What is the answer after adding the carry over (1)?	A: 5 + 1 = 6
	6 0	Q: Where do we put the 6?	A: to the left of the 0

	3. ¹1 2	Q: What is 5 × 3?	A: 15
×	4. 5	Q: Where do we put the 15?	A: to the left of the 6
	1 5 6 0		

Illustration 2.7: Multiplying Decimal Numbers *continued*

Step 2: Continue the same procedure with the next digit in the bottom number (4).

			3.	1	2
×				4.	5
		1	5	6	0
				8	0

Q: What is 4 × 2? A: 8

Q: Where do we put the 8? A: Before placing the 8, we place a 0 directly beneath the 0 from Step 1. The 8 is then placed to the left of the 0.

Q: Is there anything to carry over? A: No

			3.	1	2
×				4.	5
		1	5	6	0
			4	8	0

Q: What is 4 × 1? A: 4

Q: Where do we put the 4? A: to the left of the 8

Q: Is there anything to carry over? A: No

			3.	1	2
×				4.	5
		1	5	6	0
	1	2	4	8	0

Q: What is 4 × 3? A: 12

Q: Where do we put the 12? A: to the left of the 4

Q: Is there anything to carry over? A: No

Step 3: Add the results from Step 1 and 2.

			3.	1	2
×				4.	5
		1	5	6	0
+	1	2	4	8	0
	1	4	0	4	0

Q: What is 1560 + 12480? A: Add each column and place the sum under the column

→ 0 + 0 = 0

→ 6 + 8 = 14 (carry the 1)

→ 1 + 5 + 4 = 10 (carry the 1)

→ 1 + 1 + 2 = 4

→ 0 + 1 = 1

Step 4: As you may have noticed, Steps 1-3 are the same as when we multiplied whole numbers. Multiplying decimal numbers requires one last step.

			3.	1	2
×				4.	5
		1	5	6	0
+	1	2	4	8	0
	1	4.	0	4	0

Q: How many digits are to the right of the decimal point in 3.12? A: 2

Q: How many digits are to the right of the decimal point in 4.5? A: 1

Q: What is 2 + 1? A: 3

So, in the answer there needs to be **3 digits** to the right of the decimal.

Therefore, 3.12 × 4.5 = 14.04

EXAMPLE 2.7: Multiplying Decimal Numbers

Multiply the following numbers:

i   4.56 × 3.6
ii 65.9 × 3.42
iii 231 × 5.41

Solution:

i **4.56 × 3.6**

$$\begin{array}{rrl} & 4.56 & \longleftarrow \text{2 decimal places} \\ \times & 3.6 & \longleftarrow \text{1 decimal place} \\ \hline & 2736 & \\ + & 13680 & \\ \hline & 16.416 & \longleftarrow \text{3 decimal places} \end{array}$$

ii **65.9 × 3.42**

$$\begin{array}{rrl} & 65.9 & \longleftarrow \text{1 decimal place} \\ \times & 3.42 & \longleftarrow \text{2 decimal places} \\ \hline & 1318 & \\ & 26360 & \\ + & 197700 & \\ \hline & 225.378 & \longleftarrow \text{3 decimal places} \end{array}$$

iii **231 × 5.41**

$$\begin{array}{rrl} & 231 & \longleftarrow \text{0 decimal places} \\ \times & 5.41 & \longleftarrow \text{2 decimal places} \\ \hline & 231 & \\ & 9240 & \\ + & 115500 & \\ \hline & 1249.71 & \longleftarrow \text{2 decimal places} \end{array}$$

2.7 EXERCISES

Answers to the odd numbered exercises are available at the end of the textbook.

1. Multiply the following numbers:
   a. 14.2 × 891.5
   b. 21.47 × 6.9
   c. 67.284 × 4.3
   d. 15 × 89.33
   e. 3.6 × 41.906
   f. 2.487 × 6.4
   g. 6.24 × 94.761
   h. 7.894 × 5.434

2. Multiply the following numbers:

a. 254.1 × 17.2
b. 832.65 × 9.1
c. 45.628 × 6.2
d. 14 × 68.32
e. 5.6 × 74.398
f. 209.433 × 56.6
g. 23.65 × 102.435
h. 5.743 × 60.423

3. Karishma gets paid $13.25 per hour and she works 35 hours each week. How much does she receive each week? If she was paid bi-weekly, how much would she receive every two weeks?

4. Janet works 40 hours each week and is paid $12.50 per hour. How much does she receive each week? If she was paid bi-weekly, how much would she receive every two weeks?

5. A teacher wanted to take her class on a field trip to the science centre. Admission for each student is $13.75. If 26 students are going on the field trip, how much would the teacher have to collect in total from all students?

6. Kai wanted to change all the light fixtures in his home. He found a great deal at the local store for light fixtures that cost $44.83 each. If he bought 8 of them, how much would he pay in total?

2.8 DIVISION OF DECIMAL NUMBERS

As discussed in Chapter 1, long division is like a series of questions and answers that continue until there is no remainder, or until the desired number of decimal places is reached; this series of questions and answers allows us to reach our final answer and ensures that it is done correctly.

Before we look at an example, there are a few rules regarding division with decimal numbers that are important to keep in mind.

When doing long division, it is best to have the divisor (the number you divide by) as a whole number. When that is not the case, we can fix it simply by moving the decimal point the required number of spaces in order to ensure that the divisor is a whole number.

Note that if we move the decimal in the divisor, we also have to move the decimal the same number of places in the dividend too.

Illustration 2.8: Converting the Divisor to a Whole Number

Divisor with one decimal place:

652.46 ÷ 0.6 ⟶ moving the decimal point one place to the right we get 6,524.6 ÷ 6

The mathematics behind moving the decimal point is simply that each number was multiplied by 10.

Divisor with two decimal places:

652.46 ÷ 0.06 ⟶ moving the decimal point two places to the right we get 65,246 ÷ 6

The mathematics behind moving the decimal point is simply that each number was multiplied by 100.

EXAMPLE 2.8 (A): Dividing Decimal Numbers

Divide 432.78 by 0.4

Solution:

To convert the divisor to a whole number, move the decimal point by one place (or multiply both the divisor and dividend by 10). As a result we get, 4,327.8 ÷ 4

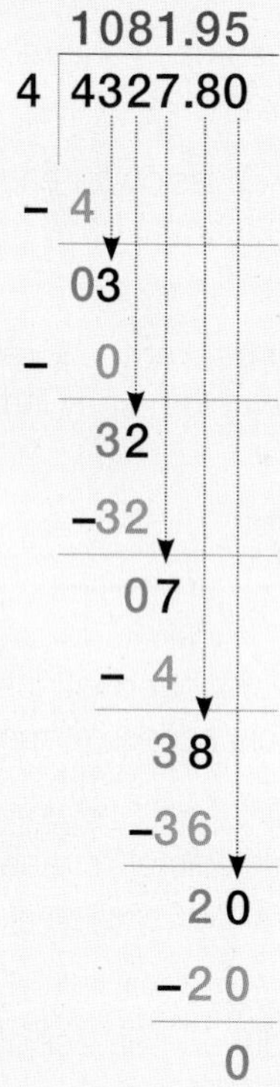

Q: How many times does 4 go into 4? A: 1
Q: What is 4 × 1? A: 4
Q: What is the remainder? A: 4 − 4 = 0
Q: What number do we bring down? A: 3
Q: How many times does 4 go into 3? A: 0
Q: What is 4 × 0? A: 0
Q: What is the remainder? A: 3 − 0 = 3
Q: What number do we bring down? A: 2
Q: How many times does 4 go into 32? A: 8
Q: What is 4 × 8? A: 32
Q: What is the remainder? A: 0
Q: What number do we bring down? A: 7
Q: How many times does 4 go into 7? A: 1
Q: What is 4 × 1? A: 4
Q: What is the remainder? A: 7 − 4 = 3
Q: What number do we bring down? A: 8
Q: How many times does 4 go into 38? A: 9
Q: What is 4 × 9? A: 36
Q: What is the remainder? A: 38 − 36 = 2
Q: What number do we bring down? A: 0
Q: How many times does 4 go into 20? A: 5
Q: What is 4 × 5? A: 20
Q: What is the remainder? A: 20 − 20 = 0

The decimal place moves straight up into the answer. Therefore, 432.78 divided by 0.4 is 1,081.95. Note how we added 0's after the decimal as needed and then stopped when there was no remainder.

EXAMPLE 2.8 (B): Dividing Decimal Numbers

Divide 57.584 by 0.06

Solution:

To convert the divisor to a whole number, move the decimal point by two places (or multiply both numbers by 100). As a result we get, 5,758.4 ÷ 6

```
     959.733
 6 | 5758.400
 - 54
   ----
    35
  - 30
   ----
     58
    -54
   ----
      44
     -42
   ----
       20
      -18
   ----
        20
       -18
   ----
         2
```

Therefore, dividing 57.584 by 0.06 we get a quotient of 959.733... which is rounded to 959.73.

Even if we are dividing a whole number by a whole number, we may still need to add a decimal point followed by zeros to the dividend. For example, when dividing 25 by 4, 4 is the divisor and 25 is the dividend. Since we know that 4 cannot go into 25 a whole number of times, we add a decimal point and zeros after the 25. The details of this can be seen in the following example.

EXAMPLE 2.8 (C): Dividing Whole Numbers and Answer is a Decimal

Divide 25 by 4.

Solution:

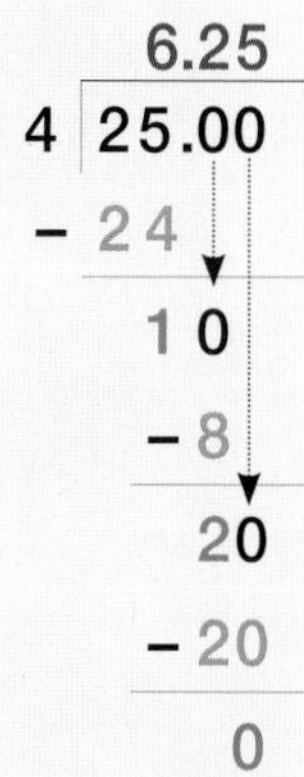

Q: How many times does 4 go into 2? A: 0

Q: How many times does 4 go into 25? A: 6

Q: What is 4 × 6? A: 24

Q: What is the remainder? A: 25 – 24 = 1

If we want the answer to be a mixed fraction, we would stop here and our answer would be $6\frac{1}{4}$ since 6 is the whole number, 1 is the remainder, and 4 is the divisor.

However, if we want a decimal answer, we continue by adding a decimal point and zeros after the whole number that is the dividend. We add a decimal point and as many zeros as needed after. Then we divide as before:

Q: What number do we bring down? A: 0

Q: How many times does 4 go into 10? A: 2

Q: What is 4 × 2? A: 8

Q: What is the remainder? A: 10 – 8 = 2

Q: What number do we bring down? A: 0

Q: How many times does 4 go into 20? A: 5

Q: What is 4 × 5? A: 20

Q: What is the remainder? A: 0

In order to round to two decimal places, it is mandatory to divide until you have three decimal places or no remainder, whichever comes first. In the above example, we reached a zero remainder and had two decimal places; therefore, the answer was complete. If the division can continue, then divide until you have three decimal places, in order to round to two decimal places.

2.8 EXERCISES

Answers to the odd numbered exercises are available at the end of the textbook.

1. Divide the following numbers:

a. 395 ÷ 0.5	b. 78.3 ÷ 0.8	c. 85.43 ÷ 5	d. 183.26 ÷ 0.04
e. 3.905 ÷ 0.6	f. 215.9 ÷ 0.04	g. 5.296 ÷ 0.02	h. 9.2304 ÷ 0.006

2. Divide the following numbers:

a. 9,314 ÷ 0.5	b. 652.1 ÷ 0.5	c. 702.52 ÷ 9	d. 184.36 ÷ 0.08
e. 7.246 ÷ 0.6	f. 947.6 ÷ 0.03	g. 31.257 ÷ 0.03	h. 4.598 ÷ 0.005

3. Four friends went out for dinner and decided to split the bill evenly. If the bill came to $132.87, how much would each person have to pay?

4. Five companies rented a venue to promote their respective products. They decided to share the cost of rent equally amongst themselves. If the total rent was $6,378.90, how much would each company have to pay?

5. A soccer coach bought a pack of a dozen soccer balls for $137.64. How much did each soccer ball cost?

6. Claire bought a large bag of flour that weighed 8.45 kg. If she planned to make three cakes of equal weight, how much flour would she use for each cake?

2.9 ESTIMATING DECIMAL NUMBERS

Estimation can be thought of as the process of finding an approximate value. This is done in situations when the exact answer to a question is not required. We often estimate values by rounding the numbers to whole numbers; however, there might be situations where you would like to know an approximate value that is closer to the exact value. When dealing with decimal numbers, we can estimate the answers to questions by rounding to different place values, depending on how close to the exact value we want our answer to be.

EXAMPLE 2.9: Estimating the Sum of Decimal Numbers

You pick up five items at the store and their prices are: $4.39, $2.80, $1.99, $2.45, and $4.79. You want to be able to estimate the approximate cost of your purchases. What is the estimated value of the amount you need to pay for these items?

Solution:

We need to estimate the sum of the numbers $4.39 + $2.80 + $1.99 + $2.45 + $4.79

The first step is to put the values in columnar format:

$4.39
$2.80
$1.99
$2.45
$4.79

The next step is to decide if we want to estimate to the nearest tenth or nearest whole number. For the purpose of this illustration we will show both.

	Rounding to the nearest whole number		Rounding to the nearest tenth	
	Actual Values	Estimated Values	Actual Values	Estimated Values
	$4.39	$4	$4.39	$4.40
	$2.80	$3	$2.80	$2.80
	$1.99	$2	$1.99	$2.00
	$2.45	$2	$2.45	$2.50
	$4.79	$5	$4.79	$4.80
Total:	$16.42	$16	$16.42	$16.50

In both cases the estimated value is close to the exact value; however, by rounding to the nearest tenth, we get a value that is closer to the exact value.

Similar procedures can be used to estimate the answers when dealing with subtraction, multiplication, and division. Round the numbers to the indicated place value, and then perform the required arithmetic operation. Compare to the actual value, if required.

2.9 EXERCISES

Answers to the odd numbered exercises are available at the end of the textbook.

For Exercises 1 to 4, estimate the sum or difference of the numbers by first rounding the numbers to the nearest whole number and nearest tenth. Compare the estimated and actual values.

1. a. 28.39 + 10.49 b. 6.66 + 9.69 c. 7.99 + 2.29 + 1.59 d. 2.25 + 5.85 + 4.50
2. a. 16.26 + 12.45 b. 7.75 + 5.99 c. 4.69 + 5.45 + 3.85 d. 3.15 + 8.75 + 12.80
3. a. 6.87 – 1.15 b. 15.23 – 6.94 c. 62.83 – 35.46 – 12.90 d. 86.12 – 28.99 – 9.15
4. a. 34.66 – 24.25 b. 45.44 – 23.82 c. 121.72 – 64.25 – 25.70 d. 99.23 – 54.99 – 23.25

For Exercises 5 and 6, estimate the answers by rounding the numbers to the nearest tenth and then performing the required arithmetic operation. Compare the estimated and actual values.

5. a. 21.35 × 42.83 b. 45.132 × 19.455 c. 25.45 ÷ 4.99 d. 125.465 ÷ 25.034
6. a. 36.79 × 15.34 b. 120.536 × 15.288 c. 54.04 ÷ 8.99 d. 250.535 ÷ 50.025

For Exercises 7 and 8, estimate the answers by rounding the numbers to the nearest hundredth and then performing the required arithmetic operation. Compare the estimated and actual values.

7. a. 89.4125 + 92.9999 b. 312.2552 – 110.1112 c. 40.5325 × 28.8999 d. 85.0455 ÷ 8.0034
8. a. 65.7811 + 78.9888 b. 245.6262 – 98.8229 c. 51.1535 × 50.5499 d. 45.4465 ÷ 5.0015

For Exercises 9 to 14, solve the estimation problems by rounding to the nearest tenth.

9. Nima wants to go on a three day trip with her friends. She decides to drive her car and wants to estimate the amount of gas she will spend. If she estimates that she will spend 25.50 L on the first day, 30.75 L on the second day, and 50.35 L on the third day, what is the approximate amount of gas she will use on this trip?

10. During the first four days of the week, Derek drove 12.25 km, 15.63 km, 9.87 km, and 17.92 km each day, respectively. If he estimates that he will drive another 45.50 km by the end of the week, what is the approximate number of kilometres that Derek will drive during the entire week?

11. Santiago had $155.50. He went to the store and purchased 5 items that cost $25.99, $19.25, $43.30, $12.89, and $52.49. Estimate how much money he will have left after paying for these items.

12. At the beginning of the month, you had a balance of $1,830.75 in your bank account. If during the month you withdrew $650.50 to spend on rent, $260.49 for food, and $367.25 for other expenses, what is the approximate balance in your bank account at the end of the month?

13. Sofiya went to the bookstore and purchased three books for $73.25 each, two notebooks for $5.99 each, a calculator for $15.89, and three pencils for $0.99 each. If she wants to estimate the total cost of these items, what would that cost be?

14. A small company has 5 employees and it pays each of them $17.25 per hour. If last week two employees worked 25.25 hours each, two employees worked 35.50 hours each, and one employee worked 40 hours, what is the approximate amount that the company will need to pay in total?

15. If you have $255.25 and you want to buy four presents of equal value, how much will each present cost you, approximately?

16. If you have $172.39 to spend equally for the next four days, estimate the amount you can spend each day.

REVIEW EXERCISES

Answers to the odd numbered exercises are available at the end of the textbook.

1. In the number 921.430865, what is the place value of each of the digits indicated below?

   a. 4 b. 8 c. 1 d. 9 e. 0
   f. 3 g. 2 h. 6 i. 5

2. In the number 613.520478, what is the place value of each of the digits indicated below?

   a. 4 b. 8 c. 1 d. 7 e. 0
   f. 3 g. 2 h. 6 i. 5

3. Express the decimal number 68.01239 in its expanded form.

4. Express the decimal number 93.20186 in its expanded form.

5. What digit in 23.308417 has the following place value?

   a. Tenths b. Tens c. Hundredths d. Thousandths
   e. Ones f. Ten thousandths g. Hundred thousandths

6. What digit in 75.654810 has the following place value?

   a. Tenths b. Tens c. Hundredths d. Thousandths
   e. Ones f. Ten thousandths g. Hundred thousandths

7. Express the following decimal numbers in their word form:

   a. 23.16 b. 560.178 c. 6.324
   d. $789.56 e. $538.09 f. $3000.05

8. Express the following decimal numbers in their word form:

   a. 78.43 b. 421.645 c. 9.321
   d. $832.21 e. $462.09 f. $2000.08

9. Express the following in their standard form:

   a. seven thousand dollars and sixty-nine cents
   b. forty-six and eight tenths
   c. one hundred and twenty-four thousandths
   d. fifty-six dollars and seventy-five cents
   e. one million, seven hundred forty-five dollars and twenty-three cents
   f. six hundred fifty dollars and eighty-nine cents

10. Express the following in their standard form:
    a. nine thousand dollars and nine cents
    b. sixty-six and seven tenths
    c. three hundred thousand and eighty-four thousandths
    d. seventy-six dollars and seventy-two cents
    e. three million, six hundred forty dollars and three cents
    f. nine hundred seventy dollars and eighty cents

11. Round 2,642.394021 to each place value indicated below:
    a. nearest thousandth
    b. nearest hundred
    c. nearest tenth
    d. nearest hundred thousandth

12. Round 53,645.182738 to each place value indicated below:
    a. nearest tenth
    b. nearest thousand
    c. nearest ten
    d. nearest hundred

13. Solve the following word problems.
    a. Julie used to drive 46.62 km each way to college every day. After she moved back home, she now drives 32.5 km each way from home to college. How many km less does she drive every week to college if she attends college five days per week?
    b. Samuel works part time at a Holiday Inn hotel to help with his school expenses. If he works 10.5 hours per week and earns $15 per hour, how much does he receive? His brother is also a college student and works 10 hours per week at a convenience store, and earns $14 per hour. Who earns the most per week and how much more do they earn?
    c. A college student had $2,500 in his account and received a few cheques from his part-time job at a restaurant in a hotel. The cheques were for $165.80, $274.60, and $94.50. If he deposited these cheques into his account, how much would he have in total?
    d. Four students rent an apartment that costs $1400 per month, which they share equally. They allow $500 each per month for food. How much does each student have to pay per month for rent and food?

14. Solve the following word problems.

    a. Sylvia, a part-time college student, spends as much time as possible at home with her three-year old daughter. On Monday she spends 3.5 hours, on Tuesday 5.5 hours, on Wednesday 3.75 hours, on Thursday 6.25 hours, and on Friday 5 hours. This helps lessen her child care expenses. Last year, Sylvia was able to spend 30 hours per week with her daughter. How many hours more, or less, did Sylvia spend with her daughter this year?

    b. Pavlo works part time as a city gardener to help his grandparents with their expenses. If he works 36 hours per week and needs to keep what he earns for 20 of those hours to cover his own expenses, how much can he give his grandparents if he earns $16 per hour?

    c. A college student had $3,500 in his account and had to pay for gas to drive between school and his part-time job. His gas bills were $40.10, $23.56, $30.00, $36.34, and $25.00. After he paid these bills, how much did he still have in his account for other expenses?

    d. Three sisters were given a travelling fund of C$6,000 from the estate of their deceased aunt. They spent $3,500 for airfare, $1,000 to stay in youth hostels, $800.50 on food, and $70.80 for souvenirs. How much, if any, did they have left?

    e. Ritu went to a thrift shop and bought two books for $50 each, three binders for $5.95 each, and four pens for $3.80 each. She wants to estimate the total cost of her purchases. How much should her estimate be if she estimates each purchase to the nearest dollar value?

CHAPTER 3

EXPONENTS, SIGNED NUMBERS, AND ORDER OF OPERATIONS

LEARNING OBJECTIVES

Studying this chapter will provide you with the knowledge needed to:

- Evaluate and simplify expressions involving exponents using rules of exponents.
- Perform arithmetic operations with exponents and signed numbers.
- Identify basic number properties.
- Identify and convert numbers from standard notation to scientific notation, and vice versa.
- Evaluate expressions using order of operations (BEDMAS).

TOPICS

3.1 EXPONENTS

Exponents are used in many disciplines, including technology and business.

In technology, exponents can be used to represent numbers in scientific notation, while in business they are often used in various mathematical calculations, such as formulas for mortgages and loans. When a number is raised to a positive exponent 'n', the resulting answer is the number multiplied by itself 'n' times.

Exponent Formula

Exponential Notation — Standard Notation

$$\overbrace{a^n} = \underbrace{\overbrace{a \times a \times a \times \ldots a}}_{n \text{ times}}$$

For example: $3^4 = 3 \times 3 \times 3 \times 3$

When it is necessary to multiply a number by itself a definitive number of times, the "exponent" or "power" can be used as shorthand to simplify notation.

For example, $2 \times 2 \times 2 \times 2 = 16$ can be written in exponential notation as 2^4. In this notation or format, 2 is the **base**; the number that is going to be multiplied by itself 4 times. 4 is referred to as the **exponent** (or power).

2^4 — 4: Exponent (or power); 2: Base

Similarly: $4 \times 4 \times 7 \times 7 \times 7$ can be written as $4^2 \times 7^3$

EXAMPLE 3.1 (A): Expressing Repeated Multiplications in Exponential Notation

Express the following repeated multiplications in exponential notation and then evaluate.

i $3 \times 3 \times 3$ ii $4 \times 4 \times 4 \times 4 \times 4$ iii $7 \times 7 \times 7 \times 7 \times 7 \times 7$

Solution:

i $\underbrace{3 \times 3 \times 3}_{3 \text{ factors of } \mathbf{3}} = \mathbf{3}^3 = 27$

ii $\underbrace{4 \times 4 \times 4 \times 4 \times 4}_{5 \text{ factors of } \mathbf{4}} = \mathbf{4}^5 = 1024$

iii $\underbrace{7 \times 7 \times 7 \times 7 \times 7 \times 7}_{6 \text{ factors of } \mathbf{7}} = \mathbf{7}^6 = 117{,}649$

EXAMPLE 3.1 (B): Expressing Exponents (Powers) in Standard Notation

Express the following powers in standard notation and then evaluate:

i 4^3 ii 5^4 iii 2^5

Solution:

i $4^3 = 4 \times 4 \times 4 = 64$

ii $5^4 = 5 \times 5 \times 5 \times 5 = 625$

iii $2^5 = 2 \times 2 \times 2 \times 2 \times 2 = 32$

3.1 EXERCISES

Answers to the odd numbered exercises are available at the end of the textbook.

In Exercises 1 and 2, express the repeated multiplications in exponential notation.

1. a. $9 \times 9 \times 9 \times 6 \times 6 \times 6 \times 6$
   b. $2 \times 2 \times 3 \times 3 \times 4 \times 4$
   c. $4 \times 4 \times 2 \times 2 \times 2 \times 2 \times 2$
   d. $2 \times 2 \times 3 \times 3 \times 4 \times 4 \times 5 \times 5$
   e. $1 \times 1 \times 5 \times 5 \times 2 \times 2 \times 2$
   f. $4 \times 4 \times 4 \times 2 \times 2 \times 2 \times 1 \times 1$

2. a. $3 \times 3 \times 2 \times 2$
   b. $9 \times 5 \times 5 \times 2 \times 2 \times 2 \times 2$
   c. $2 \times 2 \times 2 \times 2 \times 1 \times 1 \times 3 \times 3$
   d. $10 \times 10 \times 2 \times 2 \times 5 \times 3 \times 3$
   e. $5 \times 5 \times 2 \times 2 \times 10 \times 10 \times 10$
   f. $2 \times 2 \times 2 \times 5 \times 5 \times 5$

For Exercises 3 and 4, expand the exponents.

3. a. 2^7 b. 3^3 c. 10^6 d. 2^4
   e. 3^4 f. 4^4 g. 3^2 h. 5^1

4. a. 3^5 b. 5^3 c. 4^3 d. 9^2
   e. 2^5 f. 9^1 g. 5^4 h. 10^7

5. A square piece of land has each of its sides measuring 20 metres. Express the area of the piece of land using exponents and then calculate the area of the land. [Hint: Area of a square = Side^2]

6. Monique's square kitchen garden has each of its sides measuring 11 metres. Express the area of her garden using exponents and then calculate the area of the garden.

7. A cubic water tank has each of its sides measuring 5 metres. Express its volume using exponents and then calculate the volume. [Hint: Volume of a cube = Side^3]

8. Harun is building a cubic waste water treatment tank for his factory. He wants each of its sides to measure 3 metres. Express the volume of the tank using exponents and then calculate its volume.

9. If a square plate has an area of 64 square centimetres, express the area of the plate in its exponent form. What is the length of each side of the plate?

10. If the square cover on a swimming pool has an area of 49 m^2, express the area of the cover in its exponent form. What is the length of each side of the swimming pool?

11. If a cubic container contains 27 cubic metres of water, express the volume of the container in its exponent form. What is the length of each side of the container?

12. If a cubic water tank can hold a maximum of 64 metres^3 of water, express the volume of the tank in its exponent form. What is the length of each side of the tank?

3.2 ARITHMETIC OPERATIONS WITH EXPONENTS

Exponents allow us to perform arithmetic operations more easily than the standard form of a number. Since exponents are used in many different equations, it is important that we learn the basic rules that are followed to perform arithmetic operations with them.

In this section we will learn the basic rules used to perform arithmetic operations with exponents.

MULTIPLICATION OF EXPONENTS

Powers (exponents) with the same bases are multiplied by following the **Product Rule**. This rule states that to multiply powers with the same bases, their exponents should be added.

Product Rule

$$a^n \times a^m = a^{(n+m)}$$

For example:

$$2^2 \times 2^3 = (2 \times 2) \times (2 \times 2 \times 2)$$
$$= 2 \times 2 \times 2 \times 2 \times 2$$
$$= 2^{(2+3)}$$
$$= 2^5$$

EXAMPLE 3.2 (A): Simplifying Expressions Using the Product Rule

Express the following as a single exponent:

i $3^3 \times 3^5$ ii $51^5 \times 51^4$ iii $0.4^6 \times 0.4^2$

Solution:

i Using the Product Rule,

$3^3 \times 3^5$

$= 3^{(3+5)}$

$= 3^8$

ii Using the Product Rule,

$51^5 \times 51^4$

$= 51^{(5+4)}$

$= 51^9$

iii Using the Product Rule,

$0.4^6 \times 0.4^2$

$= 0.4^{(6+2)}$

$= 0.4^8$

DIVISION OF EXPONENTS

Powers with the same bases are divided by following the **Quotient Rule**. This rule states that when dividing powers with the same bases, their exponents should be subtracted.

Quotient Rule

$$a^n \div a^m = a^{(n-m)}$$

For example:

$$2^5 \div 2^3 = (2 \times 2 \times 2 \times 2 \times 2) \div (2 \times 2 \times 2)$$
$$= 2 \times 2$$
$$= 2^{(5-3)}$$
$$= 2^2$$

EXAMPLE 3.2 (B): Simplifying Expressions Using the Quotient Rule

Express the following as a single exponent:

i $4^6 \div 4^4$ ii $15^8 \div 15^5$ iii $0.5^7 \div 0.5^3$

Solution:

i Using the Quotient Rule,

$4^6 \div 4^4$

$= 4^{(6-4)}$

$= 4^2$

ii Using the Quotient Rule,

$15^8 \div 15^5$

$= 15^{(8-5)}$

$= 15^3$

iii Using the Quotient Rule,

$0.5^7 \div 0.5^3$

$= 0.5^{(7-3)}$

$= 0.5^4$

NEGATIVE EXPONENTS

Any number (base) raised to a negative exponent can also be expressed as a positive power in fractional form using the **Negative Exponent Rule**.

Negative Exponent Rule

$$a^{-n} = \frac{1}{a^n}$$

For example: $2^2 \div 2^3 = 2^{(2-3)} = 2^{-1}$ can also be expressed as $\frac{1}{2^1}$ or simply $\frac{1}{2}$

Similarly: $2^2 \div 2^3 = 2^{-1}$ can also be expressed as $(2 \times 2) \div (2 \times 2 \times 2) = \frac{4}{8} = \frac{1}{2}$

The fraction bar represents division. We will learn about fractions in Chapter 4.

ZERO (0) AS AN EXPONENT

The **Zero (0) as an Exponent Rule** states that any base with a zero as an exponent is equal to 1.

Zero (0) as an Exponent Rule

$$a^0 = 1$$

This rule can be explained as follows. We know that any number divided by itself is 1 , i.e. $5 \div 5 = 1$.

Similarly: $2^2 \div 2^2 = 1$ since $2^{(2-2)} = 2^0$, then $2^0 = 1$

These and other useful exponent rules are summarized in Table 3.2:

Table 3.2: Rules of Exponents

Rule		Example
Product Rule To multiply powers with the same bases, add the exponents.	$a^n \times a^m = a^{(n+m)}$	$2^3 \times 2^4 = 2^{(3+4)} = 2^7$
Quotient Rule To divide powers with the same bases, subtract the exponents.	$\frac{a^n}{a^m} = a^{(n-m)}$	$\frac{2^6}{2^4} = 2^{(6-4)} = 2^2$
Zero (0) as an Exponent Rule When a number is raised to the exponent 0, the resulting answer is 1.	$a^0 = 1$	$6^0 = 1$

Table 3.2: Rules of Exponents ***continued***

Rule		Example
One (1) as an Exponent Rule When a number is raised to the exponent 1, the resulting answer is the number itself.	$a^1 = a$	$6^1 = 6$
Power of a Power Rule When raising a power to a power, multiply the exponents.	$\left(a^m\right)^n = a^{(n \times m)}$	$\left(3^3\right)^4 = 3^{(3 \times 4)} = 3^{12}$
Power of a Quotient Rule When a fraction is raised to a positive exponent '*n*', the resulting answer is the fraction multiplied by itself '*n*' times, and is the same as the numerator and denominator each being raised to the power '*n*'.	$\left(\frac{a}{b}\right)^n = \left(\frac{a}{b}\right) \times \left(\frac{a}{b}\right) \times \left(\frac{a}{b}\right) \ldots \times \left(\frac{a}{b}\right) = \frac{a^n}{b^n}$	$\left(\frac{3}{4}\right)^3 = \frac{3}{4} \times \frac{3}{4} \times \frac{3}{4} = \frac{3^3}{4^3}$
Negative Exponent Rule When a number is raised to a negative exponent '$-n$', the resulting answer is the reciprocal of that number, raised to the positive exponent '*n*'.	$a^{-n} = \frac{1}{a^n}$	$2^{-3} = \frac{1}{2^3} = \frac{1}{2} \times \frac{1}{2} \times \frac{1}{2}$
Fractions with Negative Exponents Rule When a fraction is raised to a negative exponent '$-n$', the resulting answer is the reciprocal of that fraction multiplied by itself '*n*' times.	$\left(\frac{a}{b}\right)^{-n} = \left(\frac{b}{a}\right)^n$	$\left(\frac{2}{3}\right)^{-4} = \left(\frac{3}{2}\right)^4 = \frac{3}{2} \times \frac{3}{2} \times \frac{3}{2} \times \frac{3}{2}$
Fractional Exponents Rule Fractional exponents are expressed using radical notation (roots).	$a^{\frac{1}{b}} = \sqrt[b]{a}$	$8^{\frac{1}{3}} = \sqrt[3]{8} = 2$

EXAMPLE 3.2 (C): Evaluating Expressions Using the Rules of Exponents

Evaluate the following expressions:

i $5^3 \times 5^4 \div 5^5$

ii $3^2 \times 3^0$

Solution:

i $5^3 \times 5^4 \div 5^5$

$= 5^{(3 + 4 - 5)}$

$= 5^2$

$= 5 \times 5$

$= 25$

ii $3^2 \times 3^0$

$= 3^{(2 + 0)}$

$= 3^2$

$= 3 \times 3$

$= 9$

EXAMPLE 3.2 (D): Evaluating Expressions Using the Fraction Exponent Rule

Evaluate the following expression:

$64^{\frac{1}{3}}$

Solution:

$64^{\frac{1}{3}}$

$= \sqrt[3]{64}$

$= 4$

EXAMPLE 3.2 (E): Evaluating Expressions Using the Rules of Exponents

Evaluate the following expression:

$64^{\frac{1}{3}} \times 4^0$

Solution:

$64^{\frac{1}{3}} \times 4^0$

$= \sqrt[3]{64} \times 1$

$= 4 \times 1$

$= 4$

EXAMPLE 3.2 (F): Evaluating Expressions Using the Fraction Exponent Rule

Evaluate the following expressions:

i $125^{\frac{4}{3}}$ ii $9^{\frac{3}{2}}$

Solution:

i In this case, we can change this to 125 to the power of $\frac{1}{3}$, and then put that to the power of 4. This allows us to express it in radical notation (root). Since $\frac{1}{3} \times 4 = \frac{4}{3}$, we are simply expressing it differently.

Therefore,

$125^{\frac{4}{3}}$

$= \left(125^{\frac{1}{3}}\right)^4$

$= 5^4$

$= 625$

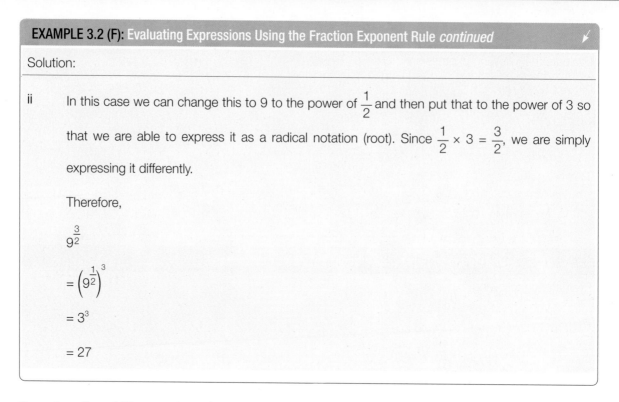

EXAMPLE 3.2 (F): Evaluating Expressions Using the Fraction Exponent Rule *continued*

Solution:

ii In this case we can change this to 9 to the power of $\frac{1}{2}$ and then put that to the power of 3 so that we are able to express it as a radical notation (root). Since $\frac{1}{2} \times 3 = \frac{3}{2}$, we are simply expressing it differently.

Therefore,

$9^{\frac{3}{2}}$

$= \left(9^{\frac{1}{2}}\right)^3$

$= 3^3$

$= 27$

To perform the addition or subtraction of powers, simply evaluate each power then perform the operation.

For example: $3^3 + 3^2 = (3 \times 3 \times 3) + (3 \times 3) = 27 + 9 = 36$

Similarly: $3^3 - 3^2 = (3 \times 3 \times 3) - (3 \times 3) = 27 - 9 = 18$

APPLICATION OF EXPONENTIAL NOTATION - SCIENTIFIC NOTATION

It is important to understand that in business and science, very large or very small numbers are expressed using scientific notation. In scientific notation, numbers are written in the form of: $a \times 10^b$, where '*a*', also known as the coefficient, is always multiplied by the base 10 to the power of '*b*'.

For example, we could say that the population of Canada is approximately 37,000,000 or we can express the number in scientific notation as 3.7×10^7.

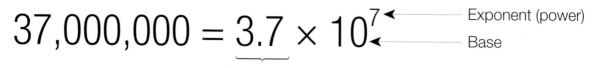

$$37{,}000{,}000 = \underbrace{3.7}_{\text{Coefficient}} \times 10^7$$

Exponent (power)

Base

The coefficient must always be a number greater than or equal to 1 and less than 10.

Did You Know?

In 2012, a petition on the White House website for the government to begin construction on a Star Wars inspired "Death Star" space station garnered over 34,000 signatures. It was estimated that the project would cost \$850 quadrillion, or \$850,000,000,000,000,000. What is this number in scientific notation?

EXAMPLE 3.2 (G): Converting Numbers from Standard Notation to Scientific Notation

i The approximate distance from the earth to the moon is 382,400 km. Express this number in scientific notation.

ii The approximate distance from the earth to the sun is 1,496,000,000 km. Express this number in scientific notation.

Solution:

i Expressing 382,400 km in scientific notation:

Step 1: Move the decimal point to the left, until the coefficient is greater than or equal to 1 and less than 10.

382,400.

Step 2: Count the number of times the decimal moved to the left. This number will be the exponent on the base of 10. Write the number in scientific notation.

$$3.824 \times 10^5$$

ii Expressing 1,496,000,000 km in scientific notation:

Step 1: Move the decimal point to the left, until the coefficient is greater than or equal to 1 and less than 10.

1,496,000,000.

Step 2: Count the number of times the decimal moved to the left. This number will be the exponent of the base of 10. Write the number in scientific notation.

$$1.5 \times 10^9$$

Note: The coefficient is rounded to one decimal place in this example.

For very small numbers, the decimal place must be moved to the right and the exponent is negative. i.e., $0.000089 = 8.9 \times 10^{-5}$

3.2 EXERCISES

Answers to the odd numbered exercises are available at the end of the textbook.

For Exercises 1 to 6, evaluate using the Exponent Rules, wherever applicable.

1. a. 3^3 b. $4^2 - 2^3$ c. $5^3 - 4^2$
   d. $3^4 + 6^0$ e. $3^2 \times 3^4$ f. $2^2 \times 2^3$

2. a. 4^2 b. $5^2 - 4^2$ c. $6^2 - 3^0$
   d. $8^0 + 5^3$ e. $5^2 \times 5^1$ f. $3^2 \times 3^0$

3. a. $3^2 \times 3^3$ b. $10^8 \div 10^6$ c. $27^7 \div 27^6$
   d. $32^5 \div 32^4$ e. $36^{\frac{1}{2}}$ f. $125^{\frac{1}{3}}$
   g. $\left(125^{\frac{1}{3}}\right)(5^0)$ h. $8^{\frac{2}{3}}$ i. $4^{\frac{3}{2}}$

4. a. $2^3 \times 2^4$ b. $9^7 \div 9^5$ c. $30^8 \div 30^6$
   d. $20^6 \div 20^4$ e. $49^{\frac{1}{2}}$ f. $8^{\frac{1}{3}}$
   g. $\left(64^{\frac{2}{3}}\right)\left(8^{\frac{1}{3}}\right)$ h. $27^{\frac{2}{3}}$ i. $8^{\frac{4}{3}}$

5. a. $\left(2^3\right)^2$ b. $\left(4^3\right)^0$ c. $\left(3^2\right)^3$
   d. $\left(1^6\right)^9$ e. $(\sqrt[3]{27})\sqrt[3]{8}$ f. $(\sqrt[3]{7})^3$

6. a. $\left(1^2\right)^3$ b. $\left(5^2\right)^1$ c. $\left(3^2\right)^0$
   d. $\left(2^2\right)^1$ e. $(\sqrt[3]{64})\sqrt[3]{1}$ f. $(\sqrt[3]{25})^3$

For Exercises 7 to 10, use the Exponent Rules to simplify, wherever possible, and express the answer in its expanded form.

7. a. $2^4 \times 2^2$ b. $3^2 \times 3^4 \times 3^2$ c. $6^2 \times 6^2 \times 6^0$ d. $4^6 \times 4^3 \div 4^4$
   e. $3^5 \div 3^2$ f. $7^8 \div 7^4 \div 7^2$ g. $8^5 \div 8^0 \div 8^2$ h. $2^7 \div 2^4 \times 2^5$

8. a. $6^5 \times 6^4$ b. $4^3 \times 4^2 \times 4^5$ c. $7^5 \times 7^0 \times 7^2$ d. $3^7 \times 3^9 \div 3^6$
   e. $2^5 \div 2^3$ f. $9^9 \div 9^3 \div 9^4$ g. $5^6 \div 5^4 \div 5^0$ h. $8^8 \div 8^4 \times 8^3$

9. a. $3^4 \times 3^2$ b. $6^2 \times 6^3 \times 6^0$ c. $5^3 + 5^2$ d. $4^2 + 4^1 - 4^0$
   e. $10^5 \div 10^3$ f. $3^3 \div 3^1 \div 3^0$ g. $4^2 + 2^2$ h. $5^3 - 3^4$

10. a. $7^3 \times 7^1$ b. $9^2 \times 9^0 \times 9^3$ c. $2^4 + 2^6$ d. $3^6 + 3^1 - 3^2$
    e. $12^2 \div 12^0$ f. $8^4 \div 8^0 \div 8^2$ g. $9^4 + 3^0$ h. $6^3 - 4^2$

In Exercises 11 and 12, convert the numbers from standard notation to scientific notation.

11. a. 369,000,000 b. 4,210,000 c. 45,000,000,000 d. 0.0001

12. a. 650,000 b. 8,000,000 c. 35,500,000 d. 54.9

In Exercises 13 and 14, convert the numbers from scientific notation to standard notation.

13. a. 2.62×10^4 b. 1.3×10^8 c. 6.99×10^6 d. 5.02×10^4

14. a. 1.3×10^3 b. 6.99×10^9 c. 9.8×10^5 d. 6.9×10^7

3.3 SIGNED NUMBERS

Numbers have a positive or negative sign in front of them. If they have a positive sign (or no sign), then their value is greater than 0. However, if they have a negative sign, then their value is less than 0.

Illustration 3.3: Number Line

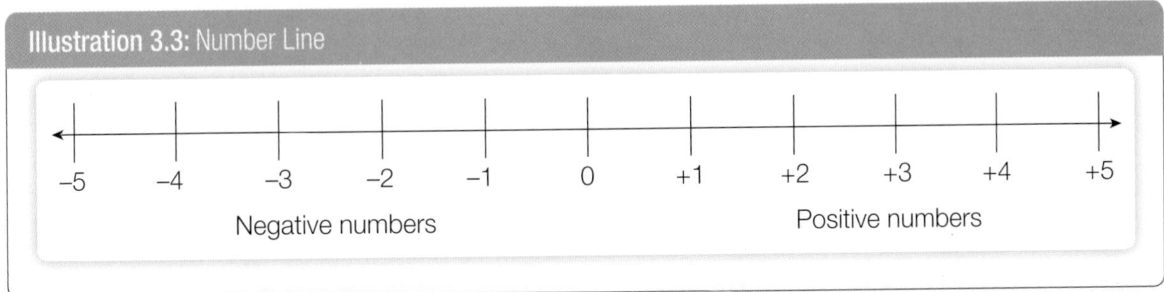

Did You Know?

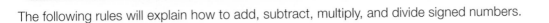

Signed number are also referred to as integers.

The following rules will explain how to add, subtract, multiply, and divide signed numbers.

ADDING SIGNED NUMBERS

- When the sign of both numbers being added is the same (positive or negative), add the numbers and keep the common sign.

For example:

$(+3) + (+4) = +7 \longleftrightarrow 3 + 4 = 7$

$(-3) + (-4) = -7 \longleftrightarrow -3 - 4 = -7$

$(-43) + (-21) = -64 \longleftrightarrow -43 - 21 = -64$

$(+43) + (+21) = +64 \longleftrightarrow 43 + 21 = 64$

- When the signs of both numbers being added are different, subtract the numbers and the result has the sign of the larger number.

For example:

$(+8) + (-2) = +6 \longleftrightarrow 8 - 2 = 6$

$(-8) + (+2) = -6 \longleftrightarrow -8 + 2 = -6$

$(-43) + (+21) = -22 \longleftrightarrow -43 + 21 = -22$

$(+43) + (-21) = +22 \longleftrightarrow 43 - 21 = 22$

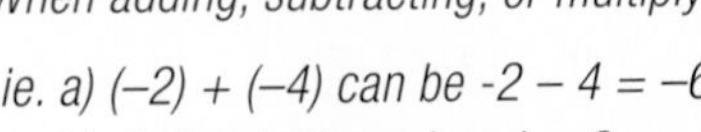

tip

When adding, subtracting, or multiplying signed numbers, you can remove the brackets.

ie. a) $(-2) + (-4)$ can be $-2 - 4 = -6$

b) $(-4) - (-3)$ can be $-4 + 3 = -1$

c) $(6) \times (-3)$ can be $6 \times (-3) = -18$

Did You Know?

At –90°F, your breath will freeze mid-air and drop to the ground!

SUBTRACTING SIGNED NUMBERS

- When subtracting signed numbers, rewrite the subtraction problem as an addition problem. This is done by adding the opposite of the number to be subtracted. Then follow the rules for adding signed numbers as previously explained.

For example:

$8 - 6 = 2 \longleftrightarrow 8 - (+6) = 2 \longleftrightarrow 8 + (-6) = 2$

$-4 - 3 = -7 \longleftrightarrow -4 - (+3) = -7 \longleftrightarrow (-4) + (-3) = -7$

$-3 - 5 = -8 \longleftrightarrow -3 - (+5) = -8 \longleftrightarrow -3 + (-5) = -8$

$(-218) - (+137) = -355 \longleftrightarrow (-218) - (+137) = -355 \longleftrightarrow -218 + (-137) = -355$

MULTIPLYING AND DIVIDING SIGNED NUMBERS

- When both numbers being multiplied or divided have the same sign (positive or negative), the answer is positive.

For example:

$(+3) \times (+4) = +12 \longleftrightarrow (+12) \div (+3) = +4$

$(-2) \times (-5) = +10 \longleftrightarrow (-10) \div (-5) = +2$

$(+24) \times (+6) = +144 \longleftrightarrow (+144) \div (+6) = +24$

$(-13) \times (-106) = +1378 \longleftrightarrow (-1378) \div (-13) = +106$

- When both numbers being multiplied or divided have different signs, the answer is negative.

For example:

$(+3) \times (-4) = -12 \longleftrightarrow (+12) \div (-3) = -4$

$(-49) \times (+5) = -245 \longleftrightarrow (-245) \div (+5) = -49$

$(-13) \times (+15) = -195 \longleftrightarrow (-195) \div (+15) = -13$

3.3 EXERCISES

Answers to the odd numbered exercises are available at the end of the textbook.

In Exercises 1 and 2, add the signed numbers.

1. a. $12 + 8$ b. $11 + (-7)$
   c. $9 + (-12)$ d. $-14 + 18$
   e. $-13 + 7$ f. $-14 + (-12)$
   g. $+328 + (-156)$ h. $-193 + 114$

2. a. $28 + 10$ b. $14 + (-9)$
   c. $2 + (-10)$ d. $-12 + 13$
   e. $-13 + 12$ f. $-18 + (-1)$
   g. $-273 + (-139)$ h. $-178 + 103$

In Exercises 3 and 4, subtract the signed numbers.

3. a. $18 - 11$ b. $10 - 13$
   c. $21 - (-1)$ d. $-19 - 12$
   e. $-9 - (-12)$ f. $-31 - (-7)$
   g. $119 - (-143)$ h. $-125 - 211$

4. a. $22 - 10$ b. $9 - 15$
   c. $17 - (-4)$ d. $-11 - 10$
   e. $-18 - (-19)$ f. $-18 - (-17)$
   g. $205 - (-102)$ h. $-147 - 241$

In Exercises 5 and 6, multiply or divide the signed numbers.

5. a. 3×5 b. $(-2)(-3)$
   c. $(+7)(-8)$ d. $(-6)(+4)$
   e. $15 \div 3$ f. $(-12) \div (-4)$
   g. $16 \div (-2)$ h. $(-20) \div 5$
   i. $105 \times (-14)$ j. $-255 \div 5$

6. a. 7×2 b. $(-4)(-9)$
   c. $(+2)(-2)$ d. $(-1)(+12)$
   e. $10 \div 5$ f. $(-14) \div (-7)$
   g. $14 \div (-2)$ h. $(-18) \div 9$
   i. $-230 \times (-12)$ j. $180 \div (-9)$

In Exercises 7 and 8, perform the arithmetic operations.

7. a. $2^3 - 4$ b. $-8 + 2^3$
   c. $-10 - 3^2$ d. $-6 + 4^3$

8. a. $4^3 - 16$ b. $-12 + 3^2$
   c. $-9 + 3^2$ d. $-15 - 5^2$

9. Jason had \$1,300 in his bank account at the beginning of the month. Throughout the month, he withdrew \$450 to pay for his rent, \$110 to pay for his transportation, and \$600 to pay for food. How much did he have left in his account? Assume that he earned no interest in the account.

10. Bisa had \$150 in her bank account. She then made deposits of \$400, \$1200, and \$56. How much did she have in her account after these deposits? Assume that she earned no interest in the account.

11. The average winter temperature in Edmonton two years ago was –11°C. However, the average winter temperature rose by 2°C last year. What was the average winter temperature last year?

12. The average winter temperature in Toronto two years ago was –5°C. However, the average winter temperature rose by 1°C last year. What was the average winter temperature last year?

13. Marco works 40 hours every week at a software company. If he worked for 5 weeks, what was the total number of hours worked?

14. Alice was paid $13 per hour for her work at a coffee shop. How much did she make last week if she worked for 35 hours?

15. Three friends equally shared the price of a take-out meal that cost $39. How much did each person have to pay?

16. Chang earned $84 for working 7 hours. How much did he earn per hour?

3.4 ORDER OF OPERATIONS (BEDMAS)

When performing operations in mathematics, it is important to follow the 'order of operations'. The set of rules that is followed when performing arithmetic operations is referred to **BEDMAS**. Each letter in 'BEDMAS' represents a mathematical operation, as follows:

B	Brackets - operations within brackets are performed first.
E	Exponents are performed next.
D M	Division and Multiplication are performed from left to right in the order that they appear.
A S	Addition and Subtraction are performed from left to right in the order that they appear.

Did You Know?

Another mnemonic device you can use to remember the order of operations is: **Please Excuse My Dear Aunt Sally** (parentheses, exponents, multiplication, division, addition, and subtraction)

The order of operations, BEDMAS, is described in the following illustration.

Illustration 3.4(A): Evaluating Expressions using Order of Operations

Evaluate the expression $(3 + 1)^2 - 5 + 5 \times 4 \div 2$

Order of Operations:	Example:
	$(3 + 1)^2 - 5 + 5 \times 4 \div 2$
1. Perform the operations within the brackets: $(3 + 1)$	$= 4^2 - 5 + 5 \times 4 \div 2$
2. Next, perform the operation with the exponent: 4^2	$= 16 - 5 + 5 \times 4 \div 2$
3. Perform the multiplication: 5×4	$= 16 - 5 + 20 \div 2$
4. Perform the division: $20 \div 2$	$= 16 - 5 + 10$
5. Perform the subtraction: $16 - 5$	$= 11 + 10$
6. Lastly, perform the addition: $11 + 10$	$= 21$

EXAMPLE 3.4: Evaluating Expressions with Multiple Arithmetic Operations

Evaluate the following expressions by following the order of operations, BEDMAS:

i $4 + 8^2 \times 15 \div 5$

ii $8 - 4 \times (4 - 2) \div (5 - 3)^2 + 3$

iii $6 + 2^2 \times [4 + (8 - 2)]^2 \div 4 - 5$

iv $5 - 3^2 \times (-2) + 10$

v $-15 \div 3 \times 7 - 8$

vi $6 + 4^2 \div 2 - (5 + 3) \times 4$

Solution:

i $4 + 8^2 \times 15 \div 5$ Evaluate the exponent

$= 4 + 64 \times 15 \div 5$ Multiply

$= 4 + 960 \div 5$ Divide

$= 4 + 192$ Add

$= 196$

ii $8 - 4 \times (4 - 2) \div (5 - 3)^2 + 3$ Perform the operations within the brackets

$= 8 - 4 \times 2 \div 2^2 + 3$ Evaluate the exponent

$= 8 - 4 \times 2 \div 4 + 3$ Multiply

$= 8 - 8 \div 4 + 3$ Divide

$= 8 - 2 + 3$ Subtract

$= 6 + 3$ Add

$= 9$

EXAMPLE 3.4 (A): Evaluating Expressions with Multiple Arithmetic Operations *continued*

Solution:

iii	$6 + 2^2 \times [4 + (8 - 2)]^2 \div 4 - 5$	Perform the operations within the inner brackets
	$= 6 + 2^2 \times (4 + 6)^2 \div 4 - 5$	Perform the operations within the outer brackets
	$= 6 + 2^2 \times 10^2 \div 4 - 5$	Evaluate the exponents
	$= 6 + 4 \times 100 \div 4 - 5$	Multiply
	$= 6 + 400 \div 4 - 5$	Divide
	$= 6 + 100 - 5$	Add
	$= 106 - 5$	Subtract
	$= 101$	
iv	$5 - 3^2 \times (-2) + 10$	Evaluate the exponent
	$= 5 - 9 \times (-2) + 10$	Multiply
	$= 5 - (-18) + 10$	Subtract (by adding the opposite)
	$= 5 + 18 + 10$	Add
	$= 23 + 10$	Add
	$= 33$	
v	$-15 \div 3 \times 7 - 8$	Divide
	$= -5 \times 7 - 8$	Multiply
	$= -35 - 8$	Subtract
	$= -43$	
vi	$6 + 4^2 \div 2 - (5 + 3) \times 4$	Perform operation within brackets
	$= 6 + 4^2 \div 2 - 8 \times 4$	Evaluate exponents
	$= 6 + 16 \div 2 - 8 \times 4$	Divide
	$= 6 + 8 - 8 \times 4$	Multiply
	$= 6 + 8 - 32$	Add
	$= 14 - 32$	Subtract
	$= -18$	

Illustration 3.4(B): Understanding the Importance of BEDMAS

Why should we use BEDMAS? Let's look at an example of what would happen if we didn't...

Penelope is the office manager at a school and needs to order dry erase markers for the classrooms. She needs 2 packages of 6 red markers, 3 packages of 6 blue markers, and 5 packages of a dozen (12) black markers. How many markers does she need in total?

Without BEDMAS:
$2 \times 6 + 3 \times 6 + 5 \times 12 = 1{,}140$

With BEDMAS:
$(2 \times 6) + (3 \times 6) + (5 \times 12)$
$= 12 + 18 + 60$
$= 90$

3.4 EXERCISES

Answers to the odd numbered exercises are available at the end of the textbook.

Evaluate Exercises 1 to 8 by following the order of operations, BEDMAS, without using a calculator.

1. a. $5 - (6 - 4)^2$ b. $6 + 3 - (5 - 2)^2$ c. $(9 + 3^2) - 2^2 + 9$ d. $[(12 + 3^2) - 4] - 4^2 + 8$
2. a. $(3 + 9) - 2 + 3$ b. $4^2 - 6 + 9 - 3$ c. $5 + 3 - (3 + 3)^2 - 1$ d. $2 + [2 + (14 - 6)]^2$
3. a. $4 \times 2 - 4 + 2$ b. $2 - 1 + (2 \times 4)^2$ c. $5(5 - 3)^2 + 2$ d. $(-2 + 4 \times 4)^2 - 3^2$
4. a. $-2 \times 4 - 3$ b. $-4 \times 3 \times (-4)$ c. $(3 + 2)^2 \times 4 - 25$ d. $-6 + 3^2 - (4 \times 3 - 9)$
5. a. $120 \div 2 \div 3$ b. $15 \div (-3) + 4$ c. $10 + 5 \div 1^2 - 3^2$ d. $50 \div 2 + 4^2 + (30 \div 3)^2$
6. a. $-20 \div 2 - (6 \div 3 + 4)$ b. $25 \div 5 + 3^2$ c. $3^2 + 8 \div 2^2 - (-2 - 4)$ d. $3^2 \div (5 + 2 - 3)^2$
7. a. $4 \times 4 \div 4 + (-2)$ b. $16 + 4 \times (8 - 4 \div 2)^2$ c. $30 \div 10 + 5 \times 2^2$ d. $(20 \div 4 \times 2)^2 - 36$
8. a. $-4 \times 6 + (90 \div 9 - 6)^2$ b. $(13 + 2 \times 3 - 9)^2 - 5^2$ c. $14 \div 2 \times 3 + 3^2$ d. $20 \times (2 \times 4 \div 2 - 2)^2$

Evaluate Exercises 9 to 16 by following the order of operations, BEDMAS, using a calculator. Round answers to the nearest hundredth.

9. a. $101 - (13 - 3)^2$ b. $-15 + 3^2 + (4 - 6)$
   c. $4^2 - 5 + (-15)$ d. $(25 - 15)^2 + 3 + 8^2$
10. a. $18 + (25 - 15)^2$ b. $(5^2 + 3)^2 - 15 \times 2 + 4$
    c. $-12^2 + 45 - (4^2 + 4)$ d. $250 - 10^2 + (12 - 6)^2$
11. a. $15 \times 3 \div (-5)^2 - 12$ b. $15(13 - 6)^2 \div (2 \times 40)^2$
    c. $23 - 13 \times (4^2 + 4) \div 3^2$ d. $-3 \times 4(28 \div 7)^2 \div 4$
12. a. $-8 \times 4^2 \div [(9 - 6)^2 \times 4]^2$ b. $(-4)(12)(-2)^2 \div 3$
    c. $16 \times (12 \div 6)^2 \times (-4)$ d. $125 \div 25 \times 15^2 \times (20 - 18)^2$
13. a. $[(12 + 6) \times (17+13)]^2 \div 4^2$ b. $[(18 - 6) \div (3 + 3)^2] \times 12$
    c. $12 + 4 \times 15 \div 25 + (21 \div 7)^2$ d. $(-18 \times 2) \times (5^2 + 3 - 4)^0$

14. a. $5(-4)^2 \div 3 + 12$
    b. $[4(15 + 5) \times 18 \div 6] \div 4^2$
    c. $4^2 - 3 \times 4 \div (2 + 3)^2 - 3$
    d. $6 \times (14 - 8)^2 \times 10 + 12^0$

15. a. $1,200[(1 + 0.025) - 1]^2$
    b. $250 \div (1 + 0.06)^2 \times 2$
    c. $3,000 \div \left(1 + 0.03 \times \frac{150}{365}\right)$
    d. $400 \times [(1 + 0.02)^2 - 1] \div 0.06$

16. a. $750[1 - (1 + 0.035)]^2$
    b. $1,500 \times (1.04)^2 \div 125$
    c. $675 \times (1 + 0.05)^2 \div 150$
    d. $2,250 \times [(1 + 0.05)^2 - 1] \times (1 + 0.04)$

REVIEW EXERCISES

Answers to the odd numbered exercises are available at the end of the textbook.

For Exercises 1 and 2 express the repeated multiplications in exponential notation.

1. a. $3 \times 3 \times 3 \times 5 \times 5 \times 5 \times 5 \times 5$
   b. $7 \times 7 \times 4 \times 4 \times 4 \times 4$
   c. $2 \times 2 \times 2 \times 6 \times 6 \times 9 \times 9 \times 9$
   d. $1 \times 1 \times 5 \times 5 \times 7 \times 7 \times 7$

2. a. $5 \times 5 \times 5 \times 1 \times 1$
   b. $9 \times 9 \times 3 \times 3 \times 3 \times 3 \times 7 \times 7$
   c. $4 \times 4 \times 4 \times 1 \times 1 \times 1$
   d. $6 \times 6 \times 8 \times 8 \times 8 \times 8 \times 8$

For Exercises 3 and 4 expand the exponents into standard notation.

3. a. 4^5 b. 8^4 c. 3^7 d. 7^4

4. a. 2^3 b. 5^6 c. 9^5 d. 6^4

Evaluate the expressions in Exercises 5 to 10 using the Exponent Rules wherever applicable. Round the number to the nearest hundredth wherever applicable.

5. a. $8^3 - 6^2$ b. $2^5 - 3^2$ c. $7^4 + 2^3$ d. $5^2 + 3^3$

6. a. $6^4 + 2^2$ b. $3^6 + 4^3$ c. $9^3 - 5^2$ d. $4^5 - 3^4$

7. a. $4^5 \times 4^3$ b. $6^7 \times 6^6$ c. $7^9 \div 7^5$ d. $9^7 \div 9^4$

8. a. $5^3 \times 5^5$ b. $8^4 \times 8^3$ c. $6^7 \div 6^6$ d. $4^8 \div 4^5$

9. a. $6^{\frac{1}{3}}$ b. $5^{\frac{3}{2}}$ c. $(4^4)^0$ d. $\left(\sqrt[3]{36}\right)^3$

10. a. $5^{\frac{1}{3}}$ b. $7^{\frac{3}{2}}$ c. $(6^3)^0$ d. $\left(\sqrt[3]{25}\right)^3$

For Exercises 11 and 12, use the Exponent Rules to simplify, wherever possible, and express the answer in its expanded form.

11. a. $3^4 \times 3^3$ b. $6^3 \times 6^4 \times 6^0$ c. $4^9 \div 4^5 \div 4^2$
    d. $7^8 \times 7^4 \div 7^7$ e. $5^2 + 8^2$ f. $7^3 - 4^3$

12. a. $5^3 \times 5^4$ b. $9^5 \times 9^7 \times 9^1$ c. $2^9 \div 2^4 \div 2^3$
    d. $4^6 \times 4^8 \div 4^5$ e. $7^3 + 3^4$ f. $5^4 - 2^3$

Convert the numbers in Exercises 13 and 14 from standard notation to scientific notation.

13. a. 425,000,000 b. 6,000,000 c. 12,000,000,000 d. 45.7

14. a. 35,000,000,000 b. 67.2 c. 9,000,000 d. 58,500,000

Convert numbers in Exercises 15 to 16 from scientific notation to standard notation.

15. a. 3.45×10^5 b. 5.7×10^6 c. 41.5×10^4 d. 9.21×10^5

16. a. 6.74×10^6 b. 53.1×10^5 c. 1.8×10^7 d. 4.75×10^4

Add or subtract the signed numbers in Exercises 17 and 18.

17. a. $14 + 7$ b. $8 + (-5)$ c. $-15 + (-5)$
d. $20 - 7$ e. $17 - (-3)$ f. $-12 - (-5)$

18. a. $13 + 5$ b. $9 + (-4)$ c. $-12 + (-8)$
d. $30 - 12$ e. $14 - (-6)$ f. $-8 - (-12)$

For Exercises 19 and 20, multiply or divide the signed numbers.

19. a. 6×7 b. $(3)(-6)$ c. $-5 \times (-5)$
d. $18 \div 6$ e. $-20 \div 4$ f. $-27 \div (-9)$

20. a. 3×11 b. $(5)(-8)$ c. $-4 \times (-7)$
d. $14 \div 2$ e. $-24 \div 8$ f. $-32 \div (-4)$

For Exercises 21 and 22, perform the arithmetic operations.

21. a. $4^3 - 28$ b. $-6 + 3^2$ c. $-18 - 2^3$ d. $9 + (-4^2)$

22. a. $2^3 - 16$ b. $-8 + 4^2$ c. $-21 - 3^2$ d. $7 + (-5^2)$

23. Ning had $1,500 in her bank account at the beginning of the week. She had to withdraw $600 for rent, $80 to pay her cellphone bill, and $120 for groceries. How much did she have left in the account? Assume that there was no interest earned in the account.

24. Victor had $600 in his wallet when he left for a city tour of Toronto. If he spent $75 at the CN Tower, $50 at Ripley's Aquarium, $35 for lunch, and $165 on shopping and souvenirs, how much did he have left?

25. Gloriana works 42 hours each week at a bank and is paid $18/hour. How much does she receive for 2 weeks of work?

26. Ashish works at a restaurant and his hours are different each week. Last week he worked 33 hours and this week he worked 41 hours. If he is paid $16/hour, how much will he receive in total for the 2 weeks?

27. The average coldest place on Earth is Antarctica. In the winter it can reach –40 degrees Celsius. If the temperature rises by 50 degrees in the summer, what would the temperature be in the summer?

28. The average temperature in Thunder Bay in December is –16 degree Celsius. In January, the temperature drops by 4 more degrees. What is the average temperature in January?

Evaluate the expressions in Exercises 29 and 30 using BEDMAS (without a calculator).

29. a. $6(5 - 2)^2 - 4 + 6$ b. $-12 + 4^2 + (5 - 9)$
c. $3^4 - 8 + (-20)$ d. $175 - 10^2 + (12 - 8)^2$

30. a. $18 + (40 - 25)^2$ b. $(6^2 + 4)^2 - 14 \times 3 + 7$
c. $-11^2 + 55 - (7^2 + 5)$ d. $175 - 10^2 + (12 - 8)^2$

CHAPTER 4

FRACTIONS

LEARNING OBJECTIVES

Studying this chapter will provide you with the knowledge needed to:

- Identify types of fractions.
- Convert improper fractions to mixed numbers.
- Convert mixed numbers to improper fractions.
- Find the reciprocal of a fraction.
- Reduce proper and improper fractions to their lowest terms.
- Reduce mixed numbers to their lowest terms.
- Find equivalent fractions.
- Convert proper and improper fractions to decimal numbers.
- Convert mixed numbers to decimal numbers.
- Perform arithmetic operations with fractions.

TOPICS

4.1 Introduction to Fractions

4.2 Addition and Subtraction of Fractions

4.3 Multiplication and Division of Fractions

4.1 INTRODUCTION TO FRACTIONS

A **fraction** is a number that is expressed as a **numerator** divided by a **denominator**. The numerator is the number on top and the denominator is the number on the bottom, as shown below:

$$\frac{3}{2} \begin{array}{l} \leftarrow \text{Numerator} \\ \leftarrow \text{Denominator} \end{array}$$

Fractions are commonly used in business. A simple example could include saying "I have completed half of the work"; half is a fraction that is represented by $\frac{1}{2}$.

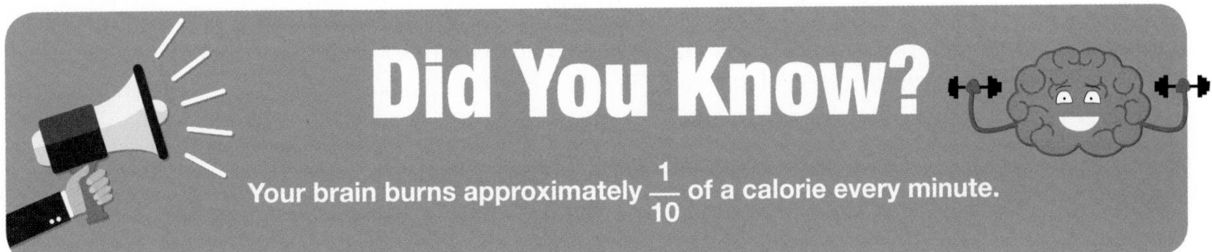

Did You Know?
Your brain burns approximately $\frac{1}{10}$ of a calorie every minute.

TYPES OF FRACTIONS

Fractions can be expressed in the following ways:

PROPER FRACTION

A **proper fraction** is a fraction in which the numerator is less than the denominator. In proper fractions, the value obtained by dividing the numerator by the denominator is less than 1.

For example: In the fraction $\frac{1}{2}$, the numerator, 1, is less than the denominator, 2; therefore, $\frac{1}{2}$ is a proper fraction. You will also notice that 1 divided by 2 is 0.5, which is less than 1.

IMPROPER FRACTION

An **improper fraction** is a fraction in which the numerator is greater than the denominator. In improper fractions, the value obtained by dividing the numerator by the denominator is greater than 1.

For example: In the fraction $\frac{7}{2}$, the numerator, 7, is greater than the denominator, 2; therefore, $\frac{7}{2}$ is an improper fraction. You will also notice that 7 divided by 2 is 3.5, which is greater than 1.

MIXED NUMBER

A **mixed number** is a number that is made up of a whole number and a proper fraction.

For example: $8\frac{1}{2}$, $12\frac{3}{5}$, $1\frac{5}{7}$ are examples of mixed numbers.

CONVERTING AN IMPROPER FRACTION TO A MIXED NUMBER

To convert an improper fraction to a mixed number, divide the numerator by the denominator to obtain a quotient and remainder. The quotient becomes the whole part of the mixed number, the remainder becomes the numerator of the fraction portion of the mixed number, and the divisor becomes the denominator of the fraction portion of the mixed number.

EXAMPLE 4.1 (A): Converting an Improper Fraction to a Mixed Number

Convert $\frac{26}{3}$ to a mixed number.

Solution:

Divide the numerator 26 by the denominator 3.

$$\begin{array}{r} 8 \leftarrow \text{Quotient} \\ 3\overline{)26} \\ -24 \\ \hline 2 \leftarrow \text{Remainder} \end{array}$$

Answer = $8\frac{2}{3}$

The quotient, 8, becomes the whole number portion of the mixed number.

The remainder, 2, becomes the numerator of the fraction portion of the mixed number.

The divisor, 3, becomes the denominator of the fraction portion of the mixed number.

Therefore, the improper fraction $\frac{26}{3}$ converted to a mixed number is $8\frac{2}{3}$.

CONVERTING A MIXED NUMBER TO AN IMPROPER FRACTION

To convert a mixed number to an improper fraction, multiply the whole number portion of the mixed number by the denominator of the fraction portion and then add the numerator to it. The result is a new numerator. The denominator will be the same as the denominator of the fraction portion of the mixed number.

EXAMPLE 4.1 (B): Converting a Mixed Number to an Improper Fraction

Convert $5\frac{3}{7}$ to an improper fraction.

Solution:

Multiply the whole number, 5, by the denominator of the fraction, 7.

$$5 \times 7 = 35$$

Add the numerator, 3, to the result.

$$35 + 3 = 38$$

38 is the new numerator, and 7 remains as the denominator of the improper fraction.

Therefore, $5\frac{3}{7}$ converted to an improper fraction is $\frac{38}{7}$.

THE RECIPROCAL OF A FRACTION

When the numerator and the denominator of a fraction are interchanged, the resulting fraction is the **reciprocal** of the original fraction.

For example: The reciprocal of $\frac{15}{2}$ is $\frac{2}{15}$

REDUCING PROPER AND IMPROPER FRACTIONS TO THEIR LOWEST TERMS

Reducing proper and improper fractions to their **lowest terms** involves dividing both the numerator and denominator of the fraction by the same non-zero number, until there is no common factor (other than 1) for the numerator and the denominator of the fraction.

For example:

$\frac{2}{4}$ reduced to its lowest terms is $\frac{2 \div 2}{4 \div 2} = \frac{1}{2}$

$\frac{3}{9}$ reduced to its lowest terms is $\frac{3 \div 3}{9 \div 3} = \frac{1}{3}$

EXAMPLE 4.1 (C): Reducing Improper Fractions to their Lowest Terms

Reduce $\frac{126}{30}$ to its lowest terms.

Solution:

$\frac{126}{30}$

$= \frac{126 \div 2}{30 \div 2}$ 126 and 30 share the common factor 2.

$= \frac{63}{15}$

$= \frac{63 \div 3}{15 \div 3}$ 63 and 15 share the common factor 3.

$= \frac{21}{5}$ This is the final answer as there is no common factor between 21 and 5 (other than 1).

Therefore, $\frac{126}{30}$ reduced to its lowest terms is $\frac{21}{5}$.

In a word problem, the improper fraction should be changed to a mixed number in lowest terms, unless you are directed in the question to leave it as an improper fraction.

Converting the answer to a mixed number in lowest terms, we obtain $4\frac{1}{5}$.

REDUCING MIXED NUMBERS TO THEIR LOWEST TERMS

To reduce mixed numbers to their lowest terms, reduce only the fractional portion to its lowest terms.

EXAMPLE 4.1 (D): Reducing Mixed Numbers to their Lowest Terms

Reduce $7\frac{6}{12}$ to its lowest terms.

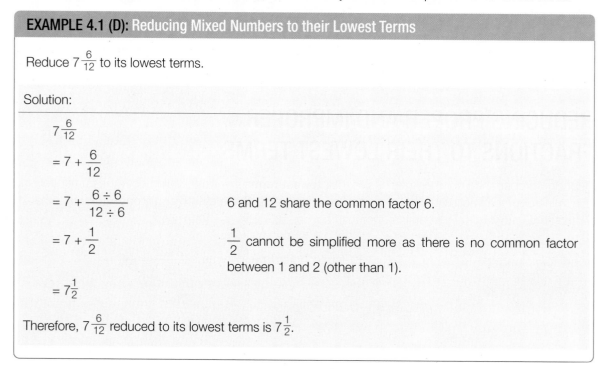

Solution:

$7\frac{6}{12}$

$= 7 + \frac{6}{12}$

$= 7 + \frac{6 \div 6}{12 \div 6}$ 6 and 12 share the common factor 6.

$= 7 + \frac{1}{2}$ $\frac{1}{2}$ cannot be simplified more as there is no common factor between 1 and 2 (other than 1).

$= 7\frac{1}{2}$

Therefore, $7\frac{6}{12}$ reduced to its lowest terms is $7\frac{1}{2}$.

EQUIVALENT FRACTIONS

The fractions obtained by dividing or multiplying the numerator and the denominator of a fraction by the same non-zero number are called **equivalent fractions**.

Illustration 4.1: Finding Equivalent Fractions

Find 2 equivalent fractions for $\frac{3}{9}$.

If we multiply both the numerator and the denominator of the fraction $\frac{3}{9}$ by 2, we obtain:

$$\frac{3 \times 2}{9 \times 2} = \frac{6}{18}$$

Now, if we divide the numerator and denominator of $\frac{6}{18}$ by 3, we obtain:

$$\frac{6 \div 3}{18 \div 3} = \frac{2}{6}$$

Therefore, $\frac{3}{9}$, $\frac{6}{18}$, and $\frac{2}{6}$ are all equivalent fractions.

You can find an equivalent fraction of a mixed number by dividing or multiplying the numerator and the denominator of the fractional portion of the mixed number by the same non-zero number.

For example: $4\frac{2}{8} = 4\frac{2 \div 2}{8 \div 2} = 4\frac{1}{4}$

CONVERTING PROPER AND IMPROPER FRACTIONS TO DECIMAL NUMBERS

To convert a proper or improper fraction to a decimal number, divide the numerator of the fraction by its denominator.

EXAMPLE 4.1 (E): Converting Fractions to Decimal Numbers

Convert the following fractions to decimal numbers:

i $\frac{1}{8}$

ii $\frac{5}{2}$

Solution:

i $\frac{1}{8} = 1 \div 8 = 0.125$

ii $\frac{5}{2} = 5 \div 2 = 2.5$

CONVERTING MIXED NUMBERS TO DECIMAL NUMBERS

To convert a mixed number to a decimal number, divide the numerator by the denominator, then add the result to the whole number.

EXAMPLE 4.1 (F): Converting Mixed Numbers to Decimal Numbers

Convert the following mixed numbers to decimal numbers:

i $2\frac{1}{4}$ ii $6\frac{7}{10}$

Solution:

i $2\frac{1}{4}$

$=2 + \frac{1}{4}$ Separate the whole number portion from the fraction portion.

$= 2 + (1 \div 4)$ Divide the numerator by the denominator.

$= 2 + 0.25$ Add the whole number and decimal portions.

$= 2.25$

ii $6\frac{7}{10}$

$= 6 + \frac{7}{10}$ Separate the whole number portion from the fraction portion.

$= 6 + (7 \div 10)$ Divide the numerator by the denominator.

$= 6 + 0.7$ Add the whole number and decimal portions.

$= 6.7$

4.1 EXERCISES

Answers to the odd numbered exercises are available at the end of the textbook.

Convert the improper fractions in Exercises 1 and 2 to mixed numbers.

1. a. $\frac{18}{4}$ b. $\frac{7}{5}$ c. $\frac{9}{4}$ d. $\frac{4}{3}$

   e. $\frac{43}{8}$ f. $\frac{5}{2}$ g. $\frac{23}{11}$ h. $\frac{15}{4}$

2. a. $\frac{27}{6}$ b. $\frac{10}{3}$ c. $\frac{12}{7}$ d. $\frac{9}{8}$

   e. $\frac{47}{4}$ f. $\frac{8}{3}$ g. $\frac{25}{12}$ h. $\frac{19}{3}$

Convert the mixed numbers in Exercises 3 and 4 to improper fractions.

3. a. $3\frac{1}{2}$ b. $6\frac{1}{4}$ c. $5\frac{2}{3}$ d. $4\frac{2}{5}$

   e. $1\frac{1}{4}$ f. $7\frac{1}{2}$ g. $5\frac{1}{5}$ h. $2\frac{1}{4}$

4. a. $4\frac{1}{3}$ b. $7\frac{1}{6}$ c. $2\frac{3}{4}$ d. $6\frac{4}{7}$

   e. $1\frac{1}{5}$ f. $5\frac{1}{3}$ g. $2\frac{1}{2}$ h. $9\frac{4}{5}$

5. Andrew scored $82\frac{1}{2}$ on his final exam. Express his score as an improper fraction.

6. Mila weighs $50\frac{2}{3}$ kg. Express her weight as an improper fraction.

7. Omar worked $\frac{27}{4}$ hours yesterday. Express the number of hours he worked as a mixed number.

8. Anya studied $\frac{13}{2}$ hours yesterday. Express her study time as a mixed number.

Find the reciprocal of the fractions in Exercises 9 and 10.

9. a. $\frac{3}{4}$ b. $\frac{9}{2}$ c. $-\frac{1}{5}$ d. $-\frac{19}{6}$

10. a. $\frac{6}{7}$ b. $\frac{1}{9}$ c. $-\frac{5}{26}$ d. $-\frac{47}{62}$

In Exercises 11 and 12, reduce the fractions or mixed numbers to their lowest terms.

11. a. $\frac{6}{12}$ b. $\frac{4}{20}$ c. $\frac{3}{18}$

    d. $\frac{12}{16}$ e. $\frac{10}{100}$ f. $\frac{15}{45}$

    g. $8\frac{2}{4}$ h. $11\frac{3}{9}$ i. $2\frac{5}{20}$

12. a. $\frac{5}{15}$ b. $\frac{6}{14}$ c. $\frac{9}{27}$

    d. $\frac{36}{48}$ e. $\frac{2}{20}$ f. $\frac{10}{25}$

    g. $5\frac{4}{8}$ h. $6\frac{4}{16}$ i. $1\frac{4}{12}$

In Exercises 13 and 14, find three equivalent fractions for each fraction given.

13. a. $\frac{1}{7}$ b. $\frac{10}{2}$ c. $4\frac{3}{5}$

14. a. $\frac{5}{20}$ b. $\frac{9}{3}$ c. $1\frac{1}{10}$

Convert the fractions in Exercises 15 and 16 to decimal numbers. Provide your answers rounded to two decimal places.

15. a. $\frac{1}{5}$ b. $\frac{3}{7}$ c. $\frac{5}{3}$ d. $7\frac{1}{3}$

    e. $2\frac{1}{2}$ f. $-\frac{3}{8}$ g. $-\frac{12}{5}$ h. $-\frac{15}{4}$

16. a. $\frac{1}{4}$ b. $\frac{4}{9}$ c. $\frac{7}{5}$ d. $9\frac{2}{5}$

e. $11\frac{3}{5}$ f. $-\frac{9}{11}$ g. $-\frac{15}{7}$ h. $-\frac{21}{6}$

17. Ruby worked $35\frac{3}{4}$ hours last week. Express the number of hours she worked as a decimal number.

18. The distance between Toronto and Waterloo is $117\frac{3}{8}$ km. Express this distance as a decimal number.

19. The price of a flight from Toronto to New York is $\$228\frac{1}{3}$. Express the price as a decimal number.

20. The time period of a loan is $8\frac{4}{11}$ years. Express the time period as a decimal number.

4.2 ADDITION AND SUBTRACTION OF FRACTIONS

Fractions must have the same denominator before they may be added or subtracted. You will learn to add and subtract fractions in cases where the denominators are the same, as well as in cases where the given fractions have different denominators.

ADDING OR SUBTRACTING FRACTIONS WHEN THE DENOMINATORS ARE THE SAME

When adding or subtracting fractions that have the same denominators:

- Add or subtract all the numerators. The result becomes the new numerator.
- The denominator will remain the same.

EXAMPLE 4.2 (A): Adding Fractions when the Denominators are the Same

Perform the arithmetic operations: $\frac{2}{10}+\frac{3}{10}+\frac{1}{10}$

Solution:

Add the numerators while keeping the denominator the same.

$$\frac{2}{10}+\frac{3}{10}+\frac{1}{10}=\frac{2+3+1}{10}=\frac{6}{10}$$

Reduce the answer to its lowest terms.

$$\frac{6\div 2}{10\div 2}=\frac{3}{5}$$

EXAMPLE 4.2 (B): Subtracting Fractions when the Denominators are the Same

Perform the arithmetic operations: $\frac{30}{18} - \frac{5}{18} - \frac{4}{18}$

Solution:

Subtract the numerators while keeping the denominator the same.

$$\frac{30}{18} - \frac{5}{18} - \frac{4}{18} = \frac{30 - 5 - 4}{18} = \frac{21}{18}$$

Reduce the answer to its lowest terms.

$$\frac{21 \div 3}{18 \div 3} = \frac{7}{6}$$

Note that when providing a solution to a word problem we should not leave an answer as an improper fraction, unless directed to do so.

Convert the answer to a mixed number.

$$\frac{7}{6} = 1\tfrac{1}{6}$$

EXAMPLE 4.2 (C): Adding Fractions and Mixed Numbers when the Denominators are the Same

Perform the arithmetic operations: $\frac{9}{2} + 2\tfrac{1}{2} + 3\tfrac{1}{2}$

Solution:

Add the whole numbers.

$$\frac{9}{2} + 2\tfrac{1}{2} + 3\tfrac{1}{2} = 5 + \frac{9}{2} + \frac{1}{2} + \frac{1}{2}$$

Add the fractions.

$$5 + \frac{9}{2} + \frac{1}{2} + \frac{1}{2} = 5 + \frac{11}{2}$$

Convert the fraction to a mixed number.

$$5 + \frac{11}{2} = 5 + 5\tfrac{1}{2} = 10\tfrac{1}{2}$$

ADDING OR SUBTRACTING FRACTIONS WHEN THE DENOMINATORS ARE DIFFERENT

To add or subtract fractions that have different denominators, it is necessary to first make all of the denominators the same. This can be done by following these steps:

- Check to see if the largest denominator is a multiple of the denominators of the other fractions.
    - If it is a multiple of the other denominators, then that number will be the denominator of the final answer.
    - If it is not a multiple of the other denominators, then the **Lowest Common Multiple** (LCM) of all the denominators (also called the Lowest Common Denominator of the fractions) will be the denominator of the final answer.
- Convert fractions to equivalent fractions with the same denominator.
- Perform the addition or subtraction as explained earlier.

Illustration 4.2: Finding the Lowest Common Multiple

Let's find the lowest common multiple (LCM) of the following numbers: 2, 4, 5.

To find the LCM, we must find the multiples of each of the numbers separately and identify the smallest multiple that they all have in common.

Multiples of 2 are 2, 4, 6, 8, 10, 12, 14, 16, 18, **20**...

Multiples of 4 are 4, 8, 12, 16, **20**, 24, 28, 32, 36, 40...

Multiples of 5 are 5, 10, 15, **20**, 25, 30, 35, 40, 45, 50...

20 is the smallest number which is a multiple of 2, 4, and 5.

Therefore, 20 is the LCM of 2, 4, and 5.

EXAMPLE 4.2 (D): Adding or Subtracting Fractions when the Largest Denominator is a Multiple of the Other Denominators

Perform the arithmetic operation: $\frac{1}{4}+\frac{11}{8}-\frac{3}{2}$

Solution:

The largest denominator, 8, is a multiple of the other denominators. Therefore, the common denominator will be 8.

Convert $\frac{1}{4}$ and $\frac{3}{2}$ to their equivalent fractions with 8 as the denominator.

$$\frac{1}{4}=\frac{1\times 2}{4\times 2}=\frac{2}{8}$$

$$\frac{3}{2}=\frac{3\times 4}{2\times 4}=\frac{12}{8}$$

Therefore, $$\frac{1}{4}+\frac{11}{8}-\frac{3}{2}=\frac{2}{8}+\frac{11}{8}-\frac{12}{8}$$

Now, as all of the denominators are the same, we can perform the arithmetic operations on the numerators:

$$\frac{2}{8}+\frac{11}{8}-\frac{12}{8}=\frac{2+11-12}{8}=\frac{1}{8}$$

EXAMPLE 4.2 (E): Adding or Subtracting Fractions by Finding the Lowest Common Multiple of the Denominators

Perform the arithmetic operation: $\frac{1}{2} + \frac{3}{5} - \frac{1}{3}$

Solution:

The largest denominator, 5, is not a multiple of the other denominators. Therefore, it is necessary to find the Lowest Common Multiple of the denominators of the three fractions.

Multiples of 2 are 2, 4, 6, 8, 10, 12, 14, 16, 18, 20, 22, 24, 26, 28, **30**..

Multiples of 5 are 5, 10, 15, 20, 25, **30**..

Multiples of 3 are 3, 6, 9, 12, 15, 18, 21, 24, 27, **30**..

The Lowest Common Multiple is 30.

Next, we convert each fraction to its equivalent fraction with a denominator of 30.

$$\frac{1}{2} = \frac{1 \times 15}{2 \times 15} = \frac{15}{30}$$

$$\frac{3}{5} = \frac{3 \times 6}{5 \times 6} = \frac{18}{30}$$

$$\frac{1}{3} = \frac{1 \times 10}{3 \times 10} = \frac{10}{30}$$

Therefore, $\frac{1}{2} + \frac{3}{5} - \frac{1}{3} = \frac{15}{30} + \frac{18}{30} - \frac{10}{30}$

Now that all of the denominators are the same, we can perform the arithmetic operations:

$$\frac{15}{30} + \frac{18}{30} - \frac{10}{30} = \frac{15 + 18 - 10}{30} = \frac{23}{30}$$

EXAMPLE 4.2 (F): Adding or Subtracting Mixed Numbers by Finding the LCM (Lowest Common Multiple) of Denominators

Perform the arithmetic operation: $2\frac{1}{4} + 4\frac{1}{3} - 1\frac{1}{2}$

Solution:

First perform the arithmetic operations on the whole numbers separately: (2 + 4 – 1) = 5

Next, find the LCM of the 3 denominators.

Multiples of 4 are 4, 8, **12**, 16, 20 ...

Multiples of 3 are 3, 6, 9, **12**, 15, 18 ...

Multiples of 2 are 2, 4, 6, 8, 10, **12**...

The LCM is 12.

EXAMPLE 4.2 (F): Adding or Subtracting Mixed Numbers by Finding the LCM (Lowest Common Multiple) of Denominators *continued*

Solution:

Next, we convert each fraction to its equivalent fraction with a denominator of 12.

$$\frac{1}{4}=\frac{1\times 3}{4\times 3}=\frac{3}{12}$$

$$\frac{1}{3}=\frac{1\times 4}{3\times 4}=\frac{4}{12}$$

$$\frac{1}{2}=\frac{1\times 6}{2\times 6}=\frac{6}{12}$$

Therefore, $\frac{1}{4}+\frac{1}{3}-\frac{1}{2}=\frac{3}{12}+\frac{4}{12}-\frac{6}{12}$

Since the denominators are now all the same, we can perform the arithmetic operations:

$$\frac{3}{12}+\frac{4}{12}-\frac{6}{12}=\frac{3+4-6}{12}=\frac{1}{12}$$

Adding back the sum of the whole numbers, the final answer is $5+\frac{1}{12}=5\frac{1}{12}$.

EXAMPLE 4.2 (G): Reducing a Final Answer from Improper Fraction to Mixed Number

Perform the arithmetic operation: $3\frac{2}{3}+5\frac{4}{5}$

Solution:

First add the whole numbers separately: 3+5 = 8

Next find the LCM of the 2 denominators:

Multiples of 3 are 3, 6, 9, 12, **15**, 18 ...

Multiples of 5 are 5, 10, **15**, 20, 25, 30 ...

The LCM is 15.

Next, we convert each fraction to its equivalent fraction with a denominator of 15.

$$\frac{2}{3}=\frac{5\times 5}{3\times 5}=\frac{10}{15}$$

$$\frac{4}{5}=\frac{4\times 3}{5\times 3}=\frac{12}{15}$$

Therefore, $\frac{10}{15}+\frac{12}{15}=\frac{22}{15}$.

Turning this improper fraction into a mixed number gives us, $1\frac{7}{15}$.

Adding back the sum of the whole numbers, the final answer is $8+1\frac{7}{15}=9\frac{7}{15}$.

EXAMPLE 4.2 (H): Reducing a Final Answer from Improper Fraction to Mixed Number

Perform the arithmetic operation: $2\frac{2}{4} + 4\frac{4}{6}$

Solution:

First add the whole numbers separately: $2 + 4 = 6$

Next find the LCM of the 2 denominators:

Multiples of 4 are 4, 8, **12**, 16, 20...

Multiples of 6 are 6, **12**, 18, 24, 30...

The LCM is 12.

Next, we convert each fraction to its equivalent fraction with a denominator of 12.

$$\frac{2}{4} = \frac{2 \times 3}{4 \times 3} = \frac{6}{12}$$
$$\frac{4}{6} = \frac{4 \times 2}{6 \times 2} = \frac{8}{12}$$

Therefore, $\frac{6}{12} + \frac{8}{12} = \frac{14}{12}$.

Turning this improper fraction into a mixed number gives us, $1\frac{2}{12}$.

You can reduce $1\frac{2}{12}$ even further because 2 can go into the 2 and 12. Therefore, $1\frac{2}{12} = 1\frac{1}{6}$.

Adding back the sum of the whole numbers, the final answer is $6 + 1\frac{1}{6} = 7\frac{1}{6}$.

EXAMPLE 4.2 (I): Subtracting a Proper Fraction from a Mixed Number

Perform the arithmetic operation: $1\frac{1}{4} - \frac{7}{8}$

Solution:

When we don't have whole numbers in both fractions, we first convert the mixed number to a fraction and then proceed.

Since $1\frac{1}{4} = \frac{5}{4}$ we can rewrite the subtraction as $\frac{5}{4} - \frac{7}{8}$.

The LCM for 4 and 8 is 8.

Next, we convert $\frac{5}{4}$ to its equivalent fraction with a denominator of 8.

$$\frac{5}{4} = \frac{5 \times 2}{4 \times 2} = \frac{10}{8}$$

Therefore, $\frac{10}{8} - \frac{7}{8} = \frac{3}{8}$.

EXAMPLE 4.2 (J): Two Methods for Adding Mixed Numbers

Calculate the number of hours that Adam worked in the week

Monday	$4\frac{1}{2}$
Tuesday	$6\frac{3}{4}$
Wednesday	$5\frac{1}{4}$
Thursday	$7\frac{1}{2}$
Friday	$5\frac{3}{4}$

Solution:

There are 2 ways to approach solving this question:

Option 1: Convert the fractions to decimals and then add

Monday	$4\frac{1}{2} = 4.50$
Tuesday	$6\frac{3}{4} = 6.75$
Wednesday	$5\frac{1}{4} = 5.25$
Thursday	$7\frac{1}{2} = 7.50$
Friday	$5\frac{3}{4} = 5.75$
Total Hours =	29.75

Option 2: Add in fraction form

$$4\frac{1}{2} + 6\frac{3}{4} + 5\frac{1}{4} + 7\frac{1}{2} + 5\frac{3}{4}$$

Add the whole numbers first $4 + 6 + 5 + 7 + 5 = 27$

The LCM for the denominators is 4 therefore convert all denominators to 4 and add the fractions

$$\frac{2}{4} + \frac{3}{4} + \frac{1}{4} + \frac{2}{4} + \frac{3}{4} = \frac{11}{4}$$

Convert the improper fraction to mixed number $\frac{11}{4} = 2\frac{3}{4}$

Add the whole number with the fraction to get a final answer of $\mathbf{27 + 2\frac{3}{4} = 29\frac{3}{4} = 29.75}$.

4.2 EXERCISES

Answers to the odd numbered exercises are available at the end of the textbook.

For Exercises 1 to 12, find the Lowest Common Multiple of the given numbers.

1. 3 and 7
2. 4 and 5
3. 4 and 6
4. 2 and 3
5. 4 and 9
6. 3 and 10
7. 6 and 8
8. 5 and 7
9. 2, 4, and 5
10. 3, 5, and 6
11. 3, 6, and 8
12. 4, 5, and 10

Perform the addition operations in Exercises 13 and 14. Reduce your answers to their lowest terms.

13. a. $\frac{3}{5}+\frac{1}{5}+\frac{6}{5}$ b. $1\frac{1}{2}+3\frac{3}{2}$ c. $\frac{9}{4}+2\frac{3}{4}+4\frac{6}{4}$
 d. $\frac{1}{3}+\frac{5}{9}+\frac{7}{6}$ e. $3\frac{3}{4}+1\frac{3}{2}$ f. $\frac{1}{5}+3\frac{1}{6}+7\frac{3}{10}$
 g. $1\frac{3}{6}+2\frac{1}{8}$ h. $3\frac{1}{2}+2\frac{1}{3}+3\frac{1}{2}$ i. $8+1\frac{2}{3}+6\frac{1}{8}$

14. a. $\frac{1}{5}+\frac{6}{5}+\frac{8}{5}$ b. $4\frac{7}{3}+7\frac{6}{3}$ c. $\frac{6}{2}+1\frac{6}{2}+2\frac{7}{2}$
 d. $\frac{1}{7}+\frac{2}{14}+\frac{3}{21}$ e. $1\frac{2}{6}+3\frac{1}{16}$ f. $\frac{5}{2}+2\frac{5}{6}+5\frac{1}{2}$
 g. $7+2\frac{8}{6}+1\frac{3}{2}$ h. $9+3\frac{3}{4}+1\frac{1}{4}$ i. $\frac{1}{2}+4\frac{9}{10}+9\frac{1}{2}$

Perform the arithmetic operations in Exercises 15 and 16. Reduce your answers to their lowest terms.

15. a. $\frac{11}{2}+\frac{1}{2}-\frac{6}{2}$ b. $5\frac{3}{4}-2\frac{1}{4}$ c. $\frac{13}{3}-3\frac{7}{3}+5\frac{8}{3}$
 d. $\frac{5}{2}-\frac{7}{9}-\frac{3}{2}$ e. $\frac{19}{5}-6\frac{1}{6}-1\frac{3}{10}$ f. $11-\frac{1}{2}+\frac{3}{7}$
 g. $2\frac{3}{6}-1\frac{1}{7}$ h. $5\frac{4}{7}-3\frac{1}{6}$ i. $7-\frac{5}{5}+\frac{1}{3}$

16. a. $\frac{12}{3}+\frac{5}{3}-\frac{4}{3}$ b. $8\frac{1}{6}-2\frac{3}{6}$ c. $\frac{15}{7}-1\frac{2}{7}+6\frac{3}{7}$
 d. $\frac{12}{4}-\frac{3}{12}-\frac{5}{4}$ e. $\frac{7}{3}-1\frac{2}{3}-2\frac{1}{9}$ f. $22-\frac{1}{3}+\frac{5}{2}$
 g. $1\frac{6}{3}-3\frac{2}{6}$ h. $\frac{1}{2}-6\frac{1}{2}-5\frac{3}{4}$ i. $7\frac{4}{6}-2\frac{3}{8}$

In Exercises 17 and 18, calculate the number of hours that each person worked in the week.

17.

DAY	WORKING HOURS
Monday	$6\frac{1}{2}$
Tuesday	$7\frac{3}{4}$
Wednesday	$6\frac{1}{4}$
Thursday	$5\frac{1}{2}$
Friday	$6\frac{3}{4}$

18.

DAY	WORKING HOURS
Monday	$8\frac{1}{4}$
Tuesday	$7\frac{1}{2}$
Wednesday	$7\frac{1}{4}$
Thursday	$6\frac{3}{4}$
Friday	$4\frac{1}{2}$

19. Troy walked $1\frac{1}{2}$ km to college, $2\frac{3}{4}$ km to the mall, and $1\frac{2}{3}$ km back home. What was the total distance covered by Troy?

20. Mary drove $123\frac{2}{3}$ km to meet her parents, then $118\frac{1}{5}$ km to meet her sister. She finally drove $56\frac{1}{2}$ km back home. What was the total distance driven by Mary?

4.3 MULTIPLICATION AND DIVISION OF FRACTIONS

MULTIPLICATION OF FRACTIONS

When dividing and multiplying fractions, you do not have to find a common denominator first. To multiply fractions, multiply the numerators of the fractions to find the single numerator, then multiply the denominators of the fractions to find the single denominator. Finally, reduce the result to the lowest terms.

To multiply mixed numbers, convert the mixed numbers to improper fractions and then follow the same procedure to multiply the fractions.

When multiplying fractions, you can also get the result in lowest terms by simplifying the individual fractions to their lowest terms before multiplying them together. This is done by dividing any numerator and denominator in the expression by a common factor.

EXAMPLE 4.3 (A): Multiplying Fractions

Multiply the following fractions. Reduce the fractions to their lowest terms before multiplying them.

i $\frac{3}{4} \times \frac{2}{3} \times \frac{1}{4}$ ii $\frac{1}{5} \times \frac{2}{7} \times \frac{15}{16}$

Solution:

i $\frac{3}{4} \times \frac{2}{3} \times \frac{1}{4}$

$= \frac{\cancel{3}^{1}}{{}_{2}\cancel{4}} \times \frac{\cancel{2}^{1}}{{}_{1}\cancel{3}} \times \frac{1}{4}$ Simplify fractions.

$= \frac{1 \times 1 \times 1}{2 \times 1 \times 4}$ Multiply numerators and denominators.

$= \frac{1}{8}$ This is the answer since it is a fraction in its lowest terms.

We could also solve this problem by first multiplying all of the numerators and all of the denominators:

$$\frac{3}{4} \times \frac{2}{3} \times \frac{1}{4} = \frac{3 \times 2 \times 1}{4 \times 3 \times 4}$$
$$= \frac{6}{48}$$

Simplifying this fraction, we get:

$$\frac{6}{48} = \frac{1}{8}$$

In both cases we end up with the same result, but it is often easier to simplify first so that we do not end up with such large numbers as the numerator and denominator.

ii $\frac{1}{5} \times \frac{2}{7} \times \frac{15}{16}$

$= \frac{1}{{}_{1}\cancel{5}} \times \frac{\cancel{2}^{1}}{7} \times \frac{\cancel{15}^{3}}{\cancel{16}_{8}}$ Simplify fractions.

$= \frac{1 \times 1 \times 3}{1 \times 7 \times 8}$ Multiply numerators and denominators.

$= \frac{3}{56}$ This is the answer since it is a fraction in its lowest terms.

DIVISION OF FRACTIONS

To divide fractions, multiply the first fraction by the reciprocal of the second fraction. Reduce the answer to its lowest terms.

To divide mixed numbers, convert the mixed numbers to improper fractions and then follow the same procedure to divide fractions.

EXAMPLE 4.3 (B): Dividing Fractions and Mixed Numbers

Divide the following fractions. Reduce the fractions to their lowest terms before dividing them.

i $\frac{1}{2} \div \frac{3}{4}$ ii $2\frac{1}{3} \div 1\frac{1}{4}$

Solution:

i $\frac{1}{2} \div \frac{3}{4}$

$= \frac{1}{2} \times \frac{4}{3}$ Multiply by the reciprocal of the second fraction.

$= \frac{1}{\cancel{2}_1} \times \frac{\cancel{4}^2}{3}$ Simplify fractions.

$= \frac{1 \times 2}{1 \times 3}$ Multiply fractions.

$= \frac{2}{3}$

ii $2\frac{1}{3} \div 1\frac{1}{4}$

$= \frac{7}{3} \div \frac{5}{4}$ Convert the mixed numbers to improper fractions.

$= \frac{7}{3} \times \frac{4}{5}$ Multiply by the reciprocal of the second fraction.

$= \frac{7 \times 4}{3 \times 5}$ Multiply fractions.

$= \frac{28}{15}$

$= 1\frac{13}{15}$ Convert the improper fraction to a mixed number.

4.3 EXERCISES

Answers to the odd numbered exercises are available at the end of the textbook.

Multiply the fractions/mixed numbers in Exercises 1 and 2. Reduce the answers to lowest terms.

1. a. $\frac{2}{5} \times \frac{3}{4} \times \frac{10}{9}$ b. $1\frac{1}{3} \times 2\frac{3}{4}$ c. $2\frac{1}{2} \times \frac{2}{15} \times \frac{3}{4}$

   d. $\frac{1}{3} \times \frac{6}{7} \times \frac{14}{12}$ e. $4\frac{1}{2} \times \frac{2}{3} \times \frac{3}{4}$ f. $2\frac{2}{3} \times 3 \times \frac{3}{4}$

   g. $2\frac{1}{4} \times \frac{4}{5} \times \frac{1}{3}$ h. $1\frac{1}{10} \times \frac{5}{6} \times \frac{12}{10}$ i. $\frac{12}{10} \times \frac{1}{3} \times \frac{5}{6} \times \frac{4}{5}$

2. a. $\frac{3}{7} \times \frac{8}{7} \times \frac{14}{12}$ b. $3\frac{1}{2} \times 1\frac{6}{8}$ c. $4\frac{1}{3} \times \frac{9}{2} \times \frac{8}{26}$

d. $\frac{1}{5} \times \frac{8}{9} \times \frac{27}{36}$ e. $3\frac{1}{6} \times \frac{5}{6} \times \frac{6}{7}$ f. $5\frac{3}{4} \times 4 \times \frac{4}{6}$

g. $3\frac{1}{2} \times \frac{2}{7} \times \frac{1}{2}$ h. $1\frac{1}{8} \times \frac{4}{5} \times \frac{10}{11}$ i. $\frac{8}{12} \times \frac{1}{2} \times \frac{7}{4} \times \frac{3}{7}$

Divide the fractions/mixed numbers in Exercises 3 and 4. Reduce the answers to lowest terms.

3. a. $3\frac{1}{2} \div \frac{21}{4}$ b. $2\frac{3}{4} \div \frac{1}{2}$ c. $5\frac{1}{4} \div \frac{3}{4}$

d. $2\frac{3}{4} \div \frac{3}{4}$ e. $1\frac{1}{3} \div 4$ f. $\frac{5}{6} \div \frac{2}{3}$

g. $1\frac{1}{6} \div 1\frac{1}{2}$ h. $8 \div \frac{12}{5}$ i. $3\frac{3}{11} \div \frac{6}{5}$

4. a. $2\frac{1}{3} \div \frac{1}{9}$ b. $7\frac{5}{8} \div \frac{1}{3}$ c. $4\frac{1}{6} \div \frac{2}{5}$

d. $3\frac{7}{8} \div \frac{7}{8}$ e. $1\frac{1}{6} \div 5$ f. $\frac{7}{8} \div \frac{3}{2}$

g. $2\frac{1}{9} \div 2\frac{1}{3}$ h. $27 \div \frac{9}{2}$ i. $10\frac{1}{2} \div \frac{7}{8}$

Perform the arithmetic operations in Exercises 5 and 6. Express your answers as decimals rounded to two decimal places.

5. a. $4\frac{3}{7} \div 2\frac{1}{7} \times \frac{1}{3}$ b. $\frac{1}{8} \times 2\frac{2}{6} \div 3\frac{1}{6}$

c. $\frac{2}{3} \div 1\frac{19}{30} \times \frac{9}{14} \div 4\frac{1}{6}$ d. $1\frac{1}{2} \div 1\frac{1}{8} \div 1\frac{8}{27} \times 4$

6. a. $2\frac{2}{3} \div 1\frac{1}{3} \times \frac{1}{2}$ b. $\frac{1}{5} \times 3\frac{3}{4} \div 1\frac{1}{4}$

c. $5\frac{1}{7} \div \frac{3}{14} \times \frac{1}{2} \div 2\frac{1}{4}$ d. $2\frac{1}{8} \div 1\frac{10}{21} \div \frac{39}{48} \times \frac{5}{7}$

7. The distance between Jenny's work and her house is $12\frac{3}{4}$ km. If she drives her car to work and back home 5 days a week, what is the distance she travels in a week? Assume that she not does not travel anywhere else other than to work and back home.

8. If Rafael lives $10\frac{1}{2}$ km from college, how far does he drive back and forth in three days?

9. Nalini works $6\frac{1}{2}$ hours per day and receives $11 per hour. How much does she earn in 5 days?

10. Juan studies $4\frac{3}{4}$ hours every night. How many hours does he study in 4 nights?

11. Jackie received \$230 last week from her work. If she worked $11\frac{3}{7}$ hours last week, how much did she earn per hour?

12. Mya received \$170 last week from her work. If she worked $8\frac{1}{2}$ hours last week, how much did she earn per hour?

13. Nida used $16\frac{1}{2}$ bags of sugar to make 3 cakes. How many bags of sugar did she need per cake?

14. It costs \$74 to rent a car for 12 hours. If Isaac wanted to rent a car for 1 hour, how much would he have to pay?

15. Usman spent \$30 on gas for driving to London from Toronto. If the distance between London and Toronto is 192 km, how far did Usman travel for \$1.00?

16. Terence worked $25\frac{1}{2}$ hours last week. If he worked 5 days per week, how many hours did he work every day?

17. John, a college student, opened a checking account at his bank with \$550. He withdrew \$18, \$115, and \$80 from this account. At the end the month, he lent two-thirds of the remaining amount to his brother.

    a. How much did John lend his brother?

    b. How much did John have left in his checking account?

18. A Toronto based insurance company has 200 employees in its office. Three-fifths of these employees graduated from a college in Toronto.

    a. How many of these employees graduated from a college in Toronto?

    b. How many did not?

REVIEW EXERCISES

Answers to the odd numbered exercises are available at the end of the textbook.

For Exercises 1 and 2, convert the improper fraction to a mixed number.

1. a. $\frac{15}{4}$ b. $\frac{9}{5}$ c. $\frac{18}{5}$ d. $\frac{5}{4}$ e. $\frac{13}{3}$

2. a. $\frac{7}{3}$ b. $\frac{20}{6}$ c. $\frac{31}{3}$ d. $\frac{9}{2}$ e. $\frac{4}{3}$

For Exercises 3 and 4, convert the mixed number to an improper fraction.

3. a. $4\frac{1}{2}$ b. $6\frac{2}{3}$ c. $5\frac{1}{4}$ d. $6\frac{6}{7}$

4. a. $1\frac{1}{6}$ b. $4\frac{3}{4}$ c. $9\frac{5}{7}$ d. $2\frac{3}{5}$

5. Vikram scored $84\frac{1}{2}$ on his final exam. Express his score as an improper fraction.

6. Lena weighs $61\frac{2}{3}$ kg. Express her weight as an improper fraction.

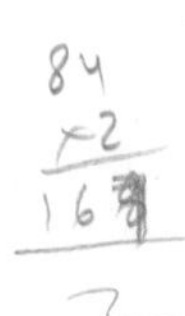

7. Aleksi worked $\frac{31}{4}$ hours yesterday. Express the number of hours he worked as a mixed number.

8. Amelia studied $\frac{15}{2}$ hours yesterday. Express her study time as a mixed number.

Find the reciprocal of the fractions in Exercises 9 and 10.

9. a. $\frac{1}{2}$ b. $\frac{3}{4}$ c. $\frac{5}{7}$ d. $\frac{4}{5}$ e. $-\frac{1}{6}$

10. a. $\frac{2}{3}$ b. $\frac{3}{5}$ c. $\frac{6}{7}$ d. $\frac{4}{9}$ e. $-\frac{2}{7}$

For Exercises 11 and 12, reduce the given fractions to lowest terms.

11. a. $\frac{5}{10}$ b. $\frac{4}{16}$ c. $\frac{3}{15}$ d. $\frac{20}{40}$ e. $7\frac{2}{4}$ f. $12\frac{3}{12}$

12. a. $\frac{6}{12}$ b. $\frac{4}{24}$ c. $\frac{3}{18}$ d. $\frac{15}{45}$ e. $4\frac{8}{10}$ f. $9\frac{4}{18}$

Find two equivalent fractions for each fraction in Exercises 13 and 14.

13. a. $\frac{3}{4}$ b. $\frac{6}{7}$ c. $\frac{2}{5}$ d. $2\frac{4}{5}$

14. a. $\frac{3}{10}$ b. $\frac{4}{9}$ c. $\frac{3}{7}$ d. $4\frac{5}{6}$

15. Miriam worked $33\frac{3}{4}$ hours last week. Express the number of hours she worked as a decimal number.

16. The distance between Toronto and Montreal is $541\frac{4}{10}$ km. Express this distance as a decimal number.

17. The price of a flight from Toronto to California is $\$428\frac{1}{3}$. Express the price as a decimal number.

18. The time period of a loan is $3\frac{5}{11}$ years. Express the time period as a decimal number.

Find the Lowest Common Multiple of the numbers given in Exercises 19 and 20.

19. a. 4 and 7 b. 3 and 5 c. 4 and 5 d. 2 and 3 e. 2, 6, and 9 f. 4, 5, and 10

20. a. 6 and 9 b. 5 and 7 c. 3 and 8 d. 3 and 7 e. 2, 5, and 10 f. 3, 6, and 9

For the expressions in Exercises 21 and 22, add and reduce to lowest terms.

21. a. $\frac{1}{4}+\frac{3}{4}+\frac{6}{4}$ b. $2\frac{2}{3}+3\frac{1}{3}$ c. $\frac{3}{5}+\frac{8}{10}+\frac{1}{4}$ d. $7+3\frac{2}{3}+4\frac{3}{5}$

22. a. $\frac{4}{6}+\frac{2}{6}+\frac{5}{6}$ b. $4\frac{4}{7}+2\frac{1}{7}$ c. $\frac{1}{3}+\frac{4}{6}+\frac{7}{9}$ d. $5+4\frac{3}{4}+3\frac{1}{6}$

For Exercises 23 and 24, perform the arithmetic operations and reduce to lowest terms.

23. a. $\frac{8}{3}+\frac{2}{3}-\frac{5}{3}$ b. $7\frac{4}{5}-3\frac{3}{5}$ c. $4\frac{3}{4}-2\frac{2}{3}$ d. $8-1\frac{1}{2}-3\frac{3}{4}$

24. a. $\frac{5}{6}+\frac{4}{6}-\frac{3}{6}$ b. $5\frac{6}{7}-3\frac{4}{7}$ c. $8\frac{4}{5}-3\frac{3}{4}$ d. $6-2\frac{1}{2}-4\frac{2}{5}$

25. Ren walked $1\frac{1}{2}$ km to school, $2\frac{3}{4}$ km to the library, and $1\frac{2}{3}$ km back home. What was the total distance Ren walked?

26. Lara drove $107\frac{2}{3}$ km to visit her parents, then $124\frac{1}{4}$ km to visit some old friends. She finally drove $74\frac{1}{2}$ km back home. What was the total distance Lara drove?

Multiply the fractions in Exercises 27 and 28 and reduce the answer to lowest terms.

27. a. $\frac{4}{5} \times \frac{6}{8} \times \frac{12}{15}$ b. $2\frac{1}{2} \times 1\frac{6}{10}$ c. $4\frac{1}{2} \times \frac{2}{3} \times \frac{6}{8}$ d. $\frac{5}{10} \times \frac{2}{3} \times \frac{6}{8} \times \frac{4}{6}$

28. a. $\frac{7}{8} \times \frac{4}{14} \times \frac{2}{4}$ b. $4\frac{1}{2} \times 3\frac{1}{3}$ c. $3\frac{3}{4} \times 6 \times \frac{2}{3}$ d. $\frac{4}{8} \times \frac{6}{4} \times \frac{1}{2} \times \frac{3}{5}$

Divide the fractions in Exercises 29 and 30 and reduce the answer to lowest terms.

29. a. $2\frac{3}{4} \div \frac{2}{6}$ b. $\frac{8}{9} \div \frac{2}{3}$ c. $5 \div \frac{6}{10}$ d. $7\frac{1}{2} \div \frac{5}{6}$

30. a. $14 \div \frac{7}{5}$ b. $3\frac{3}{4} \div \frac{10}{12}$ c. $\frac{6}{9} \div \frac{9}{6}$ d. $8\frac{1}{3} \div \frac{5}{9}$

31. The distance between Sage's work and her house is $9\frac{3}{4}$ km. If she drives her car to work and back home 5 days a week, what is the distance she travels in one week? Assume that she not does not travel anywhere else other than to work and back home.

32. If James lives $14\frac{1}{2}$ km from college, how far does he drive back and forth in three days?

33. Gina works $7\frac{1}{2}$ hours per day and receives $16 per hour. How much does she earn in 5 days?

34. Jorge studies $2\frac{3}{4}$ hours every night. How many hours does he study in 4 nights?

35. Zoe used $12\frac{3}{4}$ bags of sugar to make 4 cakes. How many bags of sugar did she need per cake?

36. It costs $58 to rent a car for 12 hours. If Marlon wanted to rent a car for 2 hours, how much would he have to pay?

37. Sergei opened a chequing account at his bank with $350. He withdrew $22, $145, and $87 from this account. At the end the month, he lent two-thirds of the remaining amount to his sister.
   a. How much did Sergei lend his sister?
   b. How much did Sergei have left in his chequing account?

38. A hotel has 180 employees. Three-fifths of these employees graduated from a college in Toronto.
   a. How many of the employees graduated from a college in Toronto?
   b. How many did not graduate from a college in Toronto?

CHAPTER 5

ALGEBRA

LEARNING OBJECTIVES

Studying this chapter will provide you with the knowledge needed to:

- Simplify algebraic expressions.
- Perform basic arithmetic operations with algebraic expressions.
- Set up algebraic equations.
- Solve for unknown variables in algebraic equations.
- Solve word problems using algebraic equations.

TOPICS

5.1 ALGEBRAIC EXPRESSIONS

Algebra requires dealing with more complex expressions, known as algebraic expressions. Working with algebraic expressions involves both numbers and variables. In this chapter, we will review the basics of algebra and we will learn how to simplify and solve a variety of algebraic expressions.

Before we begin with a complete algebraic expression, let's dissect the parts so that we understand what they each represent.

A **numerical expression** consists of a single number, or two or more numbers joined by an **operational symbol** (i.e. +, −, ×, ÷).

For example: $5 + 8$, $31 - 14$, $88 \div 11$, $4 \times (5 + 2)$ are all numerical expressions.

We see numerical expressions often and feel comfortable working with them because we recognize both the number and the operation that is to be performed. However, in **algebraic expressions** where variables are introduced, we need to take some extra steps to solve an equation.

A symbol that holds the place of an unknown value is called a **variable**.

For example: x, r, B, Δ, Ω, are all variables. The symbol that is used for the unknown does not matter as much as the value that it represents.

Sometimes, a symbol can have a number written in front of it. This number is called a **coefficient**. The coefficient and variable are connected by multiplication. Together, we refer to them as a **term**.

For example: in the term $2w$, 2 is the coefficient and w is the variable. $2w$ means $2 \times w$.

An **algebraic expression** may contain a ***numerical expression***, or an expression containing one or more ***variables***, joined by an ***operational symbol***.

For example: $h - 3$, $2w + 4w - 5w$, $8s - 3 \times 13t$ are all algebraic expressions.

DISCUSSION

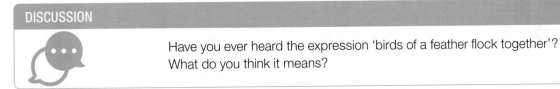

Have you ever heard the expression 'birds of a feather flock together'? What do you think it means?

SIMPLIFYING ALGEBRAIC EXPRESSIONS

To evaluate algebraic expressions, we need to first be able to simplify them.

Look at the equation below. What do you notice?

$$5p + 3p - 4p$$

All of the variables are the same and are often referred to as **like terms**; therefore, this equation can be solved as if we were solving $5 + 3 - 4$.

$5p + 3p - 4p$		$5 + 3 - 4$
$= 8p - 4p$	OR	$= 8 - 4$
$= 4p$		$= 4$

The process of simplifying is slightly different when we are working with expressions that contain more than one variable.

For example, consider the following expression: $8w + 4k - 3w + 6k$

To simplify this expression, we follow these steps:

Step 1: Group the like terms.

$8w - 3w + 4k + 6k$

When rearranging, ensure that you keep the operational symbol that is in front of the term.

Step 2: Once the like terms are grouped together, perform the operations to simplify.

$8w - 3w =$ **$5w$** and $4k + 6k =$ **$10k$**

Therefore, **$5w + 10k$** is the simplified answer.

When a variable is by itself, without a number in front, we know that there is only one (1) of that variable. For example: 'A' is the same as 1A.

Steps to simplifying algebraic equations are explained in more detail in the following illustration.

Illustration 5.1 (A): Simplifying Algebraic Expressions

Simplify the following expression: $3s + 7b + 2m - 8s + 6m + 5b + s$

Begin from the left side to group the like terms, starting with variable s.

$3s - 8s + s$

Next, group the terms containing variable b.

$3s - 8s + s + 7b + 5b$

Finally, group the terms containing variable m.

$3s - 8s + s + 7b + 5b + 2m + 6m$

Now that all the like terms are together, we can perform the operations within each group.

$3s - 8s + s = -5s + s = -4s$

Once you simplify the first variable, move on to the next one.

$-4s + 7b + 5b + 2m + 6m$

The next variable to simplify is b.

$7b + 5b = 12b$

Once the second variable is simplified, move on to the final variable.

$-4s + 12b + 2m + 6m$

The final variable is m.

$2m + 6m = 8m$

So, we get:

$3s + 7b + 2m - 8s + 6m + 5b + s$

$= 3s - 8s + s + 7b + 5b + 2m + 6m$

$= -4s + 12b + 8m$

Therefore the final, simplified expression is: **$-4s + 12b + 8m$**

EXAMPLE 5.1 (A): Simplifying Algebraic Expressions

Simplify the following expression: $-3ab + 14p + 8ab - 9p$

Solution:

$-3ab + 14p + 8ab - 9p$

Rearrange to group the like terms:

$-3ab + 8ab + 14p - 9p$

Next, perform the addition and subtraction within each group:

$5ab + 5p$

Therefore, $-3ab + 14p + 8ab - 9p$ simplifies to $5ab + 5p$.

You might have come across both the terms algebraic expressions and algebraic equations. There are differences between the two.

An **algebraic expression** is an expression that contains constants, variables, and algebraic operations. An **algebraic equation** expresses the equality between two algebraic expressions.

This difference becomes important when we simplify and solve the expressions and equations. So far, when grouping the like terms, we have not had to change the operational symbol when moving the terms around. All we did was ensure that whatever operational symbol was in front of the term moved with it. This is because there was no equal sign in the expression.

When a number is positive, we do not need to include the + symbol in front of the number, as we assume that any number that does not have a negative in front is a positive number. If a number is negative then the symbol must always be present, otherwise it will be assumed to be positive, and the calculations will be be incorrect.

Once we insert an equal sign in the expression, it becomes an equation and the rules change. The process of simplifying is still the same, but the rules regarding the operational symbols change.

When simplifying and solving algebraic equations, the terms will move from one side of the equal sign to the other. When moving from one side of the equation to the other, addition becomes subtraction and multiplication becomes division, and vice versa.

Let's practice this process and see what happens if we simplify an algebraic expression and an algebraic equation containing the same terms.

Illustration 5.1 (B): Simplifying Algebraic Expressions and Equations

Expression	Equation
$4p - 6r + 2p + 3r$	$4p - 6r = 2p + 3r$
$4p + 2p - 6r + 3r$	$4p - 2p = 3r + 6r$
$6p - 3r$	$2p = 9r$

As you can see, we end up with two different results. Therefore, it is important to ensure that you recognize when it is necessary to change the operational symbol.

EXAMPLE 5.1 (B): Simplifying Algebraic Equations

Simplify the following equation: $5r - 7g = 3g + 3r$

Solution:

$$5r - 7g = 3g + 3r$$

Group the like terms by moving the variables from one side of the equal sign to the other and changing the operational symbol:

$$5r - 3r = 3g + 7g$$

Next, perform the operations on each side of the equal sign:

$$2r = 10g$$

Therefore, $5r - 7g = 3g + 3r$ is simplified to $2r = 10g$.

EXAMPLE 5.1 (C): Simplifying Algebraic Equations with Three Variables

Simplify the following equation: $6f + 3g - 3f = 7g + 5h - 2f$

Solution:

$$6f + 3g - 3f = 7g + 5h - 2f$$

Let's start with the variable f and group the like terms by moving the variables from one side of the equal sign to the other so that they are all on the same side. We change the operational symbol when we move the variable across the equal sign:

$$6f + 3g - 3f + 2f = 7g + 5h$$

We can combine the three terms with the variable f into one: $6f - 3f + 2f = 5f$.

This gives us:

$$5f + 3g = 7g + 5h$$

Next, move all the terms with the variable g to the right-hand side:

$$5f = 7g + 5h - 3g$$

Since $7g - 3g = 4g$, the final answer simplified is:

$$5f = 4g + 5h$$

Notice that we ended up with one variable on the left-hand side of the equation and two on the right-hand side.

5.1 EXERCISES

Answers to the odd numbered exercises are available at the end of the textbook.

In Exercises 1 to 4, identify the variables in the given algebraic expressions.

1. a. $2x + 3$ b. $3x + 6y$
2. a. $4p - 4q + 2$ b. $9m + 3 - 4o$
3. a. $4 + 4y$ b. $9a + 3b$
4. a. $7w + 2k + 3l$ b. $8A - 5B + 9H$

For Exercises 5 to 14, simplify the algebraic expressions.

5. a. $9r + 3db + 5r + 7db$ b. $4ab + 6z - 4ab + 3z$
6. a. $8x + 4xy - 3x + 7xy$ b. $9q + 2op - 3q + 8op$
7. a. $12w - 6t + 4m + 3t - 7w$ b. $13t - 4w + 2k + 9t - 3k$
8. a. $4m - 7mn + 3q - 3mn + 4m$ b. $7xy - 9x + 3z - 5x + 4xy$
9. a. $B + 4s + 4B - 3s + 9z$ b. $7j - 5n - 9j + 8n + F$
10. a. $4A + 6B + C - 2B + 2C$ b. $Z - 3X + 3Z - 3XY + 4X$
11. a. $3hr + 6k - 9hr - 3sd + 4k$ b. $2fx + 8r - 9fx + 13e + 6r$
12. a. $3g - 7h + 6h + 9g - 5y$ b. $6xy - 4k + 2qr + 3k + xy - qr$
13. a. $-3ab + 14p + 8ab - 9p$ b. $-6A - 9B + 4AB + 5B + C$
14. a. $-9q - 8r - p + 6r + p - 5q$ b. $-4k + 5m - n + 2m - k$

For Exercises 15 to 24, simplify the algebraic equations.

15. a. $5r + 7g = 3g + 3r$ b. $6a + 8b = 2a + 7b$
16. a. $9A + 5B = 4B + 8A$ b. $7x + 8y = 6x + 9y$
17. a. $7m - 3n = 4n - 4m$ b. $6o - 8p = 7p - 8o$
18. a. $9x - 8z = 10x - 6z$ b. $8k - v = 4k - 5v$
19. a. $4p + 6h - 2p = 8h - 3p$ b. $5b - 4c = 9b + c + 4a$
20. a. $7m + 6n - o = 4n - 5o$ b. $9v + 5s = 6v - 3s + 2b$
21. a. $9o + 3pq - 5n = 8o + pq + 6n$ b. $-8v + 6x - 2l = v + 7x + l$
22. a. $8f + 12h - 10g = 6f - 14h + 8g$ b. $-6b - 7m + 4k = -9b + 6m - 2k$
23. a. $6A - 4B + C = -5A + 3B - 2C$ b. $M + 3N - 5P = 3M - 4N + P$
24. a. $-8C - L + H = +C - 2L + 4H$ b. $9K - 3W + 2Q = -4K + W - 5Q$

5.2 SIMPLE ALGEBRAIC EQUATIONS

In the previous section, we learned about algebraic expressions and equations and how to simplify them. In this section, we will learn how to **solve** simple algebraic equations. As we learned in the previous section, an algebraic equation expresses equality between two expressions. We cannot solve an algebraic equation until we know the values of the variables. Once we know the values for the unknown, we can evaluate the expression or equation by substituting the known values.

Illustration 5.2 (A): Substituting Known Values into Algebraic Expressions and Equations

$9y - 6s - 4y + 11s$
$= 9y - 4y - 6s + 11s$
$= 5y + 5s$
Let $y = 3$ and $s = 2$
$5(3) + 5(2)$
$= 15 + 10$
$= 25$

$8x + 3y = 5x + 5y$
$8x - 5x = 5y - 3y$
$3x = 2y$
Let $x = 4$ and $y = 6$
$3(4) = 2(6)$
$12 = 12$

DISCUSSION

In mathematics, you will often hear the words **simplify**, **evaluate**, and **solve**. What do they mean and what are the different approaches taken with each?

Often when working with algebraic equations, we are required to solve for unknown variables. There are various methods used to solve algebraic equations. In this section, we will introduce two of them.

The **direct method** involves moving numbers or variables from one side of the equal sign to the other, as we have done when simplifying algebraic equations. The important thing to remember when solving algebraic equations is that the operational symbol must change to its opposite once the term is moved from one side of the equation to the other. Solving for the unknown variables using the direct method is shown in the illustration below.

Illustration 5.2 (B): Solving for Unknown Variables Using the Direct Method – Addition and Subtraction

$B + 3 = 6$	$9 + R = 12$	$P - 4 = 6$	$Z - 4 = 2$
$B = 6 - 3$	$R = 12 - 9$	$P = 6 + 4$	$Z = 2 + 4$
$B = 3$	$R = 3$	$P = 10$	$Z = 6$

When moving a number or variable from one side of the equal sign to the other, we place it after the number that is already on that side.

For example: $B + 3 = 6$ should be $B = 6 - 3$, not $B = -3 + 6$.

Even though, in some instances, this will not affect the answer, there are cases when it will. Therefore, forming the habit in advance will help reduce errors.

Illustration 5.2 (C): Solving for Unknown Variables Using the Direct Method - Multiplication and Division

$4F = 20$	$5G = 15$	$\frac{W}{7} = 3$	$\frac{Y}{3} = 5$	$\frac{P}{9} = 4$
$F = \frac{20}{4}$	$G = \frac{15}{5}$	$W = 3 \times 7$	$Y = 5 \times 3$	$P = 4 \times 9$
$F = 5$	$G = 3$	$W = 21$	$Y = 15$	$P = 36$

Another method used to solve these equations is to **isolate the unknown variable** on one side of the equation by moving all other terms to the other side. We move a term to the other side of the equation by performing its opposite operation on both sides of the equation.

Illustration 5.2 (D): Solving for Unknown Variables by Performing the Same Operation on Both Sides of the Equation

$9 + R = 12$	$P - 4 = 6$	$5G = 15$	$\frac{W}{7} = 3$
$9 - 9 + R = 12 - 9$	$P - 4 + 4 = 6 + 4$	$5G \div 5 = 15 \div 5$	$\frac{W}{7} \times 7 = 3 \times 7$
$R = 3$	$P = 10$	$G = 3$	$W = 21$

The above examples were all **one step** algebraic equations. For these examples, it only took one step to isolate the variable and then solve for it. It might be helpful when looking at an algebraic equation to count the number of steps that it takes to isolate the variable so that we don't miss a step.

For example: $5P + 3 = 28$

When looking at this equation, you see that 3 and 5 are on the same side as the variable. To isolate the variable, both the 3 and 5 have to move to the other side of the equal sign, making this a two step equation.

The number attached to the variable should be the last one to move to the other side of the equal sign.

Illustration 5.2 (E): Solving Two Step Algebraic Equations

Solve the following algebraic equation: $5P + 3 = 28$

Step 1: $5P + 3 = 28$

$5P = 28 - 3$ Perform the subtraction before moving to the next step. We perform the subtraction first because it comes after multiplication in BEDMAS. Essentially, we are following BEDMAS backwards.

$5P = 25$

Step 2: $P = \frac{25}{5}$ Once the subtraction is complete, you can perform the division to reach the final answer. The coefficient on the variable is always the last number to be moved.

$P = 5$

DISCUSSION

Is 2 + 2 = 4 the same as 4 = 2 + 2?

Most of the equations you see will have the variable positioned on the left side of the equal sign. Because of this, we become accustomed to moving the numbers away from the variable in the direction of left to right. What happens when the variable is on the right side of the equation?

In such cases, if you are not comfortable with moving numbers/variables from right to left, you can simply flip the equation and then solve it.

$17 = 4F + 5$	is the same as	$4F + 5 = 17$
$17 - 5 = 4F$		$4F = 17 - 5$
$12 = 4F$		$4F = 12$
$\frac{12}{4} = F$		$F = \frac{12}{4}$
$3 = F$		$F = 3$

More challenging algebraic equations are those where we have to solve for the unknown in three steps. When solving algebraic expressions with multiple steps, we will move numbers/variables in *reverse* order of operations (BEDMAS).

EXAMPLE 5.2 (A): Solving Two and Three Step Algebraic Equations

Solve the following equations:

i $8S - 4 = 28$

ii $5P \div 4 + 7 = 17$

Solution:

i $8S - 4 = 28$

Step 1: $8S = 28 + 4$

$8S = 32$

We perform the addition first.

Step 2: $S = 32 \div 8$

$S = 4$

We perform the division last because the number attached to the variable is always the last number to be moved.

EXAMPLE 5.2 (A): Solving Two and Three Step Algebraic Equations *continued*

Solution:

ii $5P \div 4 + 7 = 17$

Step 1: $5P \div 4 = 17 - 7$

$5P \div 4 = 10$

We perform the subtraction first because it comes after multiplication in BEDMAS.

Step 2: $5P = 10 \times 4$

$5P = 40$

We perform the multiplication next.

Step 3: $P = 40 \div 5$

$P = 8$

We perform the division last because the number attached to the variable is always the last number to be moved.

Now that we have learned how to solve for unknown variables in algebraic equations, let's see how we can apply the direct method to **isolate variables**. There are times when there is an equation, such as $S = C + E + P$, where you may need to solve for any of the variables C, E, or P. In these instances, you may want to isolate the variable first and then solve for it.

One option would be to keep the equation in its original state and move the variables over.

$$S = C + E + P \quad \text{isolate } C$$

$$S - E - P = C$$

OR as we did previously in this section, you can flip the equation first and then move the variables accordingly.

$$S = C + E + P$$

$$C + E + P = S \quad \text{isolate } C$$

$$C = S - E - P$$

The same method applies to equations that have all operations involved, including multiplication and division.

For example, let's solve for 'r' in $I = Prt$.

P, r, and t are being multiplied, so to solve for r they must be divided on the other side of the equal sign. Since P and t are being multiplied, they can move to the other side of the equation in one step.

$$I = Prt$$

Remember that you can flip the equation first and then isolate the variable.

$$Prt = I$$

$$r = \frac{I}{Pt}$$

The next illustration combines all of the steps we have learned so far to isolate variables.

Illustration 5.2 (F): Isolating Variables in Algebraic Equations

We are given the equation $BD = R + KW$. We can isolate for the variables B, R, and K as follows:

Isolating variable B:

$$\mathbf{B}D = R + KW$$

$$\mathbf{B} = \frac{R + KW}{D}$$

Isolating variable $\mathbf{R}$:

$$BD = \mathbf{R} + KW$$

$$\mathbf{R} + KW = BD$$

$$\mathbf{R} = BD - KW$$

Isolating variable $\mathbf{K}$:

$$R + \mathbf{K}W = BD$$

$$\mathbf{K}W = BD - R$$

$$\mathbf{K} = \frac{BD - R}{W}$$

EXAMPLE 5.2 (B): Isolating Variables in Algebraic Equations

Given the equation $\frac{P}{A} - V = T$, isolate variable P.

Solution:

Solving for $\mathbf{P}$,

$$\frac{\mathbf{P}}{A} - V = T$$

$$\frac{\mathbf{P}}{A} = T + V$$

$$\mathbf{P} = (T + V)A$$

Why did we put brackets around the $T + V$ in the above example?

Let's look at it side by side with a numbers problem.

$\frac{P}{A} - V = T$	$\frac{P}{3} - 5 = 6$
$\frac{P}{A} = T + V$	$\frac{P}{3} = 6 + 5$
$P = (T + V)A$	$\frac{P}{3} = 11$
	$P = 11 \times 3$
	$P = 33$

As you can see, in the numbers problem, we were able to solve 6 + 5 = 11 before bringing over the 3. With the variables only, we must do something to indicate that once we know the numbers that represent the variables, the calculations must be done in the proper order. By putting the brackets around the $T + V$, we are indicating that $T + V$ should be completed first and then the answer should be multiplied by A.

EXAMPLE 5.2 (C): Solving Algebraic Equations

Solve for T in the equation $W = T + R$, where $W = 25$ and $R = 12$.

Solution:

$W = T + R$	Rearrange equation to solve for T.
$T + R = W$	
$T = W - R$	Substitute the known values.
$T = 25 - 12$	
$T = 13$	

5.2 EXERCISES

Answers to the odd numbered exercises are available at the end of the textbook.

Evaluate the algebraic expressions in Exercises 1 to 4, given the values for the variables.

1. $4x + 5y - 2x + 7y$, given $x = 2$ and $y = 4$.
2. $5a + 7b - 3a + 3b$, given $a = 6$ and $b = 3$.
3. $8q - 6p + 4p - 6q$, given $q = 2$ and $p = 5$.
4. $7m - 5n + 5n - 4m$, given $m = 4$ and $n = 6$.

Simplify the algebraic equations in Exercises 5 to 8, and then evaluate given the values for the variables.

5. $9k + 3l = 4k + 5l$, given $k = 4$, $l = 10$.
6. $5y + 6z = 7y - 8z$, given $y = 7$, $z = 1$.
7. $6b - 9c = 3b - 4c$, given $b = 5$, $c = 3$.
8. $5u - 8v = 7v + 9u$, given $u = -15$, $v = 4$.

Solve the equations in Exercises 9 to 16.

	a.	b.	c.	d.
9.	a. $3 + s = 7$	b. $t + 5 = 9$	c. $A + 5 = 8$	d. $Q + 8 = 3$
10.	a. $9 + g = 9$	b. $m + 9 = 8$	c. $W + 6 = 9$	d. $R + 5 = 8$
11.	a. $k - 10 = 5$	b. $g - 7 = 6$	c. $S - 9 = 7$	d. $T - 4 = 8$
12.	a. $p - 7 = 14$	b. $u - 10 = 7$	c. $M - 8 = 8$	d. $B - 9 = 5$
13.	a. $8q = 32$	b. $9k = 27$	c. $5 \times k = 30$	d. $4 \times m = 16$
14.	a. $12t = 96$	b. $6x = 48$	c. $7 \times y = 63$	d. $8 \times p = 56$

15. a. $\frac{u}{4} = 9$ b. $\frac{m}{7} = 9$ c. $\frac{g}{3} = 12$ d. $\frac{X}{9} = 8$

16. a. $\frac{W}{9} = 6$ b. $\frac{n}{5} = 15$ c. $\frac{p}{7} = 9$ d. $\frac{k}{12} = 5$

Solve the equations in Exercises 17 to 28.

17. a. $6M + 4 = 34$ b. $8A + 6 = 54$ c. $32 = 5k + 2$ d. $24 = 4n + 8$

18. a. $2P + 12 = 82$ b. $6Y + 9 = 63$ c. $21 = 3l + 3$ d. $28 = 7m + 7$

19. a. $6x - 2 = 34$ b. $4b - 8 = 44$ c. $37 = 5n - 8$ d. $64 = 8k + 4$

20. a. $8m - 6 = 42$ b. $12y - 6 = 66$ c. $45 = 6p - 9$ d. $75 = 9l - 6$

21. a. $4y \times 4 = 32$ b. $3z \times 7 = 63$ c. $98 = 7m \times 2$ d. $100 = 5u \times 2$

22. a. $9b \times 3 = 27$ b. $6w \times 3 = 90$ c. $72 = 3c \times 6$ d. $44 = 2p \times 4$

23. a. $3p \div 9 = 32$ b. $4v \div 5 = 12$ c. $49 = 2n \div 2$ d. $18 = 9r \div 3$

24. a. $9k \div 3 = 21$ b. $5d \div 2 = 15$ c. $38 = 6u \div 3$ d. $28 = 8r \div 4$

25. a. $\frac{X}{4} \times 11 + 4 = 70$ b. $\frac{Z}{2} \times 8 + 6 = 54$ c. $69 = \frac{u}{5} \times 2 - 3$ d. $58 = \frac{r}{4} \times 2 - 6$

26. a. $\frac{n}{3} \times 8 + 8 = 32$ b. $\frac{w}{6} \times 5 + 9 = 69$ c. $42 = \frac{d}{4} \times 3 - 6$ d. $46 = \frac{j}{2} \times 3 - 8$

27. a. $9Q \div 2 + 8 = 26$ b. $6b \div 4 + 6 = 42$ c. $7m \div 7 - 5 = 16$ d. $4w \div 3 + 9 = 21$

28. a. $8k \div 4 + 9 = 31$ b. $4y \div 7 + 8 = 38$ c. $5k \div 4 - 7 = 28$ d. $7k \div 9 - 4 = 31$

For Exercises 29 to 34, isolate the bold variable.

29. a. $3 + \mathbf{H} = P$ b. $\mathbf{K} + 6 = L$ c. $7 = \mathbf{W} - T$ d. $H = \mathbf{V} - 9$

30. a. $5 + \mathbf{L} = Q$ b. $\mathbf{G} + 9 = W$ c. $9 = \mathbf{V} - P$ d. $D = \mathbf{Q} - 6$

31. a. $\frac{\mathbf{R}}{H} = 9$ b. $\frac{T}{\mathbf{S}} = 3$ c. $U\mathbf{M} = 8$ d. $\mathbf{K}L = 6$

32. a. $\frac{\mathbf{J}}{L} = 8$ b. $\frac{\mathbf{O}}{P} = 3$ c. $\frac{\mathbf{W}}{X} = 9$ d. $\frac{H}{\mathbf{I}} = 11$

33. a. $WD + \mathbf{M} = P$ b. $\mathbf{W}D - M = P$ c. $\frac{\mathbf{S}}{B} - P = 18$ d. $\frac{S}{\mathbf{B}} - P = 18$

34. a. $AB + \mathbf{C} = K$ b. $\mathbf{K}L - M = L$ c. $\frac{\mathbf{L}}{K} - B = 24$ d. $\frac{A}{\mathbf{N}} - M = 31$

35. In $MB = Z - Y$, solve for B if $M = 2$, $Z = 40$, and $Y = 18$.

36. In $ZY = X - W$, solve for Z if $Y = 4$, $X = 10$, and $W = 2$.

37. In $D + KP = R$, solve for K if $D = 5$, $R = 19$, and $P = 7$.

38. In $N + MR = O$, solve for M if $N = 4$, $O = 15$, and $R = 11$.

39. In $\frac{Q}{P} = R + O$, solve for Q if $P = 12$, $R = 2$, and $O = 4$.

40. In $\frac{X}{Y} = Z + W$, solve for Y if $X = 8$, $Z = 5$, and $W = 3$.

5.3 SOLVING WORD PROBLEMS USING ALGEBRAIC EQUATIONS

In this section, we will learn how to create and solve algebraic equations using the information given in a word problem.

Before we proceed with creating an algebraic equation from a word problem, let's see some of the most common words used to represent arithmetic operations.

Table 5.3: Arithmetic Operations and their Meaning

Addition (+)	the total, more than, sum, increased, markup
Subtraction (–)	less than, sale, reduced, decreased, difference, markdown
Multiplication (×)	of, times, product
Division (÷)	ratio of, divided by

After we identify the operation that is to be used in the equation, we choose a variable to represent the unknown.

We follow these steps to solve word problems:

Step 1:	Read the problem carefully to identify the number of unknowns and the operation used in the problem.
Step 2:	Choose a variable to represent the unknown(s).
Step 3:	Create an equation that represents the relationship between the variable and the rest of the information given.
Step 4:	Solve the equation.

Using what we know, turn the following word problem into an algebraic expression.

The price of a jacket was reduced by $25.

This can be represented by the expression:

$X - \$25$

Did You Know?

The temperature can drop by almost 7°C during a total solar eclipse.

How could you express this as an algebraic expression?

EXAMPLE 5.3 (A): Creating Algebraic Expressions from Word Problems

Write the algebraic expressions for the following:

i The difference between the price of two apples and two oranges.

ii A shirt marked up by $12.

iii 5 times the sum of 8 and *G*.

Solution:

i The difference between the price of two apples and two oranges.

The word 'difference' indicates subtraction. We can choose a variable to represent apples, for example 'a', and another variable to represent oranges, for example 'o'.

Therefore,

'*The difference between the price of two apples and two oranges*' can be represented by the expression: $2a - 2o$.

ii A shirt was marked up by $12.

'Marked up' indicates addition. We choose a variable, *x*, to represent the price of the shirt.

Therefore,

'*A shirt was marked up by $12*' can be represented by the expression: x + $12.

iii 5 times the sum of 8 and *G*.

The word 'times' indicates multiplication, and 'the sum' indicates addition.

Therefore,

'*5 times the sum of 8 and G*' can be represented by the expression: $5 \times (8 + G)$, or simply $5(8 + G)$.

The same steps can be followed to create and solve more complicated word problems. This is shown in the following illustration.

Illustration 5.3: Solving Word Problems Using Algebraic Equations

The price of a set of two luggages is $145. The smaller of the two costs $65. What is the cost of the larger piece?

- After carefully reading the problem, decide what the unknown is, i.e. the larger piece of luggage = *X*.
- What do we know about *X*?

  X + the smaller piece = $145

  Therefore, *X* + $65 = $145

  X = $145 – $65

  X = $80

Therefore, the larger piece of luggage costs $80.

EXAMPLE 5.3 (B): Solving Word Problems using Algebraic Equations

A dress is on sale for $29.95. This price is $16 less than the original price. What was the original price of the dress?

Solution:

Let the unknown, the original price of the dress, be *x*.

- The problem indicates that the original price of the dress (*x*) less the discount ($16.00) is $29.95.

Therefore, the equation is: $x - \$16 = \$29.95$

$$x = \$29.95 + \$16.00$$

$$x = \$45.95$$

Therefore, the original price of the dress was $45.95.

Now, let's apply this method to even more complex word problems.

EXAMPLE 5.3 (C): Solving Word Problems using Algebraic Equations

Jack made $3,000 this month which included his base salary of $1,200 plus commission that he made from the sale of computers. For each computer he sold, he made $50 commission. How many computers did he sell?

Solution:

- Our unknown is the number of computers sold, *X*.
- What do we know about *X*?

X is only based on the amount of commission Jack made and not the entire amount he received for the month.

The amount of commission Jack made is: $3,000 – $1,200 = $1,800

Therefore, the equation is $X = 1{,}800 \div 50$

$$X = 36$$

Therefore, the number of computers sold was 36.

5.3 EXERCISES

Answers to the odd numbered exercises are available at the end of the textbook.

Write the algebraic expressions for Exercises 1 to 14.

1. A number increased by two.
2. Three more than a number.
3. A number decreased by two.
4. Five less than a number.
5. Two fourths of a number.
6. Six times a number.
7. The price of a computer was increased by $59.
8. Number of students at a college increased by 1,230 from last year.
9. The highest temperature this winter is 3° C less than last summer.
10. A shirt was marked down by $5.
11. The price of a pair of shoes tripled.
12. The number of items sold at a store doubled.
13. A rope of a certain length is cut into nine pieces.
14. The total price of a dinner is split between four friends.

For Exercises 15 to 24, write the algebraic equations and solve.

15. The sum of two numbers is 126. If one of the numbers is 67, what is the other number?
16. Sixty-nine is the total of three numbers. If one number is 13, and the second number is 19, what is the third number?
17. What number when decreased by 49 results in 82?
18. The difference between two positive numbers is 98. If one of the numbers is 57, what is the other number?
19. The average temperature this summer was 4° C warmer than the average temperature last summer. If the average temperature last summer was 23° C, what was the average temperature this summer?
20. This year, Andria, a real estate agent, sold 12 houses more than last year. If last year she sold 89 houses, how many did she sell this year?
21. Cindy paid $120 for the purchase of two items. If one item cost her $49.50, what was the price of the other item?
22. Aaron paid a total of $125.50 for a pair of shoes and a pair of pants. If the pants cost $36.25, how much did the shoes cost?
23. A professor has 240 students enrolled in his classes. If he teaches 6 classes in total, how many students are there in each of his classes if each class is the same size?
24. $700 is split between Cathy, Ben, and Abey. Cathy received $140, and the remaining is split equally between Ben and Abey. How much did each of them receive?

REVIEW EXERCISES

Answers to the odd numbered exercises are available at the end of the textbook.

For Exercises 1 and 2, identify the variables.

1. a. $4x + 7$ b. $6x + 3k$ c. $2p - 4r + 1$
   d. $5n + 8 - 4b$ e. $9z + 2w + 4s$ f. $3G - 5H + 4F$

2. a. $8 + 5G$ b. $H + 4j$ c. $5L + 4W + 1$
   d. $10x + 5b - z$ e. $A + 5t$ f. $8Y + 101X$

Simplify the algebraic expressions in Exercises 3 to 6.

3. a. $5k + 3tp + 2r + 6tp$ b. $2bn + 4w - 4bn + 2w$

4. a. $11z - 4y + 6j + 3y - 7z$ b. $15f - 8a + 7g + 9f - 3g$

5. a. $9H + 4E + 3C - 2E + C$ b. $3S - 2X + 5S - 7LP + 6X$

6. a. $6v - 5h + 4h + 9v - 3i$ b. $8cd - 5T + 4gh + 3T + cd - gh$

Simplify the algebraic equations in Exercises 7 to 12.

7. a. $6t + 7w = 3w + 4t$ b. $3a + 4f = 8a + 5f$

8. a. $3g - 4n = 5n - 2g$ b. $7r - 5q = 7q - 8r$

9. a. $5y + 8s - 2y = 3s - 6y$ b. $6c - 2a = 9c + a + 4a$

10. a. $8u + 3gh - 3n = 4u + gh + 7n$ b. $-3f + 5x - 4z = f + 7x + z$

11. a. $5e + 14j - 9g = 6e - 8j + 10g$ b. $-4a - 7k + 8p = -6a + 4k - 2p$

12. a. $-3D - K + 6T = +D - 5K + T$ b. $4W - 3M + 6Q = -7M + M - 4Q$

For Exercises 13 to 16, evaluate the algebraic expressions given the values of the variables.

13. $3x + 4y - 5x + 6y$, *given* $x = 3$ *and* $y = 2$.

14. $4f + 6b - 3f + 2b$, given $f = 6$ and $b = 4$.

15. $8g - 4p + 7p - 5g$, given $g = 5$ and $p = 3$.

16. $5m - 3t + 5t - 3m$, given $m = 4$ and $t = 7$.

For Exercises 17 to 20, simplify the algebraic equation then evaluate given the values of the variables.

17. $7h + 3n = 4h + 6n$, *given* $h = 3$, $n = 3$.

18. $4y + 6k = 7y - 3k$, given $y = 3$, $k = 1$.

19. $3r - 8c = 7r - 3c$, given $r = -5$, $c = 4$.

20. $8p - 5v = 7v + 9p$, given $p = 12$, $v = -1$.

For Exercises 21 to 26, solve the equation.

21. a. $7 + j = 9$ b. $m - 4 = 8$ c. $K + 6 = 11$ d. $b - 3 = 8$

22. a. $P - 10 = 4$ b. $g + 3 = 6$ c. $S - 5 = 7$ d. $q + 6 = 15$

23. a. $8f = 24$ b. $5k = 40$ c. $4 \times g = 32$ d. $7 \times m = 28$

24. a. $12d = 84$ b. $4z = 64$ c. $5 \times y = 75$ d. $6 \times w = 48$

25. a. $\frac{r}{4} = 8$ b. $\frac{j}{5} = 7$ c. $\frac{v}{5} = 8$ d. $\frac{C}{7} = 6$

26. a. $\frac{W}{5} = 6$ b. $\frac{e}{6} = 9$ c. $\frac{p}{3} = 12$ d. $\frac{k}{11} = 7$

Solve each of the equations in Exercises 27 to 32.

27. a. $6K + 2 = 38$ b. $5g + 4 = 49$ c. $37 = 6p - 5$ d. $62 = 8k + 6$

28. a. $6j + 12 = 78$ b. $7H + 5 = 54$ c. $32 = 6c - 4$ d. $75 = 9z + 12$

29. a. $5y \times 4 = 60$ b. $45 = 3t \times 5$ c. $49 = 2k \div 2$ d. $5h \div 3 = 15$

30. a. $3b \times 3 = 27$ b. $80 = 4d \times 5$ c. $8 = 6h \div 9$ d. $7a \div 4 = 14$

31. a. $\frac{t}{5} \times 6 + 4 = 70$ b. $37 = \frac{k}{3} \times 5 - 8$ c. $4f \div 6 - 12 = -6$ d. $8z \div 3 + 7 = 23$

32. a. $\frac{b}{8} \times 6 + 8 = 56$ b. $80 = \frac{j}{2} \times 4 - 4$ c. $3e \div 6 - 14 = -10$ d. $5b \div 3 - 4 = 11$

For Exercises 33 to 36, isolate the bold variable in each of the expressions.

33. a. $7 + \mathbf{J} = P$ b. $4 = \mathbf{K} - Q$ c. $\frac{\mathbf{G}}{Z} = 6$ d. $\mathbf{H}L = 5$

34. a. $2 + \mathbf{M} = V$ b. $6 = \mathbf{A} - T$ c. $\frac{\mathbf{D}}{H} = 2$ d. $\mathbf{E}F = 3$

35. a. $JY + \mathbf{M} = K$ b. $\mathbf{R}D - N = P$ c. $\mathbf{A}H - O = 12$ d. $U\mathbf{B} - R = 9$

36. a. $ZC + \mathbf{F} = K$ b. $\mathbf{N}W - M = S$ c. $\mathbf{R}G - B = 18$ d. $J\mathbf{Q} - Z = 25$

Express the phrases in Exercises 37 to 45 as algebraic expressions.

37. A number increased by four.

38. Six more than a number.

39. A number decreased by eight.

40. A number less than three.

41. Seven fifths of a number.

42. Five times a number.

43. The number of baskets sold at a store doubled.

44. A cake is cut into nine pieces.

45. The total price of a meal is split between three friends.

Express the phrases in Exercises 46 to 51 as algebraic equations and solve.

46. The sum of two numbers is 142. If one of the numbers 73, what is the other number?

47. Ninety-two is the total of three numbers. If one number is 18, and the second number is 41, what is the third number?

48. What number, when decreased by 36, results in 74?

49. The difference between two positive numbers is 56. If one of the numbers is 28, what is the other number?

50. A professor has 260 students enrolled in his classes. If he teaches 5 classes in total and they have equal number of students, how many students are there in each of his classes?

51. $650 is split between Martha, Henry, and Penelope. Martha received $246, and the remaining is split equally between Henry and Penelope. How much did each of them receive?

CHAPTER 6

AVERAGES, PERCENTS, PERCENT CHANGES, AND APPLICATIONS

LEARNING OBJECTIVES

Studying this chapter will provide you with the knowledge needed to:

- Calculate arithmetic average and weighted average of a set of numbers.
- Convert percents to decimal numbers and decimal numbers to percents.
- Calculate percent changes.
- Solve different word problems involving percents and percent changes.
- Calculate payroll for employees who receive an hourly rate, annual salary, and commission.

TOPICS

6.1 AVERAGES

ARITHMETIC AVERAGE

The **average** of a set of numbers is a measure of the middle value of that set of numbers. The simple **arithmetic average** (or 'average') is calculated by adding up all the numbers and dividing the result by the number of items. This is represented by the following formula:

Arithmetic Average Formula

$$Average = \frac{Sum\ of\ all\ numbers}{Total\ number\ of\ items}$$

Did You Know?

If your dog lives to age 11, you will probably have spent around $13,000 on it - on average how much will you spend each year?

EXAMPLE 6.1 (A): Calculating the Arithmetic Average of a Set of Numbers

Calculate the arithmetic average of 2, 5, 8, 10, and 15.

Solution:

Using the formula,

$$Average = \frac{Sum\ of\ all\ numbers}{Total\ number\ of\ items}$$

$$= \frac{2 + 5 + 8 + 10 + 15}{5}$$

$$= \frac{40}{5}$$

$$= 8$$

Therefore, the arithmetic average of the set of numbers is 8.

EXAMPLE 6.1 (B): Practical Application of Averages

Samantha, a college student, worked part-time at a grocery store. Her weekly wages last month were \$350, \$270, \$280, and \$300, respectively. What was her average weekly wage last month?

Solution:

Using the formula,

$$Average = \frac{Sum\ of\ all\ numbers}{Total\ number\ of\ items}$$

$$= \frac{350 + 270 + 280 + 300}{4}$$

$$= \frac{1{,}200}{4}$$

$$= \$300$$

Therefore, her average weekly wage for last month was \$300.

WEIGHTED AVERAGE

If items on a list have different relative values, the **weighted arithmetic average** (also referred to as weighted average) is determined. In the arithmetic average, each number in the set contributes equally to the average, whereas in the weighted average, some numbers contribute more than others. In other words, each number has a different weight. Each number is multiplied by its weighting factor (which represents its importance or relative value). The result is then divided by the number of items.

Weighted Average Formula

$$Weighted\ Average = \frac{Sum\ of\ weighted\ numbers}{Total\ number\ of\ items}$$

EXAMPLE 6.1 (C): Practical Application of Weighted Averages

The Coffee House sells a variety of blends of coffee. Last month, the manager decided to create his own house blend from a variety of coffees in the store. He blended:

- 25 kg of high mountain Jamaican coffee that sells for \$30 per kg
- 12 kg of Arabian coffee that sells for \$20 per kg
- 13 kg of Columbian coffee that sells for \$16 per kg

How much should The Coffee House charge for the house blend to earn a consistent amount of profit per kg?

EXAMPLE 6.1 (C): Practical Application of Weighted Averages *continued*

Solution:

$$\text{Average Price per kg} = \frac{\text{Total Price}}{\text{Total Weight}}$$

$$= \frac{(25\text{ kg})(\$30.00) + (12\text{ kg})(\$20.00) + (13\text{ kg})(\$16.00)}{(25\text{ kg} + 12\text{ kg} + 13\text{ kg})}$$

$$= \frac{750.00 + 240.00 + 208.00}{50}$$

$$= \$23.96\text{ per kg}$$

Therefore, The Coffee House should sell the house blend coffee for $23.96 per kg.

EXAMPLE 6.1 (D): Practical Application of Weighted Averages

Shelly, a college student, enjoys going to concerts. While in college, she went to 5 concerts that cost $25 each, 3 concerts that cost $30 each, and 12 concerts that cost $10 each. What was the average amount she spent per concert?

Solution:

$$\text{Average Price per Concert} = \frac{\text{Total Cost of Concerts}}{\text{Number of Concerts}}$$

$$= \frac{(5)(\$25.00) + (3)(\$30.00) + (12)(\$10.00)}{5 + 3 + 12}$$

$$= \frac{125.00 + 90.00 + 120.00}{20}$$

$$= \$16.75\text{ per concert}$$

Therefore, the average amount she spent per concert was $16.75.

DISCUSSION

Can you think of other applications where the weighted average would need to be calculated?

6.1 EXERCISES

Answers to the odd numbered exercises are available at the end of the textbook.

Calculate the arithmetic average of the sets of numbers in Exercises 1 and 2.

1. a. 22, 12
   b. 2, 5, 7, 9, 7
   c. 10, 11, 15
   d. 12, 18, 24, 6

2. a. 8, 4
   b. 1, 6, 5, 12, 11
   c. 18, 21, 24
   d. 7, 9, 2, 2

3. Carissa took 5 courses in her first semester, 4 in her second semester, 5 in her third semester, and 6 in her fourth semester. Calculate the average number of courses she took per semester.

4. Meghan received a grade of 80% in English, 95% in Mathematics, 90% in Marketing, and 75% in Computer Application. What was her average grade for that semester?

5. Demar, a professor at a college, was teaching six math sections this semester. He had 35, 40, 23, 28, 33, and 33 students in sections A, B, C, D, E, and F, respectively. What was the average number of students he had per section?

6. Elijah worked as a graphic designer at a company. In April, if he worked 40 hours in the first week, 35 hours the next week, 38 hours the following week, and 39 hours the last week, calculate the average number of hours he worked per week.

In Exercises 7 to 14, round the answers to the nearest cent, wherever applicable.

7. Many college students use different types of pens, pencils, and markers. William used 3 pens costing $7 each, 2 coloured pens costing $2 each, 3 pencils costing 10 cents each, and 3 markers costing $3 each. What was the average price of his items?

8. A store sells laptops, notebooks, and desktop computers. Last week, a salesperson sold 6 laptops at $1,500 each, 7 notebooks at $850 each, and 7 desktop computers at $1,100 each. What was the average price of the items sold?

9. In a marketing company, 17 employees are paid $15 per hour, 13 employees are paid $18 per hour, and 10 employees are paid $20 per hour. Determine the average hourly rate of the employees.

10. A publishing company pays its employees based on the positions they hold. 5 employees are paid $10 per hour, 2 employees are paid $23 per hour, and 2 employees are paid $30 per hour. Determine the average hourly rate of the employees.

11. A marketing student had to obtain a loan from her parents to buy her textbooks. Two textbooks cost $100 each, one cost $90, and another two cost $70 each. Calculate the average cost per textbook.

12. Miguel was hired by a company that gave company shares as a special bonus. In January of this year, Miguel received 25 shares, in February he received 15 shares, and in March he received 30 shares. If each share was valued at $20, how much did he receive per month on average?

13. Yuan is a student with a part-time job. The number of hours he works per week varies. Find his average wage per week if he earned the following amounts per week for the last 30 weeks:

    - $50 per week for the first 4 weeks
    - $70 per week for the next 10 weeks
    - $100 per week for the next 2 weeks
    - $200 per week for the next 5 weeks
    - $150 per week for the final 9 weeks

14. A professor asked her students what salary they would expect to start at after college. The responses she received were as follows:

    - 3 students expected to start at $20,000 per year
    - 2 students expected to start at $40,000 per year
    - 5 students expected to start at $36,000 per year
    - 6 students expected to start at $42,000 per year
    - 4 students expected to start at $30,000 per year

    What was the average salary students expected to start at after finishing college?

6.2 PERCENTS

Percent is a common term that we use throughout our lives.

Percent is the relationship of a number to 100, or the ratio of a number to 100.

For example, $\frac{13}{100}$ is the ratio of 13 to 100.

We learn more about ratios in Chapter 7.

Did You Know?
"Cent" is the French word for hundred. Therefore, "percent" (%) means "per hundred."

If an item at a store is listed for $100, and the HST in Ontario for this item is $13, we could say that the ratio of tax to the list price is $\frac{13}{100}$ or 13%.

CONVERTING PERCENTS TO DECIMALS AND DECIMALS TO PERCENTS

When using percents mathematically, it is important to understand the transition of a percent to a decimal number and vice versa.

> To convert a percent to a decimal number, move the decimal point two spaces to the **left**, or **divide** by 100, and drop the '%' symbol.

It is important to note that even when we do not see the decimal point in all percents, it does not mean that it is not there. We often drop the decimal as it is not needed, but it is good to know its location, especially when you need to convert from a percent to a decimal.

For example: 23% is the same as 23.0%

To convert 23% (or 23.0%) to a decimal number, move the decimal point two spaces to the left (the spaces represent the number of zeroes in 100). This is equivalent to dividing by 100 and removing the % symbol.

$$23.0\% = 0.23 \quad \text{or} \quad \frac{23}{100} = 0.23$$

Therefore, 23% becomes 0.23.

Did You Know?

Mobster Charles "Lucky" Luciano was arrested 25 times but convicted only once. What was his arrest rate expressed as a decimal?

EXAMPLE 6.2 (A): Converting Percents to Decimal Numbers

Convert the following percents to decimal numbers:

i 16% ii 74% iii 80% iv 58%

Solution:

i **Converting 16% to a decimal number:**

Moving the decimal point to the left: OR Dividing by 100:

16% = 0.16 $\frac{16}{100} = 0.16$

ii **Converting 74% to a decimal number:**

Moving the decimal point to the left: OR Dividing by 100:

74% = 0.74 $\frac{74}{100} = 0.74$

iii **Converting 80% to a decimal number:**

Moving the decimal point to the left: OR Dividing by 100:

80% = 0.8 $\frac{80}{100} = 0.8$

iv **Converting 58% to a decimal number:**

Moving the decimal point to the left: OR Dividing by 100:

58% = 0.58 $\frac{58}{100} = 0.58$

Now that we know how to convert a decimal to a percent, let's try the process with percents that have decimals already in them, or percents that are more than 99% or less than 10%.

For example: When converting 154% to a decimal number, we get: 154.0% = 1.54

Note that 154% or 154.0% becomes 1.54 since we only move the decimal two spaces to the left.

A common error in this case is to move the decimal three spaces and turn 154% to 0.154, but remember that when converting percents to decimal numbers, we always move the decimal point two spaces to the left.

Similarly: When converting 6% to a decimal number, we get: 6.0% = 0.06

Note that 6% or 6.0% becomes 0.06 since we move the decimal two spaces to the left.

In this instance, when the decimal was moved, there was an empty space to the left of the 6; this became ._6. Anytime there is a space, we must fill it with a zero!

Similarly:

- 3.5% becomes 0.035
- 0.5% becomes 0.005
- 14.8% becomes 0.148
- 0.03% becomes 0.0003
- 320% becomes 3.20
- 1,478% becomes 14.78

Over the years, we develop a comfort level with numbers that we see often, but do not realize the many forms they can take until we expand our minds into business and science applications. These may not be common percents that you encounter on a daily basis, but that does not make them wrong. As long as you follow the rule of moving the decimal two spaces to the left, your answer will be correct.

EXAMPLE 6.2 (B): Converting Percents to Decimal Numbers

Convert the following percents to decimal numbers:

i 1% ii 58.4% iii 100% iv 803%

Solution:

i **Converting 1% to a decimal number:**

Moving the decimal point to the left: OR Dividing by 100:

1% = 0.01

$$\frac{1}{100} = 0.01$$

ii **Converting 58.4% to a decimal number:**

Moving the decimal point to the left: OR Dividing by 100:

58.4% = 0.584

$$\frac{58.4}{100} = 0.584$$

iii **Converting 100% to a decimal number:**

Moving the decimal point to the left: OR Dividing by 100:

100% = 1.0 or 1

$$\frac{100}{100} = 1$$

iv **Converting 803% to a decimal number:**

Moving the decimal point to the left: OR Dividing by 100:

803% = 8.03

$$\frac{803}{100} = 8.03$$

Now that we have converted percents to decimals, let's reverse the action and turn decimals to percents.

To convert decimal numbers to percents, move the decimal point two spaces to the **right**, or **multiply** the decimal number by 100 and then add the percent '%' symbol.

For example: To convert 0.85 to a percent, multiply by 100 or move the decimal point two spaces to the right and add the percent symbol.

0.85 = 85% or 0.85 × 100 = 85%

EXAMPLE 6.2 (C): Converting Decimal Numbers to Percents

Convert the following decimal numbers to percents:

i 0.93 ii 0.14 iii 0.68 iv 0.32

Solution:

i **Converting 0.93 to a percent:**

Moving the decimal point to the right: OR Multiplying by 100:

0.93 = 93% 0.93 × 100 = 93%

ii **Converting 0.14 to a percent:**

Moving the decimal point to the right: OR Multiplying by 100:

0.14 = 14% 0.14 × 100 = 14%

iii **Converting 0.68 to a percent:**

Moving the decimal point to the right: OR Multiplying by 100:

0.68 = 68% 0.68 × 100 = 68%

iv **Converting 0.32 to a percent:**

Moving the decimal point to the right: OR Multiplying by 100:

0.32 = 32% 0.32 × 100 = 32%

As in our previous examples, when converting percents to decimals, there are often times when the numbers are not 'common' and therefore need more thought and caution when converting from one form to another.

For example: 0.4 becomes 40%: when you move the decimal two spaces to the right, there is an empty space created immediately to the right of the 4 that must be filled with a zero.

Similarly:

- 0.03 becomes 3%
- 2.4 becomes 240%
- 6 or 6.0 becomes 600%
- 0.002 becomes 0.2%
- 73 becomes 7,300%

EXAMPLE 6.2 (D): Converting Decimal Numbers to Percents

Convert the following decimal numbers to percents:

i 0.21 ii 0.775 iii 0.03 iv 2.5

Solution:

i **Converting 0.21 to a percent:**

Moving the decimal point to the right: 0.21 = 21%

OR

Multiplying by 100: 0.21 × 100 = 21%

ii **Converting 0.775 to a percent:**

Moving the decimal point to the right: 0.775 = 77.5%

OR

Multiplying by 100: 0.775 × 100 = 77.5%

iii **Converting 0.03 to a percent:**

Moving the decimal point to the right: 0.03 = 3%

OR

Multiplying by 100: 0.03 × 100 = 3%

iv **Converting 2.5 to a percent:**

Moving the decimal point to the right: 2.5 = 250%

OR

Multiplying by 100: 2.5 × 100 = 250%

Illustration 6.2 (A): The Portion-Rate-Base (PRB) Triangle

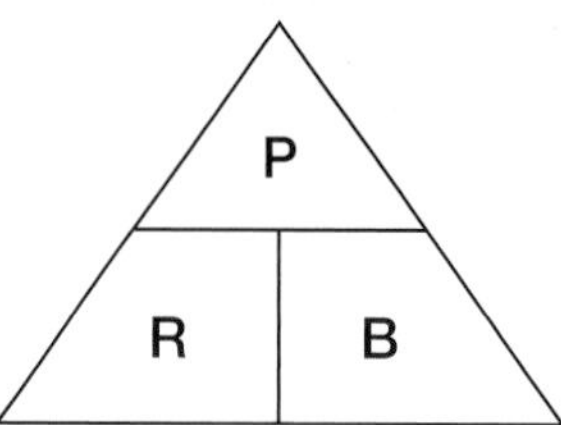

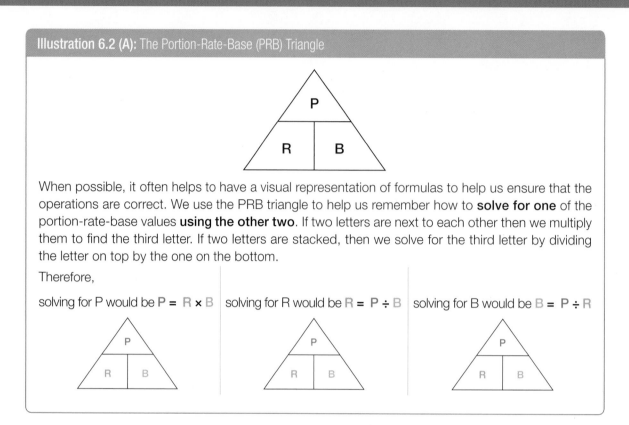

When possible, it often helps to have a visual representation of formulas to help us ensure that the operations are correct. We use the PRB triangle to help us remember how to **solve for one** of the portion-rate-base values **using the other two**. If two letters are next to each other then we multiply them to find the third letter. If two letters are stacked, then we solve for the third letter by dividing the letter on top by the one on the bottom.

Therefore,

solving for P would be **P = R × B**	solving for R would be **R = P ÷ B**	solving for B would be **B = P ÷ R**
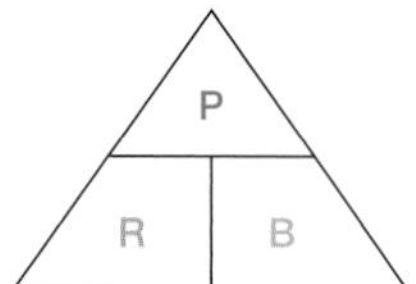	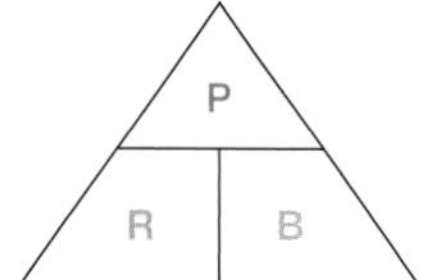	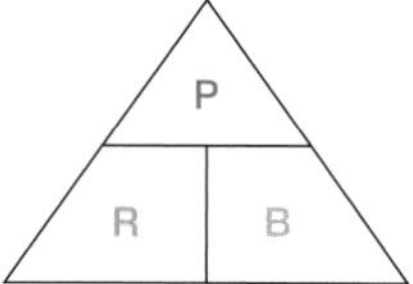

SOLVING PERCENT PROBLEMS

When we use percents in a mathematical equation, we need to first convert to a decimal and then solve the equation.

Anytime we are finding a percent **'of'** something, the operation will always be multiplication.

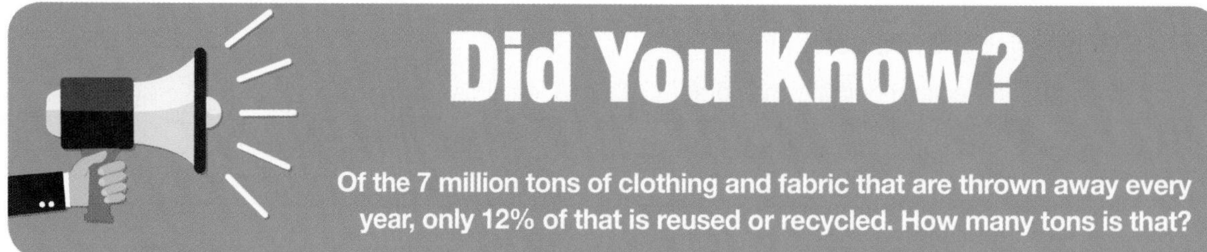

Did You Know?
Of the 7 million tons of clothing and fabric that are thrown away every year, only 12% of that is reused or recycled. How many tons is that?

There are three different approaches to percent problems. To find the right approach, it is helpful to answer the following questions:

- Is the percent problem a '*percent of*' question?

  For example: What amount of tax was paid on a shirt that cost $47.50 if the tax was 8%?

- Is the percent problem a '*percent increase*' question?

  For example: How much is the total price of a sweater that costs $34.99 plus 13% tax?

- Is the percent problem a '*percent decrease*' question?

  For example: What would Peter pay for a pair of shoes that cost $83.75 but are now on sale at 35% off?

Before doing the math, read the question to see if you are simply finding the percent of something or if there are more steps required to solve the question.

You will always begin by finding the percent as the first step. What is important is knowing whether to stop there, or to continue on for a complete and correct answer. Reading the question carefully will make it clear if more steps are required.

Illustration 6.2 (B): Solving Percent Problems

A store owner paid $32.00 for a coat and marked the price up by 48%.

What is the new price of the coat?

What is 48% of $32.00?

0.48 × 32.00

By converting the percent to a decimal, we can now find the amount of the markup:

48% converted to a decimal number is 0.48

Markup = 0.48 × 32.00 = $15.36

$15.36 is the amount of markup, or the dollar value of 48% of $32.00, not the new price of the coat. You must either add or subtract this amount from the original price in order to have the final answer.

In this case, we add this amount to the cost of the coat is because the item was marked up, and therefore, the price increased.

The coat had an original price of $32.00 with a markup of $15.36. In order to find the new price of the coat, we must add the two amounts together:

New Price = 32.00 + 15.36 = $47.36

Therefore, the new price of the coat is $47.36.

When there is an increase in percent, we can add 1 to the decimal or 100% to the percent and that will allow you to solve for the final answer with no need to add. By adding 1 or 100%, we ensure that 100% of the original price is included in the equation, and therefore eliminate the final step of adding.

For example:

If the cost of the coat was $32.00 with an increase of 48%, then the answer will include both the original cost of the coat, 100%, and the markup of 48%.

148% of 32.00

1.48 × 32

Therefore, 1.48 × 32.00 = $47.36

Illustration 6.2 (C): Solving Percent Problems

Katie was waiting for Boxing Day to buy a pair of boots she wanted. If the original price of the boots was $148.00 and they are now on sale at 63% off, what is the sale price?

What is 63% of $148.00?

0.63 × 148

If an item is on sale or discounted, then the item is marked down.

By converting the percent to a decimal number, we can find the amount of the markdown.

Markdown = 0.63 × 148.00 = $93.24

$93.24 is the amount of the markdown, or the dollar value of 63% of $148.00, not the final sale price.

To find the final sale price, you must subtract $93.24 from the original price:

Sale Price = 148.00 – 93.24 = $54.76

Therefore, the new price of the boots is $54.76.

6.2 EXERCISES

Answers to the odd numbered exercises are available at the end of the textbook.

In Exercises 1 and 2, convert the percents to decimal numbers.

1. a. 3% b. 30% c. 300% d. 95% e. 13%
   f. 5.5% g. 250.3% h. 36.6% i. 15.2% j. 75.5%

2. a. 7% b. 15% c. 200% d. 104% e. 98%
   f. 2.3% g. 189.9% h. 14.1% i. 19.0% j. 25.5%

In Exercises 3 and 4, convert the decimal numbers to percents.

3. a. 0.13 b. 0.90 c. 0.63 d. 0.5 e. 6.0
   f. 0.33333 g. 2.55 h. 36.0 i. 0.15 j. 0.0075

4. a. 0.21 b. 0.101 c. 0.87 d. 0.1 e. 9.01
   f. 0.0222 g. 4.44 h. 90.0 i. 0.44 j. 0.8888

Find the missing values in the tables for Exercises 5 and 6.

5.

	Decimal	Percent
a.	0.13	
b.		33%
c.	0.2555	
d.		25.2%
e.	1.085	
f.		103.7%

6.

	Decimal	Percent
a.		18%
b.	0.455	
c.		99.9%
d.	0.7777	
e.		201.01%
f.	2.067	

For Exercises 7 to 16, round your answer to two decimal places, wherever applicable.

7. How much tax is charged on an item that costs $163.99, if the tax rate is 13%?

8. What is 27% of $74.50?

9. Karen was paid $14.00/hour at her job. She received a raise of 7%. What was the amount of the raise? What was her new hourly rate?

10. A clothing store paid $22.00 for a sweater and marked up the price by 54%. What was the amount of the markup? What was the price of the sweater after the increase?

11. A family went for dinner at a restaurant and the bill came to $78.42. They wanted to leave a tip of 15%. How much was the tip? What was the total amount they paid?

12. Taxes on a dress costing $115.00 are 13%. How much are the taxes? How much will the dress cost in total?

13. A store decided to have a huge sale and clear out their winter items. If a snowboard costing $233.00 went on sale at 65% off, what is the new price of the snowboard?

14. A furniture store put a desk on sale at 45% off. The original price of the desk was $358.50. What is the price of the desk now? How much will the desk cost after 13% taxes are added to the 'sale' price?

15. During a winter storm, only 62% of students attend classes. If there are 1,300 students in the school, how many make it to class and how many do not?

16. Rachel receives $2,350 pay each month from her job. If she spends 29% on rent and 11% on food, how much does she have remaining after her expenses?

6.3 PERCENT CHANGES

We are in a constant state of change, whether we are growing taller, changing jobs, or moving from one place to another. Sometimes we have to be able to distinguish the differences in changes that occur. Below we give some examples of how this is done.

When something changes by a 'percent', then we need to understand it as **percent change**. This means that we have an 'original' value, an increase or decrease to this original value, and a new or final value.

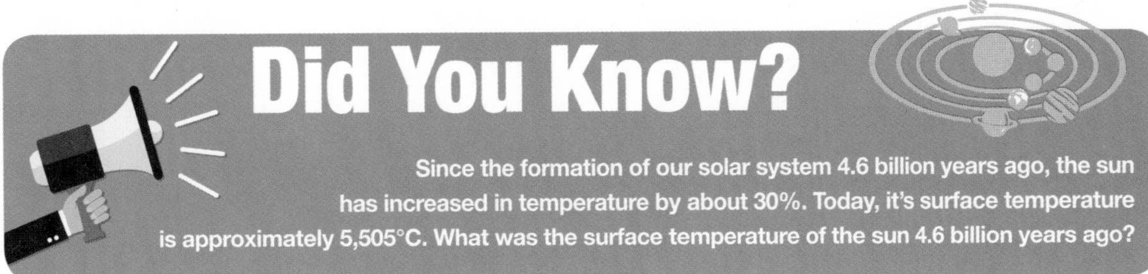

Did You Know?
Since the formation of our solar system 4.6 billion years ago, the sun has increased in temperature by about 30%. Today, it's surface temperature is approximately 5,505°C. What was the surface temperature of the sun 4.6 billion years ago?

If we are given the percent increase or decrease in percent change problems, then we can solve for the missing information. The method we would use looks like this:

Value Change Formula

Original Value +/– Percent of the Original Value = Final Value

or

$$X +/- \%(X) = Y$$

This method to solve percent problems is described in the following examples.

EXAMPLE 6.3 (A): Calculating the Final Value given the Percent Increase

The population of a small town was 2,350 last year. After a company moved their head office close by, the population increased by 6%. What is the increased population of the town?

Solution:

We know the original value (population last year): 2,350

Using X +/– % (X) = Y, we have,

$$2{,}350 + 6\%(2{,}350) = Y$$
$$2{,}350 + 0.06(2{,}350) = Y$$
$$2{,}350 + 141 = Y$$
$$2{,}491 = Y$$

Therefore, the increased population of the town is 2,491.

EXAMPLE 6.3 (B): Calculating the Original Value given the Percent Increase

Eli made $3,285 this month in commission. This is an increase of 15% from his commission last month. How much commission did he make last month?

Solution:

We know the final value (this month's commission); therefore, the original value (last month's commission) is our unknown.

$$X + 15\%(X) = \$3{,}285.00$$
$$X + 0.15X = 3{,}285.00$$
$$1.15X = 3{,}285.00$$
$$X = 3{,}285.00 \div 1.15$$
$$X = 2{,}856.521739... = \$2{,}856.52$$

Therefore, Eli made $2,856.52 in commission last month.

EXAMPLE 6.3 (C): Calculating the Original Value Given the Percent Decrease

Hasan's Hardware sold 460 hammers this month. Compared to last months' sales, this is a decrease of 20%. How many hammers were sold last month?

Solution:

We know the final value; therefore, the original value is unknown.

$$X - 20\% (X) = 460$$
$$X - 0.20X = 460$$
$$0.80X = 460$$
$$X = 460 \div 0.80$$
$$X = 575$$

Therefore, 575 hammers were sold last month.

EXAMPLE 6.3 (D): Estimating Using Percent Change (when we know the percentage)

A group of friends went out for dinner and the final bill, including taxes, came to $104.00. If they wanted to add 20% for a tip, estimate the tip amount and then calculate the total amount of the bill including the tip.

Solution:

When estimating an answer, it helps to round the numbers involved, so in this case we can round $104 to $100. Therefore, we need to find 20% of 100. Sometimes it helps to find 10% of an amount first. In this case 10% of 100 is 10. We can then multiply that by 2 since we need 20%. Therefore, 20% of 100 is $20 and that is the estimated amount of the tip. If we add that to the bill then we estimate the total to be $104 + $20 = $124.00

To check how close we are to the answer we can use the formula:

$$104 + 0.20(104) = Y$$
$$104 + 20.80 = Y$$
$$Y = 124.80$$

There was a difference of only $0.80 between the estimated value and the real value, which shows how close we were to the correct answer. Well done!

EXAMPLE 6.3 (E): Using Value Change Formula with Taxes (when we know X)

Deborah has been saving to buy a new laptop for school. The price of the laptop is $419.00 and taxes are 15%. How much will she have to pay in total for the laptop?

Solution:

We know the original value is $419 and that there is an increase of 15% due to the taxes. Remember to change the decimal to a percent (15% = 0.15).

Therefore:

$$419 + 15\%(419) = Y$$
$$419 + 0.15(419) = Y$$
$$419 + 62.85 = Y$$
$$Y = 481.85$$

Therefore, she will have to pay a total of $481.85 for the laptop.

EXAMPLE 6.3 (F): Using Value Change Formula with Taxes (when we know Y)

If the total amount paid for a pair of running shoes was $92.50, how much of that was the 13% tax?

Solution:

We know the final value is $92.50 and that there was an increase due to taxes being added and included in the total amount.

Therefore:

$$X + 13\%(X) = 92.50$$
$$X + 0.13X = 92.50$$
$$1.13X = 92.50$$
$$X = 92.50 \div 1.13$$
$$X = 81.86$$

Therefore, $81.86 is the amount BEFORE the taxes were added. So, $92.50 – $81.86 = $10.64 was the amount of taxes.

We can even double-check this by multiplying 81.86 by 1.13 → 81.86 × 1.13 = 92.50.

To find the percent change between an original value and a final value, you must first find the difference between the two values. Once you have done that, divide the difference by the original value and turn that into a percent.

Percent Change Formula

$$\textit{Percent Change} = \frac{\textit{Final Value} - \textit{Original Value}}{\textit{Original Value}} \times 100\%$$

Using this method to find the percent change is shown in the following examples.

EXAMPLE 6.3 (G): Calculating the Percent Increase

The population of a town changed from 4,176 last year to 4,325 this year. What was the percent change in population?

Solution:

$$\text{Percent Change} = \frac{\text{Final Value} - \text{Original Value}}{\text{Original Value}} \times 100\%$$

$$= \frac{4{,}325 - 4{,}176}{4{,}176} \times 100\%$$

$$= \frac{149}{4{,}176} \times 100\%$$

$$= 0.035680\ldots \times 100\%$$

$$= 3.57\% \text{ (increase)}$$

Therefore, there was a 3.57% increase in the population of the town from last year.

EXAMPLE 6.3 (H): Calculating the Percent Decrease

A clothing store sold 258 shirts this month. Last month they sold 344 shirts. What was the percent change in the sale of shirts?

Solution:

$$\text{Percent Change} = \frac{\text{Final Value} - \text{Original Value}}{\text{Original Value}} \times 100\%$$

$$= \frac{258 - 344}{344} \times 100\%$$

$$= \frac{-86}{344} \times 100\%$$

$$= -0.25 \times 100\%$$

$$= -25\% \text{ or } 25\% \text{ decrease}$$

Therefore, there was a 25% decrease in the sale of shirts from last month.

DISCUSSION

Come up with your own examples where you would calculate the percent change.

EXAMPLE 6.3 (I): Estimating Using Percent Change (when we don't know the percentage)

The area around a new school is growing in population quickly and the number of students attending the school has changed. Last year there were 388 students attending the school and this year there are now 465 students attending the school. Estimate the percent change of the number of students attending the school.

Solution:

To estimate the percent change, we should first figure out the difference in the number of students attending. Last year there were 388 and this year there are 465, therefore, the difference is 465 – 388 = 77 students. When calculating percent change, we always compare the difference to the 'original' value, in this case, the number of students last year.

If we started with 388 students and there was a change of 77 students, what percentage do we estimate that is? When estimating, it helps to round the numbers involved and in this case we can round 388 to 400. Next, let's see how many students 10% of 400 is. 10% of 400 is 40 which is not close enough to 77 students, so we know the percent change must be more than 10%. Let's try and double that (10% × 2 = 20%) to see how close that gets us, 40 × 2 = 80. 80 is much closer to 77 so we can safely say that the change is approximately 20%. The final step is to decide if the change was an increase or a decrease. To do this we compare the original value (388) to the final value (465). We see that the number has increased, therefore, our estimation is that the number increased by 20%. Now we can check how close our estimate is to the actual answer by using the formula.

$$\textit{Percent Change} = \frac{\textit{Final Value} - \textit{Original Value}}{\textit{Original Value}} \times 100\%$$

$$= \frac{465 - 388}{388} \times 100\%$$

$$= \frac{77}{388} \times 100\%$$

$= 19.85\%$ and if we round that to a whole number it is 20%

Great estimating!

EXAMPLE 6.3 (J): Using Percent Change Formula with Taxes

A boat costs \$9,530, but with taxes added the total came to \$10,959.50. What was the percent change in the cost of the boat? What was the tax rate?

Solution:

$$\textit{Percent Change} = \frac{\textit{Final Value} - \textit{Original Value}}{\textit{Original Value}} \times 100\%$$

$$= \frac{10{,}959.50 - 9{,}530}{9{,}530} \times 100\%$$

$$= \frac{1{,}429.50}{9{,}530} \times 100\%$$

$$= 0.15 \times 100\%$$

$$= 15\%$$

So, there was a 15% increase after taxes were added which means the tax rate was 15%.

Here is a helpful table for changing fractions to percent to decimals:

Table 6.3: Fraction-Decimal-Percentage Conversion Table

Fraction	Percentage	Decimal
$\frac{1}{2}$	50%	0.50
$\frac{1}{3}$	33.33% or 33%	0.33
$\frac{2}{3}$	66.67% or 67%	0.67
$\frac{3}{3}$	100%	1.00 or 1
$\frac{1}{4}$	25%	0.25
$\frac{2}{4}$	50%	0.50
$\frac{3}{4}$	75%	0.75
$\frac{4}{4}$	100%	1.00 or 1
$\frac{1}{5}$	20%	0.20
$\frac{2}{5}$	40%	0.40
$\frac{3}{5}$	60%	0.60
$\frac{4}{5}$	80%	0.80
$\frac{5}{5}$	100%	1.00 or 1
$\frac{1}{10}$	10%	0.10
$\frac{2}{10}$	20%	0.20
$\frac{3}{10}$	30%	0.30
$\frac{4}{10}$	40%	0.40
$\frac{5}{10}$	50%	0.50
Etc...		

6.3 EXERCISES

Answers to the odd numbered exercises are available at the end of the textbook.

Find the missing values in the tables in Exercises 1 and 2. Round answers to the nearest hundredth.

		Original Value	Percent Change	Final Value
1.	a.	15.50	25%	
	b.		11.25%	222.50
	c.		15%	312.00
	d.	35.50	−13%	
	e.		−15.50%	110.10
	f.		−23%	350.00

		Original Value	Percent Change	Final Value
2.	a.	89.90	32%	
	b.		22.5%	329.00
	c.		47%	439.00
	d.	175.50	−15%	
	e.		−32%	90.10
	f.		−40%	410.00

3. Last year, the number of students enrolled at a college was 13,585. If this number increased by 10%, what is the number of students enrolled at the college this year? Round up to the nearest whole number.

4. Brad's salary increased by 6%. If his salary was $43,500 initially, what is his new salary?

5. The average temperature this summer was 26° C. If the average temperature decreased by 12% from last summer, what was the average temperature last year?

6. If Carmen's hourly rate of pay increased by 4% to $17.50, what was her original hourly rate of pay?

7. If a pair of shoes went on sale from $80 to $59, what was the percent change in the price of the shoes?

8. A company's revenue was $356,000 last year. This year, their revenue is $412,000. What is the percent change in the company's revenue?

Find the missing values in the tables in Exercises 9 and 10.

		Final Value	*Original Value*	*Final Value – Original Value*	*% Change*
9.	a.	11	10		
	b.	9	10		
	c.		8	2	
	d.		7	−3	
	e.	25		−5	
	f.	100		10	

	Final Value	Original Value	Final Value – Original Value	% Change
g.		20		20%
h.		115		–35%

	Final Value	Original Value	Final Value – Original Value	% Change
10. a.	25	21		
b.	14	17		
c.		32	8	
d.		53	–19	
e.	69		–20	
f.	97		23	
g.		89		18%
h.		312		–80%

11. Determine the percent increase in the hourly rate of pay if last year you were making $12.00/hour, and this year you are making $14.50/hour.

12. Your mutual fund investment went from $20/share to $15/share. What percent increase or decrease did you experience?

13. The price of gasoline went from $1.20/litre to $1.18/litre. What is the percent change in the price of gasoline?

14. The sales at a store were $25,200 last year and $23,500 this year. What is the percent change in sales from last year?

15. A town's population increased by 253 from last year. If last year the town's population was 13,255, what is the town's population this year? What was the percent change in the population?

16. Last year, the value of a house was $515,000. This year, the value increased by $15,000. What is the new value of the house, and what is the percent change in value?

17. Taxes at a vacation resort are 23% in total. If the resort's base cost per room is $180 per night, how much is the cost in total per night including taxes?

18. A tour of an island near Cancun, Mexico costs $65 per person. In addition to this, taxes are 20% per person. What is the total cost per person, including taxes?

19. Sadie and Hana went out for dinner and the bill came to $32.78 after taxes. If the taxes were 15%, what was the amount owing before taxes?

20. A pair of winter boots cost $74.85 + 13% in taxes. What was the total cost of the boots with taxes included?

21. The price of a bike was $325 but with the taxes included the total came to $370.50. What was the amount and percentage of taxes on the bike?

22. A day-pass for Treetop Trekking is $45. There is a charge of 15% taxes on top of the $45 fee. What will you pay for a pass including taxes for 2 people?

23. Paula went shopping for groceries for the week. She was charged 5% GST on her purchases. If the total amount, including taxes, was $63.78, how much did she pay in taxes?

24. A package trip to Niagara-on-the-Lake for 2 days cost $489 plus tax. This includes 2-night accommodations and visits to popular landmarks. If the taxes are 23%, what is the total cost of the package?

25. Complete the fraction to percent to decimal conversions:

FRACTION	PERCENTAGE	DECIMAL
$\frac{1}{2}$		
	65%	
		0.08
	25%	
$\frac{3}{8}$		
		1.35
		0.4
$\frac{1}{3}$		

26. Complete the fraction to percent to decimal conversions:

FRACTION	PERCENTAGE	DECIMAL
$\frac{3}{4}$		
		0.05
	17%	
	10%	
		2.22
		0.007
$\frac{7}{8}$		
$\frac{1}{6}$		

6.4 PAYROLL

An important part of employment is the remuneration we receive for the services we provide. All companies have a system to keep track of all employees and their compensation. The number of employees, their payment periods, and the amount of payment is referred to as **payroll**. Payment can be made in various ways, such as:

- Hourly rate
- Annual salary
- Commissions

In this section, we will explore the different ways employees are compensated for their work and the ways to calculate their pay.

HOURLY RATE

A common option for organizations that employ part-time employees is to pay them an **hourly rate** or wage. This option allows employers to pay their employees on an hour-by-hour basis. The hourly rate of pay can differ from one organization to another. However, in Canada the minimum hourly wage is set for employees. The minimum hourly wages in Canada as of January 1st, 2019 are shown in the exhibit below.

Exhibit 6.4: Minimum Hourly Wages Across Canada in 2019

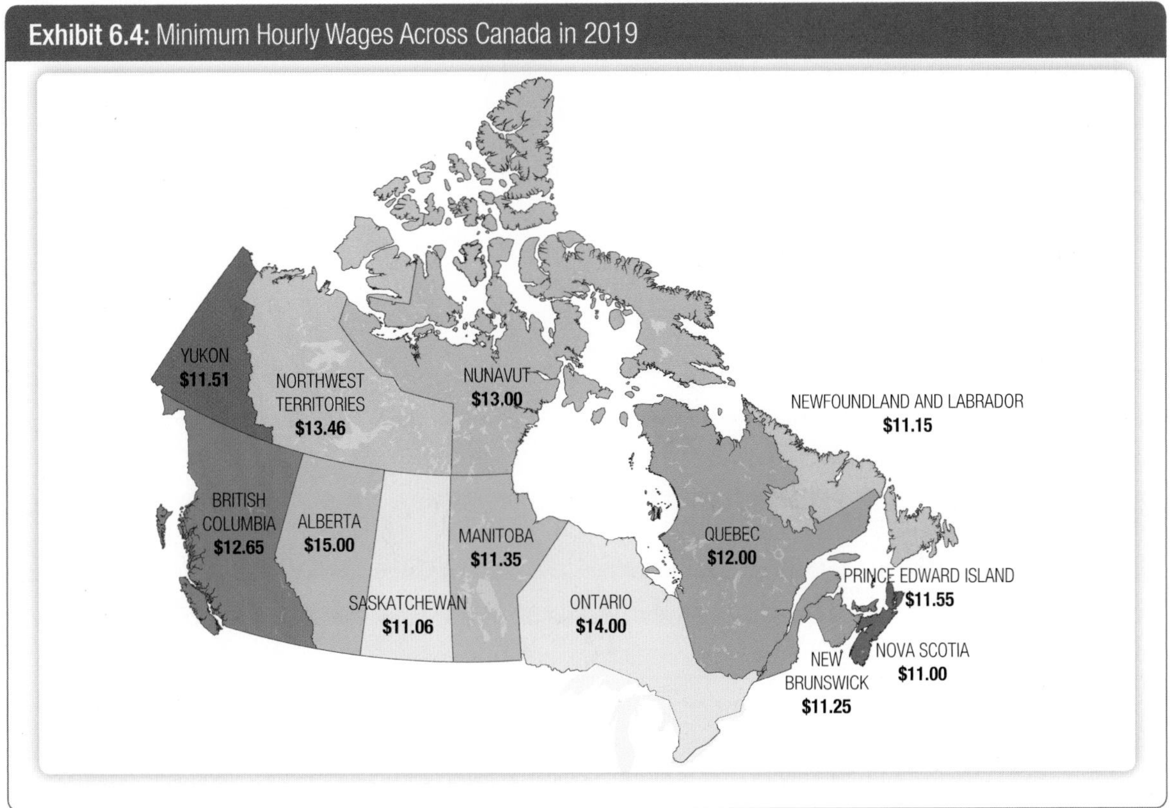

The total payment for a time period is calculated by multiplying the total number of hours worked by the hourly rate of pay.

Hourly Rate - Payment for Pay Period Formula

Payment for Pay Period = Hourly Wage × Total Number of Hours Worked

The number of hours is not fixed for these employees, and could vary from week to week, or even day to day. However, for most employees, the maximum number of hours worked per week is limited to 44 hours, and the number of work hours in a day is 8 hours. When employees are requested to work more than the set number of hours per week, they are paid an overtime amount. The overtime rate of pay is usually one and a half times the regular hourly rate; however, there are companies that also pay two times the regular hourly rate as the overtime rate.

EXAMPLE 6.4 (A): Calculating the Payment per Period, Given the Hourly Rate and the Total Number of Hours Worked

Ravinder works at a coffee shop and is paid an hourly wage of $11.75. Last week Ravinder worked 16 hours and this week he worked 21 hours. How much will Ravinder get paid for the total hours he worked during these two weeks?

Solution:

Total Number of Hours Worked for two weeks = 16 + 21 = 37.

Using the formula,

Payment for Pay Period = Hourly Wage × Total Number of Hours Worked

Payment for Pay Period = $11.75 × 37

Payment for Pay Period = $434.75

Therefore, Ravinder is paid $434.75 for these two weeks of work.

Let's take a look at an example where we know the total payment and the hours worked for the pay period, but do not know the hourly rate.

EXAMPLE 6.4 (B): Calculating the Hourly Rate of Pay, Given the Payment per Period and the Total Number of Hours Worked

Janice received $411.20 for a week in which she worked 32 hours. How much was her hourly rate of pay?

Solution:

Using the formula,

Payment for Pay Period = Hourly Wage × Total Number of Hours Worked

$411.20 = Hourly Wage × 32

$$\text{Hourly Wage} = \frac{\$411.20}{32}$$

Hourly Wage = $12.85

Therefore, Janice's hourly rate of pay was $12.85.

If we know how much was received in a payment period as well as the hourly wage, then the total hours worked can also be calculated.

EXAMPLE 6.4 (C): Calculating the Total Number of Hours Worked, Given the Hourly Rate and the Payment per Period

Farhan was paid an hourly rate of $14.25 and received $954.75 once every two weeks. How many hours did Farhan work in that pay period?

Solution:

Using the formula,

$$\text{Payment for Pay Period} = \text{Hourly Wage} \times \text{Total Number of Hours Worked}$$

$$\$954.75 = \$14.25 \times \text{Total Number of Hours Worked}$$

$$\text{Total Number of Hours Worked} = \frac{\$954.75}{\$14.25}$$

$$\text{Total Number of Hours Worked} = 67$$

Therefore, Farhan worked 67 hours in that pay period.

ANNUAL SALARY

Most employees that are hired to work on a full-time basis are paid an **annual salary**. The salary is then paid out to the employee on a set frequency that allows the employee to organize their funds throughout the year.

The most common pay periods are as follows:

Table 6.4: Pay Periods for Annual Salary

Payment Type	Payment Frequency	Payments Per Year
weekly payments	once per week	52
bi-weekly payments	once every two weeks	26
semi-monthly payments	twice per month	24
monthly payments	once per month	12

In order to calculate the payment for a particular time period, we must divide the annual salary by the payments per year:

Annual Salary Payment - Pay Period Formula

$$\textit{Payment for Pay Period} = \frac{\textit{Annual Salary}}{\textit{Payments per Year}}$$

EXAMPLE 6.4 (D): Calculating Payment per Pay Period Given Annual Salary and Payment Frequency

Sandra is paid an annual salary of $43,000. How much does Sandra receive if:

i Payments are made weekly?

ii Payments are made bi-weekly?

iii Payments are made semi-monthly?

iv Payments are made monthly?

Solution:

i **Weekly payments**

Using the formula:

$$\text{Payment for Pay Period} = \frac{\text{Annual Salary}}{\text{Payments per Year}}$$

$$= \frac{43{,}000.00}{52}$$

$$= 826.923076... = \$826.92$$

Therefore, when payments are made weekly, Sandra will receive $826.92 per pay period.

ii **Bi-weekly payments**

Using the formula:

$$\text{Payment for Pay Period} = \frac{\text{Annual Salary}}{\text{Payments per Year}}$$

$$= \frac{43{,}000.00}{26}$$

$$= 1{,}653.846154... = \$1{,}653.85$$

Therefore, when payments are made bi-weekly, Sandra will receive $1,653.85 per pay period.

iii **Semi-monthly payments**

Using the formula:

$$\text{Payment for Pay Period} = \frac{\text{Annual Salary}}{\text{Payments per Year}}$$

$$= \frac{43{,}000.00}{24}$$

$$= 1{,}791.666667... = \$1{,}791.67$$

Therefore, when payments are made semi-monthly, Sandra will receive $1,791.67 per pay period.

EXAMPLE 6.4 (D): Calculating Payment per Pay Period Given Annual Salary and Payment Frequency *continued*

iv **Monthly payments**

Using the formula:

$$\text{Payment for Pay Period} = \frac{\text{Annual Salary}}{\text{Payments per Year}}$$

$$= \frac{43{,}000.00}{12}$$

$$= 3{,}583.333333... = \$3{,}583.33$$

Therefore, when payments are made monthly, Sandra will receive $3,583.33 per pay period.

Often employees that receive an annual salary will work 'overtime', which is considered work done above the hours included in the annual salary. Overtime is paid on an hourly basis and added to the amount received from the salary. Organizations will vary on the calculation of overtime, but the most common rate would be 'time and a half' (1.5) or 'double time' (2).

Hourly and Overtime Wage Formulas

$$\text{Weekly Pay} = \frac{\text{Annual Salary}}{52}$$

$$\text{Hourly Wage} = \frac{\text{Weekly Pay}}{\text{\# of Hours per Week}}$$

$$\text{Overtime Wage} = \text{Hourly Wage} \times \text{Overtime Rate}$$

EXAMPLE 6.4 (E): Calculating Overtime Pay for a Weekly Pay Period

Patricia works for a storage company. She receives an annual salary of $43,800 and works 37.5 hours/week. Occasionally, she works overtime when the company's services are in high demand. How much would Patricia receive in a weekly pay period where she worked 6 hours of overtime at time-and-a-half?

Solution:

$$\text{Weekly Pay} = \frac{\$43{,}800.00}{52} = 842.307692... = \$842.31$$

$$\text{Hourly Wage} = \frac{\$842.31}{37.5} = 22.4616... = \$22.46/\text{hour}$$

$$\text{Overtime Wage} = \$22.46 \times 1.5 = \$33.69/\text{hour}$$

$$\text{Total Pay} = \text{Overtime Wage} \times \text{Hours of Overtime} + \text{Weekly Pay}$$

$$= \$33.69(6) + \$842.31$$

$$= \$202.14 + \$842.31$$

$$= \$1{,}044.45$$

Therefore, Patricia would receive $1,044.45 for a week in which she worked 6 hours of overtime.

Note that we have rounded each step to two decimal places and will continue to follow this method for multi-step questions. However, you can choose to keep as many decimals as you'd like for the intermediate steps and round only in the last step.

COMMISSION

Those that are employed in organizations that focus on sales will often be paid by commission. Commission based pay is meant to reward employees for the total sales they make for a given period, based on the percent of commission that is offered. Commission based income can be applied in various ways, such as commission only, tiered commission, and base + commission.

COMMISSION ONLY

Employees such as real estate agents and those involved in car sales will earn their income based solely on the commission they receive from their total sales. To calculate total commission, we need to know the total sales as well as the percent of commission.

Total Commission Formula

$$\text{Total Commission} = \text{Commission Percent} \times \text{Total Sales}$$

EXAMPLE 6.4 (F): Calculating Total Commission for Commission Only Based Income

Brenda is a real estate agent and is currently finalizing the closing of a home sale where she will earn 2.45% commission on the sale of a home worth $675,000. How much commission will Brenda earn?

Solution:

$$\begin{aligned}\text{Total Commission} &= \text{Commission Percent} \times \text{Total Sales}\\ &= 2.45\% \times \$675{,}000.00\\ &= 0.0245 \times 675{,}000.00\\ &= \$16{,}537.50\end{aligned}$$

Therefore, Brenda will receive $16,537.50 in commission from the sale of the house.

TIERED COMMISSION

As an incentive to sell more, often a company will offer 'tiered' commission to its employees. This means that there will be an increase in the percent of commission earned depending on the amount of sales made.

EXAMPLE 6.4 (G): Calculating Total Commission for Tiered Commission Based Income

Hans works for a computer store and receives commission based monthly pay. He receives 2.25% on the first $7,000 of sales, 3.75% on the next $10,000 of sales, and 5% on all remaining sales.

i How much commission did Hans receive last month on total sales of $35,000?

ii How much commission will Hans earn this month if his total sales are $16,500?

EXAMPLE 6.4 (G): Calculating Total Commission for Tiered Commission Based Income *continued*

Solution:

i

$$\begin{aligned}\text{Total Commission} &= 2.25\% \times \$7{,}000.00 + 3.75\% \times \$10{,}000.00 + 5\% \times (\$35{,}000.00 - \$7{,}000.00 - \$10{,}000.00)\\ &= 2.25\% \times 7{,}000.00 + 3.75\% \times 10{,}000.00 + 5\% \times 18{,}000\\ &= 0.0225(7{,}000.00) + 0.0375(10{,}000.00) + 0.05(18{,}000.00)\\ &= 157.50 + 375.00 + 900.00\\ &= \$1{,}432.50\end{aligned}$$

Therefore, Hans received $1,432.50 in commission for last month's sales of $35,000.

ii

$$\begin{aligned}\text{Total Commission} &= 2.25\% \times 7{,}000.00 + 3.75\% \times 9{,}500\\ &= 0.0225(7{,}000.00) + 0.0375(9{,}500.00)\\ &= 157.50 + 356.25\\ &= \$513.75\end{aligned}$$

Therefore, he will earn $513.75 in commissions on sales of $16,500.

BASE + COMMISSION

Another payment option that some organizations utilize is the base + commission model. This allows an employee to receive a base pay PLUS the ability to earn more money based on the sales made during the payment period.

EXAMPLE 6.4 (H): Calculating Total Pay for Base + Commission Based Income

Priyanka worked in a shoe store that paid her $11.50/hour + 6.50% commission on sales that exceed $6,000. How much did Priyanka receive in a week where she worked 32 hours and sold $14,000 worth of shoes in total?

Solution:

$$\begin{aligned}\text{Total Pay} &= \text{Total Hourly Pay} + \text{Commission}\\ &= \$11.50(32) + 0.065(\$14{,}000.00 - \$6{,}000.00)\\ &= 368.00 + 520.00\\ &= \$888.00\end{aligned}$$

Therefore, Priyanka received $888.00.

6.4 EXERCISES

Answers to the odd numbered exercises are available at the end of the textbook.

For all of the below exercises, round your answer to two decimal places wherever applicable.

1. Sabrina works as a freelancer and is paid $15 per hour for a website development project. If she is paid every four weeks and worked 47 hours in the first week, 30 hours in the second week, and 32 hours in the third and fourth weeks last month, calculate her gross pay.

2. Ayesha, an accountant in a bookkeeping firm, works for 39 hours a week and is paid $35 per hour. Calculate her monthly payment, assuming each month has 4 weeks.

3. Satomu, a lawyer at a top legal consulting firm, received a remuneration of $9,650 for two weeks in which he worked 26 hours per week. How much is his hourly rate?

4. Ana works as a chef at Royale Cuisine Ltd. and earns $1,530 for 36 hours of work in a week. What is her hourly rate?

5. Lola, a newly graduated architect, is offered jobs from two different companies:

   Option 1: $76 per hour; 42 hours of work every week

   Option 2: $85 per hour; 39 hours of work every week

   If she will be paid on a monthly basis, which offer has a higher pay per period assuming each month has 4 weeks?

6. Job Outsourcing Inc. is looking for one editor and one writer for a newspaper company. The salaries are as follows:

   Writer: $1,085 for a 28-hour workweek

   Editor: $1,215 for a 30-hour workweek

   Which job has a higher hourly rate? By how much?

7. Alyana, an IT specialist, is paid $39 per hour and earns $6,800 for a monthly pay period. How many hours does she work every pay period?

8. Jin, a broadcaster on NewsTV, has an hourly rate of $78 and receives $4,865 for a weekly pay period. How many hours does she work in a week?

9. A famous computer company offered Richard a job that pays $49,500 per annum in which he is required to work 35 hours a week. Calculate his gross pay for a pay period if he's paid:

   a. monthly

   b. semi-monthly

   c. bi-weekly

   d. weekly

10. A car manufacturing company pays each technician $55,600 per annum. How much does each technician receive if the pay period is bi-weekly?

11. Due to a successful project launch, Genie is promoted as the Vice President of Business and Development of a company. Her $70,000 salary is increased by 20%. She is paid on the 1st and 15th of each month. How much will she receive per pay period?

12. Czarina decided to apply as a senior hairstylist in a well-known salon. If she is offered an annual salary of $57,500, compute her semi-monthly gross pay. If her employer changes her pay period to monthly instead of semi-monthly, what monthly payment will she receive?

13. Simone graduated with honours at her university. She was offered advertising jobs at two big companies:

    Company A: $1673.08, paid on a weekly basis

    Company B: $3076.92, paid on a bi-weekly basis

    Which company offers higher weekly earnings? By how much?

14. Builders Inc. promoted Naresh as the head of the architecture department. From $74,000, his salary increased by 25%. If his employer pays him weekly, calculate his total earnings per pay period.

15. Paloma works as an event coordinator and earns an annual salary of $56,900. She works overtime when their company has additional events. How much will she receive in a weekly pay period if she worked 50 hours? Assume that she is only required to work for 40 hours and the overtime factor is $1\frac{1}{2}$.

16. Luis, a chemical engineer, receives an annual salary of $77,600 and has 33-hour workweeks. If he worked 14 hours of overtime during his last pay period to assist with the shipping of building equipment, calculate his gross pay per period. Assume that his overtime factor is $1\frac{1}{2}$ and he is paid on a weekly basis.

17. Tasty Cola Corp. is paying each factory worker an annual salary of $33,500. Each worker works 45 hours per week, paid bi-weekly, and occasionally has overtime work when soda is in high demand. What is their pay per period if all of them have 7 hours of overtime, in one pay period, at time and a half?

18. Mitesh, a corporate secretary, has an annual salary of $48,500, has 36-hour workweeks and is paid bi-weekly. If his overtime factor is time and a half, calculate his gross pay for the pay period if he worked a total of 89 hours.

19. Yvette, a real estate agent, sells a house for $350,000. If she receives a commission of 2.3%, how much commission will she earn?

20. Giang sells cars at a car dealership in Vancouver. This month, she sold 5 cars valued at $35,000, $18,000, $22,000, $57,000, and $16,000, respectively. If her entire income is based on commission, and she receives 3.75% commission on all car sales she makes, what is her income this month?

21. Jana works part-time in a shoe store in the mall and receives commission every month. She receives 10% commission for her first $2,000 worth of sales, 15% commission on the next $3,000 worth of sales, and 20% commission on all sales that exceed $5,000. How much commission does she receive in a month where she sells $5,950 worth of shoes?

22. Mateo works in an electronics store and is paid commission for his monthly sales. This month he sold $14,300 worth of electronics. If he makes 4% on his first $5,000 of sales, 6% on his next $5,000 of sales, and 8% on all remaining sales, what is the total commission he made this month?

23. Victoria works in sales at a toy store during the summer and earns $11.75/hour. As an incentive to its employees, the toy store pays them a 2.5% commission for monthly sales that exceed $2,500. If Victoria works 80 hours and sells $3,700 worth of toys this month, what is her total pay for the month?

24. Petra works as a personal trainer at her local gym. She is paid $13.00/hour and receives a commission of 5% on all personal training sales she makes that exceed $5,000 each month. Calculate her total pay if she works 65 hours and makes $6,100 worth of sales this month.

REVIEW EXERCISES

Answers to the odd numbered exercises are available at the end of the textbook.

Calculate the arithmetic average of the sets of numbers in Exercises 1 and 2.

1. a. 24, 16 b. 3, 4, 9, 8, 6 c. 12, 14, 16 d. 14, 11, 20, 8

2. a. 7, 5 b. 1, 4, 9, 7, 1 c. 19, 14, 27 d. 5, 13, 4, 6

3. Brooke took 5 courses in her first semester, 6 in her second semester, 4 in her third semester, and 6 in her fourth semester. Calculate the average number of courses she took per semester.

4. Hamza received a grade of 82% in English, 94% in Mathematics, 88% in Marketing, and 76% in Computer Application. What was his average percent grade for all 4 subjects?

5. Evan was teaching five classes this semester. He had 33, 41, 27, 25, and 35 students in sections A, B, C, D, and E respectively. What was the average number of students he had per section? Round up to the nearest whole number.

6. Wanda works as a computer technician. In April, she worked 38 hours in the first week, 34 hours the second week, 40 hours the third week, and 39 hours the fourth week. Calculate the average number of hours she worked per week in April.

In Exercises 7 to 10, round the answers to the nearest cent, wherever applicable.

7. Jamal had to buy supplies for school. He bought 4 black pens costing $3 each, 3 red pens costing $4 each, 6 pencils costing 20 cents each, and 3 markers costing $3.50 each. What was the average price of his items?

8. A store sells laptops, notebooks, and desktop computers. Last week, a salesperson sold 4 laptops at $750 each, 7 notebooks at $475 each, and 5 desktop computers at $1,200 each. What was the average price of the items sold?

9. A landscaping company has 21 employees who are paid $18 per hour, 11 employees who are paid $21 per hour, and 7 employees who are paid $25 per hour. Determine the average hourly rate of the employees.

10. A small advertising company has 8 employees who are paid $22 per hour, 6 employees who are paid $28 per hour, and 3 employees who are paid $35 per hour. Determine the average hourly rate of the employees.

In Exercises 11 and 12, convert the percents to decimal numbers.

11. a. 5% b. 28% c. 420% d. 73% e. 61% f. 7.8%

12. a. 9% b. 14% c. 185% d. 107% e. 52% f. 3.4%

In Exercises 13 and 14, convert the decimal numbers to percents.

13. a. 0.21 b. 0.70 c. 0.41 d. 0.3 e. 8.0 f. 0.414141

14. a. 0.14 b. 0.402 c. 0.64 d. 0.6 e. 1.09 f. 0.0777

15. Complete the table.

Fraction	Percent	Decimal
$\frac{1}{2}$		
	48%	
		0.07
	25%	

16. Complete the table.

Fraction	Percent	Decimal
	8%	
		1.46
$\frac{1}{4}$		
		0.2

For Exercises 17 to 46, round to your answer two decimal places, wherever applicable.

17. How much tax is charged on an item that costs $121.99, if the tax rate is 13%?

18. What is 41% of $79.50?

19. Hilda was paid $16.00/hour at her job. She received a raise of 9%. What was the amount of the raise? What was her new hourly rate?

20. A clothing store paid $18.00 for a sweater and marked up the price by 47%. What was the amount of the markup? What was the price of the sweater after the increase?

21. A family went for dinner at a restaurant and the bill came to $94.72. They wanted to leave a tip of 15%. How much was the tip? What was the total amount they paid?

22. During a snow day, only 73% of students attended classes. If there are 2,600 students in the school, how many made it to class and how many did not?

23. Shara receives $3,650 pay each month from her job. If she spends 24% on rent and 13% on food, how much does she have remaining after her expenses?

24. Taxes at a vacation resort are 21% in total. If the resort's base cost per room is $165 per night, how much is the cost in total per night including taxes?

25. Last year there were 21,425 students enrolled at a college. If this number increased by 10% from last year, what is the number of students enrolled at the college this year?

26. Anthony's salary increased by 4%. If his salary was $47,500 initially, what is his new salary?

27. The average temperature this summer was 24° C. If the average temperature decreased by 8% from last summer, what was the average temperature last year?

28. If Anika's hourly rate of pay increased by 6% to $19.50, what was her original hourly rate of pay?

29. If a pair of boots went on sale from $120 to $79, what was the percent change in the price of the shoes?

30. A company had a revenue of $650,000 last year. This year, their revenue was $840,000. What was the percent change in the company's revenue?

31. Paula works as a freelance writer and is paid $25 per hour. If she is paid every four weeks and worked 41 hours in the first week, 35 hours in the second week, and 27 hours in the third and fourth weeks last month, calculate her gross pay.

32. Ava, a bookkeeper, works 36 hours a week and is paid $35 per hour. Calculate her monthly earnings.

33. Malikai, a top consultant, received a remuneration of $12,450 for two weeks in which he worked 32 hours per week. How much is his hourly rate?

34. Ana works as a chef and earns $5,375 for 42 hours of work in a week. Compute her hourly rate.

35. A company offered Derek a job that earns $52,500 per annum in which he is required to work 38 hours a week. Calculate his gross pay for a pay period if he's paid
    a. monthly
    b. semi-monthly
    c. bi-weekly
    d. weekly

36. A manufacturing company pays each technician $62,300 per annum. How much does each technician receive if the pay period is bi-weekly?

37. Brianna is promoted to Vice President of Research and Development of a company. Her salary of $65,000 is increased by 27%. She is paid on the 1st and 15th of each month. How much will she receive per pay period?

38. ABC Inc. promoted William as the head of the Marketing department. From $59,500, his salary increased by 24%. If his employer pays him weekly, calculate his total earnings per pay period.

39. Nadine earns an annual salary of $53,700. She works overtime when their company has special projects. How much will she receive in a weekly pay period if she worked 48 hours? Assume that she is only required to work for 40 hours and the overtime factor is $1\frac{1}{2}$.

40. Gurjot receives an annual salary of $71,300 and has a 37-hour workweek. If he worked 14 hours of overtime during his last pay period, calculate his gross pay per period. Assume that his overtime factor is $1\frac{1}{2}$ and he is paid on a weekly basis.

41. Mariella sells a house for $750,000. If she receives a commission of 2.3%, how much commission will she earn?

42. George sells cars at a car dealership in Ottawa. This month, he sold 5 cars valued at $32,000, $16,000, $24,500, $41,000, and $27,000, respectively. If his entire income is based on commission, and he receives 4.15% commission on all car sales he makes, what is his income this month?

43. Cynthia works part-time in a shoe store and receives commission every month. She receives 12% commission for her first $2,500 of sales, 17% commission on the next $3,000 of sales, and 22% commission on all sales that exceed $5,500. How much commission does she receive in a month where she sells $6,850 worth of shoes?

44. Tejas works part-time in an electronics store and is paid commission for his monthly sales. This month he sold $31,300 worth of electronics. If he makes 3.5% on his first $8,000 of sales, 5.5% on his next $15,000 of sales, and 8.5% on all remaining sales, what is the total commission he made this month?

45. Mehvish works in sales at a craft store during the summer. She receives $15.75/hour, and as an incentive, all sales that exceed $4,500 in a month receive a commission of 3.5%. If she works 60 hours and sells $8,400 worth of toys this month, what is her total pay for the month?

46. Tanya works as an esthetician at a salon. She is paid $24.00/hour, and receives a commission of 7.5% on all sales she makes that exceed $15,000 each month. Calculate her total pay if she works 65 hours and makes $21,800 worth of sales this month.

CHAPTER 7

RATIOS AND PROPORTIONS

LEARNING OBJECTIVES

Studying this chapter will provide you with the knowledge needed to:

- Identify ratios and proportions.
- Reduce ratios to lowest terms.
- Solve for unknown terms in proportions.

TOPICS

7.1 RATIOS

A **ratio** can be defined as a relationship between two or more quantities. For example, if the number of females in a classroom is 12 and the number of males is 15, then we can say that the ratio of females to males in the classroom is 12 to 15.

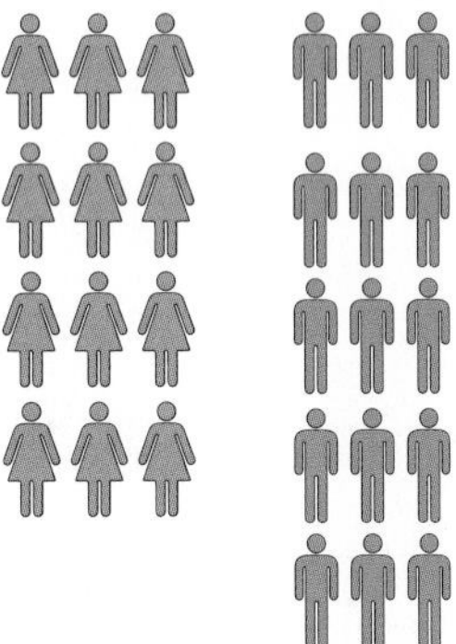

12 females : 15 males

"12 : 15" is referred to as a ratio. The numbers 12 and 15 are the **terms** of the ratio, and we put a colon between the terms to present them in ratio form. Changing the order of the terms in a ratio results in a different ratio, i.e. 12 : 15 ≠ 15 : 12. For a ratio to have meaning, both terms must be non-zero. Ratios can also contain more than 2 terms.

For example: If you have US$10, C$5, and £2, then the ratio of the different amounts you have is:

US$: C$: £ = 10 : 5 : 2

Did You Know?

In Shakespeare's collective works, he used 31,534 distinct words. Of those words, he used 14,376 only once. What is the ratio of words Shakespeare used once to words he used more than once?

Later in this chapter we will be solving proportions. To assist in solving, we can visually represent the ratio in a way that looks like a fraction, ie. $\frac{12}{15}$. This is not to be confused with expressing the ratio as a mathematical fraction but rather simply putting the right side of the ratio below the left. If we are to actually express the ratio as a fraction, that would require that we ensure the 'total' parts of the ratio are represented in the denominator.

If we want to express how many females are in the class in fraction form, it would be $\frac{12}{27}$. The 27 is obtained as a result of including all the females and all the males in the total count of students in the class. Therefore, total females is expressed as $\frac{12}{27}$ and total males is expressed as $\frac{15}{27}$.

Did You Know?
Your tongue can detect sweetness in a solution of 1 part sugar to 200 parts water.

SIMPLIFYING RATIOS

Just as we can simplify fractions, we can simplify ratios to their lowest terms.

Illustration 7.1(A): Simplifying Ratios

Andrew has completed 5 courses out of 35. Express the ratio of his completed courses to total number of courses in simplest form.

Completed Courses : Total Number of Courses	5 : 35
Divide each term by 5	1 : 7

Therefore, 5 : 35 = 1 : 7

1 : 7 is called an **equivalent ratio** of 5 : 35 as they are equal when reduced to lowest terms.

A ratio is generally (but not always) expressed in its lowest terms. Ratios are expressed without units.

USING RATIOS TO SHARE QUANTITIES

Illustration 7.1(B): Understanding Parts and Total Parts of a Ratio

It is important that we understand that a ratio is split into 'parts', as was shown in our example of the males and females in a classroom. The 'parts' of 12 females and 15 males equal 27 in total. When we are using ratios to solve a problem around quantities, we need to ensure that the parts are added together and that each portion is considered as a part of the total.

Ratios can be used to share quantities as illustrated in the following examples:

EXAMPLE 7.1 (A): Using Ratios to Share Quantities Between Two People

Ann and Ben invested $10,000 in the ratio of 2 : 3. How much did they each invest?

Solution:

They distributed this investment in 2 + 3 = 5 parts.

$$\text{Ann's investment} = \frac{2}{5} \times \$10{,}000.00 = \$4{,}000.00$$

$$\text{Ben's investment} = \frac{3}{5} \times \$10{,}000.00 = \$6{,}000.00$$

Therefore, Ann invested $4,000 and Ben invested $6,000.

EXAMPLE 7.1 (B): Using Ratios to Share Quantities Among Three People

Marina, Quincy, and Khalid invested $50,000 in the ratio of 1 : 2 : 3 to start a business. What was the amount each person invested?

Solution:

They distributed this investment in 1 + 2 + 3 = 6 parts.

$$\text{Marina's investment} = \frac{1}{6} \times \$50{,}000.00 = 8{,}333.333333... = \$8{,}333.33$$

$$\text{Quincy's investment} = \frac{2}{6} \times \$50{,}000.00 = 16{,}666.666666... = \$16{,}666.67$$

$$\text{Khalid's investment} = \frac{3}{6} \times \$50{,}000.00 = \$25{,}000.00$$

Therefore, Marina, Quincy, and Khalid invested $8,333.33, $16,666.67, and $25,000.00, respectively.

USING RATIOS TO DETERMINE UNIT RATES

Given a ratio between two quantities, you can determine the ratio of the first term to a *single unit* of the second term, also known as the **unit rate**. For example, the kilometres a car travels per hour is a unit rate because it represents the distance traveled in a single hour.

EXAMPLE 7.1 (C): Using a Ratio as a Unit Rate

Saul worked 5 hours and earned $80. Calculate his hourly rate of pay.

Solution:

Earning $80 for working 5 hours expressed as ratio is,

80 : 5

To find the hourly rate, we simply divide the total amount earned by the quantity of hours provided.

Since $\frac{80}{5} = 16$, Saul's hourly rate of pay is $16/hr. We can also think of this as reducing the ratio 80 : 5 to its lowest terms, 16 : 1.

7.1 EXERCISES

Answers to the odd numbered exercises are available at the end of the textbook.

Reduce the ratios in Exercises 1 and 2 to their lowest terms.

1. a. 2 : 4 b. 6 : 18 c. 12 : 22
   d. 16 : 24 e. 21 : 24 f. 200 : 125
   g. $\frac{4}{3} : 2$ h. 2 : 4 : 8 i. 50 : 30 : 25

2. a. 3 : 9 b. 5 : 35 c. 14 : 16
   d. 15 : 20 e. 9 : 18 f. 300 : 180
   g. $\frac{8}{6} : 4$ h. 3 : 9 : 18 i. 70 : 40 : 80

3. Write the following as ratios and simplify to lowest terms:
   a. A college hired 20 professors for 600 students.
   b. A student has worked an average of 6 hours per day this year, whereas he worked 4 hours per day last year.
   c. A college graduate earned three times as much per hour as his brother who did not have a college diploma.
   d. A textbook for an english course costs twice as much as the one for a math course.
   e. Elisa works 40 hours per week, Julie works 35 hours per week, and Samantha works 30 hours per week.
   f. Deepak earns $15 per hour, Ashish earns $12 per hour, and their little brother Krishna earns $8 per hour.

4. Write the following as ratios and simplify to lowest terms:
   a. A restaurant hired 5 chefs and 25 waiters.
   b. A financial consultant worked an average of 40 hours per week this year, whereas he worked 35 hours per week last year.
   c. A senior manager earns four times as much per hour as a junior manager.
   d. A large coffee costs five-fourths as much as a medium one.
   e. Min, Hugo, and Sonal study 12, 16, and 20 hours per week, respectively.
   f. Ingrid, Foluke, and David earn $2,700, $3,300, and $3,900 every month, respectively.

5. Amy and Kevin invested $24,000 in their bakery. If the ratio of their investments is 2 : 3 respectively, how much did each invest?

6. Pascal and Jasmine shared the profit of $16,000 from their company last month. If they shared the profit in the ratio of 5 : 8 respectively, how much did each receive?

7. Carson and Hannah invested $5,000 in their lamp manufacturing business. If the ratio of their investments was 3 : 5 respectively, how much did each invest?

8. Naomi and Sylvain invested $3,000 in furniture for their office. If the ratio of their investments was 2 : 5 respectively, how much did each invest?

9. Tanya and Matilde invested $4,000 in their ice cream specialty store. If the ratio of their investments was 3 : 7 respectively, how much did each invest?

10. Lakeem, Vincent, and Nolan invested $20,000 to upgrade the machinery for their business in the ratio of 2 : 3 : 4 respectively. How much did each invest?

11. Chris, Lacey, and Nadia invested a total of $30,000 for their new timeshare property in the ratio of 3 : 4 : 5 respectively. How much did each invest?

12. Kim, Lisa, and Yuna bought a condo in Florida for $100,000 and invested in the ratio of 1 : 2 : 7 respectively. How much did each invest?

13. If John worked 12 hours and earned $200, was was his hourly wage?

14. If Bhavin drove 150 km in 2 hours, what was his speed in km/hr?

7.2 PROPORTIONS

When two ratios are equivalent, we say that they are **proportional** to each other.

For example: The ratios 4 : 6 and 20 : 30 are proportional to each other.

We can verify this as follows:

$4 : 6 = 20 : 30$

$\frac{4}{6} = \frac{20}{30}$ Write as fractions.

$\frac{2}{3} = \frac{2}{3}$ Simplify to lowest terms.

As the ratios are equal when reduced to lowest terms, they are proportional.

SOLVING FOR AN UNKNOWN TERM IN A PROPORTION

If any term in a proportion is unknown, we can write the ratios as fractions and cross-multiply to calculate the unknown term.

Did You Know?

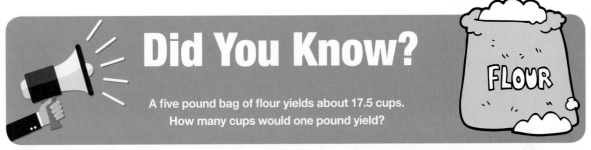

A five pound bag of flour yields about 17.5 cups. How many cups would one pound yield?

Illustration 7.2: Solving for an Unknown Term in a Proportion

In the proportion equation 3 : *k* = 4 : 9, find the value of the unknown term '*k*'.

$3 : k = 4 : 9$

$\frac{3}{k} = \frac{4}{9}$ Write ratios as fractions.

$(3)(9) = (4)(k)$ Cross-multiply.

$27 = 4k$ Simplify.

$\frac{27}{4} = k$

$k = 6.75$

Therefore, 3 : 6.75 = 4 : 9

We can check our answers by converting the ratios to percents by dividing the first term of each ratio by the second term of each ratio and multiplying by 100% and seeing if they are equal.

$3 \div 6.75 = 0.444444... \times 100\ \% = 44.44\%$

$4 \div 9 = 0.444444... \times 100\ \% = 44.44\%$

EXAMPLE 7.2 (A): Finding the Unknown in a Proportion

Find the unknown term in the proportion 6 : 11 = 7 : x and confirm that the ratios are in proportion by converting both into percents.

Solution:

$6 : 11 = 7 : x$

$\frac{6}{11} = \frac{7}{x}$ Write ratios as fractions.

$(6)(x) = (7)(11)$ Cross-multiply.

$6x = 77$ Simplify.

$x = \frac{77}{6}$

$x = 12.833333...$

Convert 6 : 11 and 7 : 12. 833333... to percents to check if they are equal.

$6 : 11 = \frac{6}{11} = 0.545454... = 54.55\%$

$7 : 12.833333... = \frac{7}{12.833333...} = 0.545454... = 54.55\%$

Therefore, 6 : 11 = 7 : 12.833333...

EXAMPLE 7.2 (B): Solving Word Problems Using Proportions

Dalia goes to the market and buys 4 apples and 10 oranges. If next week she buys 6 apples, how many oranges should she buy to keep the ratio of apples to oranges in proportion?

Solution:

Step 1: Identify the ratio.

4 apples and 10 oranges

Therefore, the ratio is 4 : 10.

Step 2: Choose a variable for each term in the ratio.

A is apples and O is oranges

Therefore, the ratio can be expressed as A : O.

Step 3: Complete the proportion.

Review the question and complete the proportion by inserting the information you know into the ratio A : O.

she buys 6 apples

Therefore, A : O can be replaced with 6 : O.

EXAMPLE 7.2 (B): Solving Word Problems Using Proportions *continued*

Solution:

We now have a proportion with an unknown.

$4 : 10 = 6 : O$

$\frac{4}{10} = \frac{6}{O}$ Write ratios as fractions.

$(4)(O) = (6)(10)$ Cross-multiply.

$4O = 60$ Simplify.

$O = \frac{60}{4}$

$O = 15$

Therefore, Dalia should buy 15 oranges.

SOLVING FOR TWO UNKNOWN TERMS IN A PROPORTION

In a proportion with three terms $x : y : z = p : q : r$, the relationship among the terms can be expressed as:

$$\frac{x}{y} = \frac{p}{q} \text{ or } \frac{y}{z} = \frac{q}{r} \text{ or } \frac{x}{z} = \frac{p}{r}$$

When there are three terms, you can solve for two unknowns in a proportion.

EXAMPLE 7.2 (C): Solving for Two Unknown Terms in a Proportion

Find the values of the unknown terms in the following proportions.

i. $3 : 4 : x = k : 8 : 16$

ii. $a : 8 : 5 = 6 : b : 2$

Solution:

i. $3 : 4 : x = k : 8 : 16$

Express the equation as relationships amongst the terms.

$\frac{3}{4} = \frac{k}{8}$ $\frac{4}{x} = \frac{8}{16}$ $\frac{3}{x} = \frac{k}{16}$

To solve for x and k, select the two relationships that contain only one variable, x or k, but not both.

$\frac{3}{4} = \frac{k}{8}$ $\frac{4}{x} = \frac{8}{16}$

$(3)(8) = (k)(4)$ $(4)(16) = (8)(x)$ Cross multiply.

$24 = 4k$ $64 = 8x$ Simplify.

$\frac{24}{4} = k$ $\frac{64}{8} = x$

$k = 6$ $x = 8$

Therefore, $3 : 4 : 8 = 6 : 8 : 16$.

EXAMPLE 7.2 (C): Solving for Two Unknown Terms in a Proportion *continued*

Solution:

ii. $a : 8 : 5 = 6 : b : 2$

Express the equation as relationships amongst the terms.

$$\frac{a}{8} = \frac{6}{b} \qquad \frac{8}{5} = \frac{b}{2} \qquad \frac{a}{5} = \frac{6}{2}$$

To solve for a and b, select the two relationships that contain only one variable, a or b, but not both.

$$\frac{a}{5} = \frac{6}{2} \qquad \frac{8}{5} = \frac{b}{2}$$

$(a)(2) = (6)(5)$ $\quad$ $(8)(2) = (b)(5)$ $\quad$ Cross multiply.

$2a = 30$ $\quad$ $16 = 5b$ $\quad$ Simplify.

$$a = \frac{30}{2} \qquad \frac{16}{5} = b$$

$a = 15$ $\quad$ $b = 3.2$

Therefore, $15 : 8 : 5 = 6 : 3.2 : 2$.

7.2 EXERCISES

Answers to the odd numbered exercises are available at the end of the textbook.

For Exercises 1 to 6, solve for the unknown variable.

1. a. $3 : 4 = x : 15$ $\quad$ b. $x : 4 = 12 : 8$
2. a. $2 : 5 = x : 10$ $\quad$ b. $x : 6 = 9 : 18$
3. a. $5 : x = 15 : 30$ $\quad$ b. $4 : 6 = 16 : x$
4. a. $6 : x = 12 : 18$ $\quad$ b. $7 : 8 = 28 : x$
5. a. $2 : 9 = x : 27$ $\quad$ b. $4 : x = 20 : 30$
6. a. $4 : 12 = 12 : x$ $\quad$ b. $x : 7 = 18 : 42$
7. Jason spent $22 to buy 18 staplers for his students. How many staplers can he buy with $33?
8. If Hani received $560 for working 35 hours, how many hours does she have to work to receive $640?
9. It takes 15 minutes to walk 850 metres. At that rate, how long would it take to walk 1,300 metres? Round to two decimal places.
10. A vehicle requires 76 litres of gas to cover 600 km. How many litres of gas will it require to cover 1,200 km?
11. Ana paid $45.50 in taxes for the purchase of a $350 item. How much taxes will she have to pay for an item that costs $425?

12. Gigi bought 4 kg of apples for $13. How many kilograms of apples can she buy with $15?

13. If C$1.00 = €0.6889, how much will you receive for converting C$2,000 to euros?

14. If C$1.00 = ¥94.9668, how much will you receive for converting C$2,000 to Japanese yen?

15. Convert 200 British pounds to euros if 1 British pound = €2.0308.

16. Convert US$500 to Canadian dollars, if the exchange rate is US$1.00 = C$1.2980.

17. Aaliyah went to the States and spent $435 Canadian dollars. How much did she spend in US dollars if the exchange rate was C$1.00 = US$0.7696? Round to the nearest cent.

18. Kata is planning to travel to Australia and has saved C$2,000. How many Australian dollars will she receive when she converts her savings, if the exchange rate is C$1.00 = A$1.0438?

For Exercises 19 to 22, solve for the unknowns in the proportions.

19. a. $4 : 6 : 9 = x : y : 18$ b. $3 : 4 : 8 = x : y : 24$

20. a. $3 : 8 : 12 = x : 24 : y$ b. $5 : 6 : 7 = x : 18 : y$

21. a. $6 : 10 : 16 = 26 : x : y$ b. $8 : 12 : 16 = 12 : x : y$

22. a. $8 : 9 : 12 = x : 26 : y$ b. $12 : 14 : 18 = x : 49 : y$

23. Three friends, Saleh, Mali, and Erin, invested in their business in the ratio 2 : 3 : 4, respectively. If Saleh invested $2,500, how much did Mali and Erin invest?

24. Adesh invested his savings in mutual funds, fixed deposits, and GICs in the ratio of 3 : 4 : 2, respectively. If he invested $3,500 in mutual funds, how much did he invest in fixed deposits and GIC?

25. Raha, Leo, and Shawna decided to start their own business and invested their savings in the business in the ratio of 3 : 2 : 4, respectively. They agreed to share the profits of the business based on the ratio of their investments. If in the first year they had profits of $12,000, how much did each of them receive?

26. Three friends rent an office space together and pay for it in the ratio of 2 : 4 : 5, respectively, based on the space they occupy. If the rent is $4,500 per month, how much does each of the friends pay?

REVIEW EXERCISES

Answers to the odd numbered exercises are available at the end of the textbook.

Reduce the ratios in Exercise 1 and 2 to their lowest terms.

1. a. 6 : 9 b. 5 : 30 c. 14 : 24 d. 150 : 185 e. $\frac{5}{4} : 2$ f. 4 : 8 : 16 g. 70 : 40 : 55

2. a. 4 : 8 b. 6 : 36 c. 16 : 28 d. 130 : 165 e. $\frac{3}{2} : 2$ f. 5 : 15 : 40 g. 85 : 30 : 60

For Exercises 3 to 6, write the ratios and reduce them to lowest terms.

3. A school hired 18 teachers for 540 students.

4. Simran has worked an average of 8 hours per day this year, whereas he worked 6 hours per day last year.

5. Ashley works 35 hours per week, Cam works 30 hours per week, and Leena works 40 hours per week.

6. Isaiah earns $18 per hour, Keesha earns $20 per hour, and Ryan earns $16 per hour.

7. Angela and Rhea invested $28,000 in their coffee shop. If the ratio of their investments is 3 : 4 respectively, how much did each invest?

8. Gloria and Philip shared the profit of $14,000 from their company last month. If they shared the profit in the ratio of 4 : 7 respectively, how much did each receive?

9. Chris, Puja, and Mohammad invested $30,000 to upgrade their equipment for their business in the ratio of 3 : 5 : 4 respectively. How much did each invest?

10. James, Luda, and Svetlana invested a total of $42,000 for the home they own as a rental property in the ratio of 6 : 4 : 3 respectively. How much did each invest?

For Exercises 11 and 12, find the missing term and confirm the ratios are in proportion.

11. a. $5 : 4 = x : 8$ b. $x : 8 = 12 : 4$ c. $2 : 10 = x : 5$ d. $x : 3 = 18 : 9$

12. a. $5 : x = 20 : 32$ b. $4 : 5 = 28 : x$ c. $3 : x = 12 : 21$ d. $7 : 9 = 35 : x$

13. It takes 20 minutes to walk 1,200 metres. At that rate, how long would it take to walk 1,600 metres?

14. A vehicle requires 55 litres of gas to cover 550 km. How many litres of gas will it require to cover 800 km?

15. Briana paid $34.45 in taxes for the purchase of a $265 item. How much taxes will she have to pay for an item that costs $385?

16. Carmen bought 5 kg of lemons at $3 per kg. How many kilograms of lemons can she buy with $28?

17. If C$1.00 = €0.5749, how much will you receive for converting C$1,500 to euros?

18. If C$1.00 = ¥81.9347, how much will you receive for converting C$3,000 to Japanese yen?

19. Gurmeet went to New York and spent $785 Canadian dollars. How much did she spend in US dollars, if the exchange rate was C$1.00 = US$0.7794?

20. Damon was planning to travel to New Zealand and saved CAD\$2,500 for the trip. How many New Zealand dollars will he receive when he converts from Canadian dollars, if the exchange rate is C\$1.00 = NZD\$1.1465?

For Exercises 21 and 22, solve for the unknowns in the proportions.

21. a. $2 : 3 : 6 = a : b : 24$ b. $4 : 5 : 6 = z : b : 18$ c. $3 : 5 : 7 = w : 15 : y$

22. a. $6 : 12 : 16 = 28 : x : y$ b. $4 : 10 : 14 = 12 : x : k$ c. $9 : 12 : 8 = b : 26 : y$

23. Three colleagues, Tom, Agnes, and Caroline, invested in their business in the ratio 3 : 4 : 5, respectively. If Tom invested \$3,500, how much did Agnes and Caroline invest?

24. Johanna invested her savings in an RRSP, a mutual fund, and a GIC in the ratio of 4 : 2 : 3, respectively. If she invested \$6,500 in the mutual fund, how much did she invest in the RRSP and the GIC?

25. Brandon, Haley, and Samora decided to start their own business and invested in the ratio of 5 : 3 : 4, respectively. They agreed to share the profits based on the ratio of their investments. If in the first year they had profits of \$15,000, how much did each of them receive?

26. Three companies rent office space together and pay for it in the ratio of 6 : 4 : 7 respectively, based on the space they occupy. If the rent is \$8,500 per month, how much does each company pay?

CHAPTER 8

SIMPLE AND COMPOUND INTEREST

LEARNING OBJECTIVES

Studying this chapter will provide you with the knowledge needed to:

- Calculate the amount of simple interest when the time period is provided in years, months, and days.
- Calculate the principal, rate, and time by re-arranging the simple interest formula.
- Calculate the maturity value and the principal value of simple interest loans and investments.
- Calculate the amount of compound interest when the compounding frequency is annually, semi-annually, quarterly, monthly, and daily.
- Calculate the future value and principal value of loans and investments using compound interest.

TOPICS

8.1 SIMPLE INTEREST

CALCULATING THE AMOUNT OF SIMPLE INTEREST

Lenders of money (for example, financial institutions or money lenders) charge **interest** for the use of their money. If **simple interest** is charged, the interest is based on the original loan amount. Simple interest is generally charged for short periods of time.

The amount of simple interest is calculated by multiplying the original loan or investment by the simple interest rate and the time period.

Simple Interest Formula

$$I = Prt$$

- **Interest** (I) is the amount of money earned on an investment or charged on a loan.
- **Principal** (P) is the amount of money invested or loaned.
- **Rate** (r) is the interest rate earned on the investment or charged on a loan. It is usually expressed as a rate per annum (p.a.). The rate is often given as a percent. We must first convert it to a decimal before inputing it into the formula.
- **Time** (t) is the interest period, usually expressed in years. The interest period can be given in days, months, or years. Before inputing it into the formula, we must first convert it to years.

EXAMPLE 8.1 (A): Calculating Simple Interest

Calculate the amount of simple interest earned on the following investments.

i $3,300 at 3.90% p.a. for 3 years ii $6,500 at 4% p.a. for 8 months iii $2,000 at 4.30% p.a. for 162 days

Solution:

i P = $3,300.00 r = 3.90% p.a. = 0.039 p.a. t = 3 years

Using the Simple Interest Formula:

$I = Prt$

$I = 3{,}300.00 \times 0.039 \times 3$

$= \$386.10$

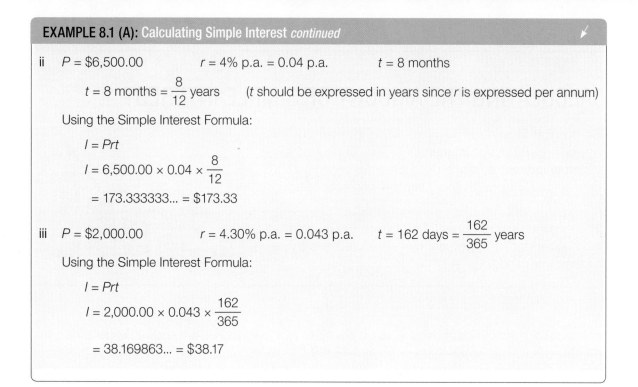

EXAMPLE 8.1 (A): Calculating Simple Interest *continued*

ii $P = \$6{,}500.00$ $r = 4\%$ p.a. $= 0.04$ p.a. $t = 8$ months

$t = 8 \text{ months} = \frac{8}{12} \text{ years}$ (t should be expressed in years since r is expressed per annum)

Using the Simple Interest Formula:

$$I = Prt$$

$$I = 6{,}500.00 \times 0.04 \times \frac{8}{12}$$

$$= 173.333333... = \$173.33$$

iii $P = \$2{,}000.00$ $r = 4.30\%$ p.a. $= 0.043$ p.a. $t = 162 \text{ days} = \frac{162}{365} \text{ years}$

Using the Simple Interest Formula:

$$I = Prt$$

$$I = 2{,}000.00 \times 0.043 \times \frac{162}{365}$$

$$= 38.169863... = \$38.17$$

CALCULATING PRINCIPAL, RATE, AND TIME

By re-arranging the simple interest formula, $I = Prt$, we can find the unknown values for the principal, rate, and time of a loan. This is illustrated in the following examples.

EXAMPLE 8.1 (B): Calculating the Principal Amount

If the simple interest amount charged on a loan was \$250 and the interest rate was 3.50% p.a. for 15 months, what was the amount of principal borrowed?

Solution:

$I = \$250.00$ $r = 3.50\%$ p.a. $= 0.035$ p.a. $t = 15 \text{ months} = \frac{15}{12} \text{ years}$

Rearranging the simple interest formula, $I = Prt$, to solve for P:

$$P = \frac{I}{rt}$$

$$P = \frac{250.00}{0.035 \times \frac{15}{12}}$$

$$= 5{,}714.28714... = \$5{,}714.29$$

Therefore, the amount of principal borrowed was \$5,714.29.

EXAMPLE 8.1 (C): Calculating the Interest Rate

At what annual simple interest rate will $5,000 earn $800 in interest in 1.5 years?

Solution:

P = $5,000.00 I = $800.00 t = 1.5 years

Rearranging the simple interest formula, $I = Prt$, to solve for r:

$$r = \frac{I}{Pt}$$

$$r = \frac{800.00}{5{,}000.00 \times 1.5}$$

$$= 0.106666... \times 100\%$$

$$= 10.666667... = 10.67\% \text{ p.a.}$$

Therefore, the annual simple interest is 10.67% p.a.

EXAMPLE 8.1 (D): Calculating the Time Period

How long will it take for $6,000 to earn $1,450 at 4.10% p.a. simple interest? Express your answer in years and months, rounded up to the next month.

Solution:

P = $6,000.00 I = $1,450.00 r = 4.10% p.a. = 0.041 p.a.

Rearranging the simple interest formula, $I = Prt$, to solve for t:

$$t = \frac{I}{Pr}$$

$$t = \frac{1{,}450.00}{6{,}000.00 \times 0.041}$$

$$= 5.894308... \text{ years}$$

To express the answer in years and months, we need to multiply the decimal portion of the number by 12 (the number of months in a year).

t = 5 years and (0.894308... × 12) months

= 5 years and 10.731707... months

= 5 years and 11 months (rounded up to the next month)

Therefore, it will take 5 years and 11 months for $6,000 to earn $1,450 in interest at a simple interest rate of 4.10% p.a.

CALCULATING MATURITY VALUE

The **maturity value** (S), also referred to as the future value, is the sum of the principal and interest.

$$S = P + I$$

Substituting the simple interest formula, $I = Prt$, in the above formula, we get

$$S = P + Prt = P(1 + rt)$$

Maturity Value Formula

$$S = P(1 + rt)$$

Rearranging, we get the Principal Value Formula.

Principal Value Formula

$$P = \frac{S}{1 + rt}$$

EXAMPLE 8.1 (E): Calculating the Maturity Value

Find the maturity value (or future value) of an investment of $10,000 for 10 months at 6.7% p.a. simple interest.

Solution:

$P = \$10{,}000.00$ $\quad r = 6.7\%$ p.a. $= 0.067$ p.a. $\quad t = 10$ months $= \frac{10}{12}$ years

Using the Maturity Value Formula:

$$S = P(1 + rt)$$

$$S = 10{,}000.00\left(1 + 0.067 \times \frac{10}{12}\right)$$

$$= 10{,}000.00\ (1.055833...)$$

$$= 10{,}558.333333... = \$10{,}558.33$$

Therefore, the maturity value is $10,558.33.

Remember: We perform multiplication before addition in BEDMAS

EXAMPLE 8.1 (F): Calculating the Principal Given the Maturity Value

What is the principal (or present value) that will grow to $12,500 in 2 years at a simple interest rate of 5% p.a.

Solution:

$S = \$12{,}500.00$ $\quad r = 5\%$ p.a. $= 0.05$ p.a. $\quad t = 2$ years

Using the Principal Value Formula:

$$P = \frac{S}{1 + rt}$$

$$P = \frac{12{,}500.00}{1 + (0.05 \times 2)}$$

$$= \frac{12{,}500}{1.1}$$

$$= 11{,}363.636363... = \$11{,}363.64$$

Therefore, the principal value is $11,363.64.

8.1 EXERCISES

Answers to the odd numbered exercises are available at the end of the textbook.

1. Harry borrowed $7,500 from his parents before starting college. They agreed on a simple interest rate of 4.45% p.a. on the loan. How much simple interest will he have to pay them in 3 years when he graduates?
2. Minjia was short some money to furnish her new café, so she borrowed $4,500 from a friend and agreed to pay a simple interest of 4% p.a. If she plans to settle the loan in 7 months, how much simple interest will she have to pay?
3. Ben was ready to purchase an apartment, but was short $3,000 on the down payment. A friend lent him the money on the condition that Ben pays him simple interest at the rate of 3.50% p.a. and allows him to sleep on the couch on occasion. How much simple interest does Ben owe his friend in 150 days, when he is ready to settle the loan?
4. Julia invested $12,000 from her savings in a friend's landscaping business. Her friend agreed to pay her simple interest at 5.50% p.a. for 3.5 years. How much interest will Julia earn at the end of 3.5 years?
5. Having $5,000 saved up from a summer job, Preeti decides to invest it at 3.50% p.a. simple interest for 100 days, after which she will need the money for school. How much simple interest will Preeti earn in this time?
6. Raheem lent $3,670 to his younger brother for 18 months to help with college expenses. The brothers agreed that Raheem would receive simple interest of 2% p.a. How much interest will Raheem receive?
7. If Thomas borrowed $9,000 from a friend at 5.40% p.a. over 20 months, how much simple interest does he owe?
8. Vivian lent her daughter $2,000 at 3.80% p.a. over 16 months. How much simple interest is she owed?
9. Jenna borrowed money for 6 months at 4.60% p.a. If the simple interest she owed accumulated to $309.78, what was the principal amount that she borrowed?
10. Carlos was owed $1,000 simple interest on an amount he lent for 11 months at 9% p.a. What was the principal amount that he lent?
11. If $2,600 earns $21 in 86 days, what is the annual simple interest rate?
12. If $1,500 earns $17 in 75 days, what is the annual simple interest rate?
13. If Ghulam wants to earn interest of $1,345 on a $10,000 investment for 2.5 years, what rate of simple interest does he require?
14. If Tatiana wants to pay no more than $1,600 in interest on a loan of $17,000 that she has taken for 1.5 years, what is the maximum simple interest rate she can agree on?
15. How many days will it take $2,900 to earn $43.55 in simple interest at 17% p.a.?
16. How many days will it take for $7,000 to earn $700 in simple interest at 10% p.a.?
17. How many years are needed for $1,000 to earn $400 in simple interest at 8% p.a.? Express your answer in years and months, rounded up to the next month, if applicable.
18. How many years are needed for $3,000 to earn $520 in simple interest at 8% p.a.? Express your answer in years and months, rounded up to the next month.
19. Find the annual rate of simple interest needed for $20,000 to earn $4,345 in 3.5 years.
20. Find the annual rate of simple interest needed for $14,000 to earn $2,765 in 2.5 years.

21. Michael invested $5,600 for 200 days at a simple interest rate of 4% p.a. Calculate the maturity value of his investment.

22. Rebecca borrowed $2,800 for 150 days at simple interest of 3% p.a. Calculate the maturity value of the loan.

23. Hamza borrowed $10,900 for 14 months at 6.40% p.a. simple interest to take care of his expenses while his new business became profitable. What is the maturity value of his debt?

24. Lilliana lent a friend $4,000 for 18 months at 5.50% p.a. simple interest. What is the maturity value of the loan?

8.2 COMPOUND INTEREST

When interest is **compounded**, it represents the process in which interest begins to accumulate on both the principal and previously accrued interest. This is different than simple interest, where the interest only accumulates on the principal.

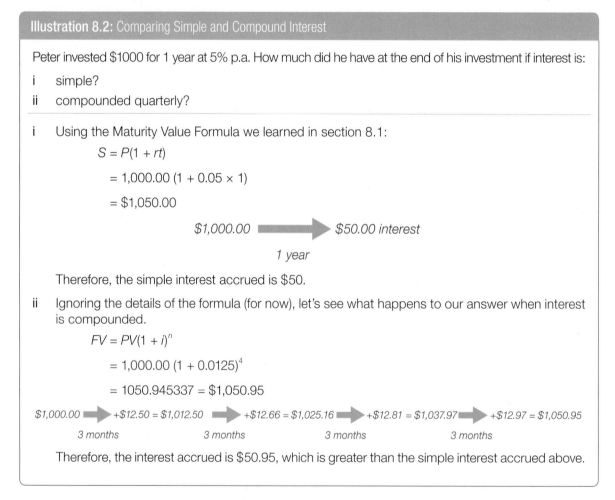

Illustration 8.2: Comparing Simple and Compound Interest

Peter invested $1000 for 1 year at 5% p.a. How much did he have at the end of his investment if interest is:

i simple?

ii compounded quarterly?

i Using the Maturity Value Formula we learned in section 8.1:

$$S = P(1 + rt)$$
$$= 1{,}000.00\,(1 + 0.05 \times 1)$$
$$= \$1{,}050.00$$

$1,000.00 → *$50.00 interest*

1 year

Therefore, the simple interest accrued is $50.

ii Ignoring the details of the formula (for now), let's see what happens to our answer when interest is compounded.

$$FV = PV(1 + i)^n$$
$$= 1{,}000.00\,(1 + 0.0125)^4$$
$$= 1050.945337 = \$1{,}050.95$$

$1,000.00 → *+$12.50 = $1,012.50* → *+$12.66 = $1,025.16* → *+$12.81 = $1,037.97* → *+$12.97 = $1,050.95*

3 months *3 months* *3 months* *3 months*

Therefore, the interest accrued is $50.95, which is greater than the simple interest accrued above.

Before we begin to break down how the compound interest equation functions, it is important to understand what compounding actually does. As you saw in Illustration 8.2, the investment that had the compounded interest accrued $0.95 more than the investment that had simple interest. The reason for this is because, with the compound interest example, interest began accruing on the interest already earned by the 3 month mark, or quarterly. Essentially, the interest that had accrued up until the 3 month mark was added to the principal, resulting in the remaining interest accruing on the principal + interest from the previous compounding period.

In basic terms, simple interest is the interest that accrues on the principal on an annual basis whereas compound interest is the interest that accrues on the principal *and* on itself at a pace set by the compounding frequency.

CALCULATING FUTURE VALUE AND PRINCIPAL VALUE

Let's dissect the compound interest equation to understand the components and how they fit together.

Future Value Formula

$$FV = PV(1 + i)^n$$

- **Future Value** (*FV*), also known as Face Value, Maturity Value, or Accumulated Value, is the amount of the investment/loan including the interest that has accrued.
- **Principal Value** (*PV*), also known as Loan, Prior/Earlier Value, or Pre-Interest Value, is the amount of the investment/loan before any interest has accrued. When the Future Value is known, Principal Value can be calculated using the following formula:

Principal Value Formula

$$PV = \frac{FV}{(1 + i)^n}$$

- **Periodic Interest Rate** (*i*) is the interest rate earned on the investment or charged on the loan per compounding period.
- **Number of Compounding Periods** (*n*) is the number of compounding periods over the entire term of the investment or loan.

The periodic interest rate (*i*) is calculated using the following formula:

Periodic Interest Rate Formula

$$i = \frac{j}{m}$$

- **Annual Interest Rate** (*j*) is the interest rate earned on the investment or charged on the loan, per annum (p.a.)
- **Compounding Frequency per Year** (*m*) is the number of times that interest accrues per year. This can be:
  - annually (once per year)
  - semi-annually (twice per year or every 6 months)
  - quarterly (four times per year or every 3 months)
  - monthly (twelve times per year or every month)
  - daily (365 times per year, or every day)

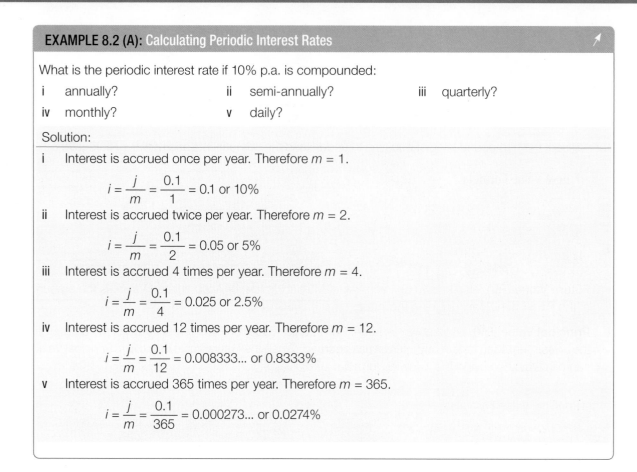

EXAMPLE 8.2 (A): Calculating Periodic Interest Rates

What is the periodic interest rate if 10% p.a. is compounded:

i annually? ii semi-annually? iii quarterly?

iv monthly? v daily?

Solution:

i Interest is accrued once per year. Therefore $m = 1$.

$$i = \frac{j}{m} = \frac{0.1}{1} = 0.1 \text{ or } 10\%$$

ii Interest is accrued twice per year. Therefore $m = 2$.

$$i = \frac{j}{m} = \frac{0.1}{2} = 0.05 \text{ or } 5\%$$

iii Interest is accrued 4 times per year. Therefore $m = 4$.

$$i = \frac{j}{m} = \frac{0.1}{4} = 0.025 \text{ or } 2.5\%$$

iv Interest is accrued 12 times per year. Therefore $m = 12$.

$$i = \frac{j}{m} = \frac{0.1}{12} = 0.008333... \text{ or } 0.8333\%$$

v Interest is accrued 365 times per year. Therefore $m = 365$.

$$i = \frac{j}{m} = \frac{0.1}{365} = 0.000273... \text{ or } 0.0274\%$$

The number of compounding periods per term (n) is calculated using the following equation:

Number of Compounding Periods

$$n = m \times t$$

- **Compounding Frequency per Year** (m) is the number of times interest accrues per year.
- **Time** (t) is the interest period in years.

These calculations are used when calculating the Future Value or Principal Value of a loan or an investment, as shown in the following examples.

EXAMPLE 8.2 (B): Calculating Future Value

Sheila invests $3,500 into a 2-year GIC that earns 3.25% compounded quarterly. How much will Sheila have at the end of the 2-year term? How much interest will the GIC earn?

Solution:

$PV = \$3,500.00$ $j = 3.25\% = 0.0325$ $m = 4$ (quarterly) $t = 2$ years

Calculating the periodic interest rate:

$$i = \frac{j}{m} = \frac{0.0325}{4} = 0.008125$$

EXAMPLE 8.2 (B): Calculating Future Value *continued*

Solution:

Calculating the number of compounding periods per term:

$$n = m \times t = 4 \times 2 = 8$$

Substituting the known values in the Future Value formula:

$$FV = PV(1 + i)^n$$

$$= 3{,}500.00\,(1 + 0.008125)^8$$

$$= 3{,}734.075726... = \$3{,}734.08$$

Remember to use the principals of BEDMAS and perform operations in the brackets first (1 + 0.008125), then the exponent (8), then multiply by 3,500.

Therefore, at the end of the 2-year term, Sheila will have $3,734.08.

To find out how much interest the GIC will earn, we find the difference between the Future Value and the Principal Value.

$$I = FV - PV = 3{,}734.08 - 3{,}500.00 = \$234.08 \text{ interest}$$

Therefore, the amount of interest earned from the GIC will be $234.08.

Similarly, we can calculate the initial investment or loan by using the Principal Value formula, as demonstrated in the following example.

EXAMPLE 8.2 (C): Calculating Principal Value

Brian needs to save $18,000 for a down payment on a house. How much should he invest today if the investment offers 4.50% compounded monthly for 4 years? How much interest will Brian earn over the 4 years?

Solution:

$FV = \$18{,}000.00$ $\quad j = 4.50\% = 0.045$ $\quad m = 12$ (monthly) $\quad t = 4$ years

Calculating the periodic interest rate:

$$i = \frac{j}{m} = \frac{0.045}{12} = 0.00375$$

Calculating the number of compounding periods per term:

$$n = m \times t = 12 \times 4 = 48$$

Substituting the known values in the Principal Value formula:

$$PV = \frac{FV}{(1 + i)^n}$$

$$PV = \frac{18{,}000.00}{(1 + 0.00375)^{48}}$$

$$= 15{,}039.92627... = \$15{,}039.93$$

EXAMPLE 8.2 (C): Calculating Principal Value *continued*

Solution:

Therefore, to accumulate $18,000.00 at the end of 4 years, Brian should invest $15,039.93 today.

To find the amount of interest earned on this investment, we find the difference between the Future Value and the Principal Value.

$$I = FV - PV = 18{,}000.00 - 15{,}039.93 = \$2{,}960.07$$

Therefore, the amount of interest earned on this investment is $2,960.07.

8.2 EXERCISES

Answers to the odd numbered exercises are available at the end of the textbook.

1. What is the periodic interest rate, rounded to 2 decimal places, if 6% p.a. is compounded
   a. annually? b. semi-annually? c. quarterly?
   d. monthly? e. daily?
2. What is the periodic interest rate, rounded to 2 decimal places, if 7.25% p.a. is compounded
   a. annually? b. semi-annually? c. quarterly?
   d. monthly? e. daily?
3. What is the number of compounding periods per term if an investment earns 8% compounded monthly and the term is 2.5 years?
4. What is the number of compounding periods per term if an investment earns 4.25% compounded annually and the term is 6 years?
5. What is the number of compounding periods per term if an investment earns 10% compounded quarterly and the term is 9 months?
6. What is the number of compounding periods per term if an investment earns 8% compounded daily and the term is 6 months?
7. Ali borrowed $15,000 at 4.20% compounded monthly to buy a car. If the loan is for 3 years, how much does he owe at the end of the term? How much interest is accrued?
8. If Louis lent his nephew $10,000 at 3% compounded annually for 4.5 years, how much will he receive at the completion of the term? How much of it is interest?
9. If the compound frequency per term of an investment is 96 and the term is 8 years, how often is the investment compounded?
10. If the compound frequency per term of an investment is 26 and it's compounded quarterly, how long is the term?
11. Nima received a loan of $3,600 at 5% compounded daily. She pays it back in full in 1.5 years. How much interest does she pay at the end of the term?
12. Sasha invests a portion of her paycheque. If she invests $1,100 for 18 months at a rate of 5.50% compounded annually, how much interest will she have earned at the end of the 18 months?
13. What is the future value of $1,800 compounded quarterly at 6.25% for 15 months?
14. What is the future value of $1 compounded semi-annually at 2.10% for 50 years?

15. Moira wants to have $60,000 saved by her 60th birthday in 7 years. If she invests at 6% compounded quarterly, how much does she need to invest today to reach her goal? How much interest will she make?

16. Elaine lent her sister money at a rate of 8.70% compounded monthly. 8 months later, Elaine received $3,000 from her sister when she paid back the loan in full. How much did Elaine lend her sister? How much interest did she make?

17. Sakina needs to save $4,800 in the next 1.5 years. How much must she invest today, at a rate of 3.70% compounded annually?

18. Aria needs to save $2,200 in 6 months to pay for tuition. How much must she invest today, at a rate of 2.75% compounded semi-annually?

19. What is the principal value compounded monthly at 9.10% that accumulates to $17,000 in 10.25 years?

20. What is the principal value compounded semi-annually at 3.50% that accumulates to $1,000,000 in 50 years?

REVIEW EXERCISES

Answers to the odd numbered exercises are available at the end of the textbook.

1. Simon borrowed $5,800 from his parents before starting college. They agreed on a simple interest rate of 3.75% p.a. on the loan. How much simple interest will he have to pay them in 4 years when he graduates?

2. Joy needed to furnish her new apartment, so she borrowed $2,500 from a friend and agreed to pay a simple interest rate of 4.25% p.a. If she plans to settle the loan in 9 months, how much simple interest will she have to pay?

3. Having saved $3,500 from a part-time job, Kayla decided to invest it at 3.60% p.a. simple interest for 90 days, after which she will need the money for school. How much simple interest will Kayla earn during this time?

4. Umar lent $2,350 to his younger sister for 20 months to help with college expenses. They agreed that Umar would receive simple interest of 2.35% p.a. How much interest will Umar receive?

5. Rita borrowed some funds for 7 months at 5.25% p.a. If the simple interest she owed accumulated to $321.85, what was the principal amount that she borrowed?

6. Christopher was owed $1,200 simple interest on an amount he lent for 10 months at 7.40% p.a. What was the principal amount that he lent?

7. If $1,800 earns $16 in 74 days, what is the annual simple interest rate?

8. If $2,600 earns $31 in 97 days, what is the annual simple interest rate?

9. If Tiago wants to earn interest of $442 on a $12,000 investment for 1.5 years, what rate of simple interest does he require?

10. If Alisha wants to pay no more than $1,600 in interest on a loan of $19,500 that she has taken for 2.5 years, what is the maximum simple interest rate she can agree on?

11. How many days will it take $3,700 to earn $29.85 in simple interest at 14% p.a.?

12. How many days will it take for $6,300 to earn $110 in simple interest at 9% p.a.?

13. How many years are needed for $2,800 to earn $450 in simple interest at 11% p.a.? Express your answer in years and months, rounded up to the next month, if applicable.
14. How many years are needed for $5,000 to earn $760 in simple interest at 9% p.a.? Express your answer in years and months, rounded up to the next month.
15. Find the annual rate of simple interest needed for $30,000 to earn $2,750 in 2.5 years.
16. Find the annual rate of simple interest needed for $15,000 to earn $1,650 in 3.5 years.
17. Marcus invested $4,900 for 220 days at a simple interest rate of 3.95% p.a. Calculate the maturity value of his investment.
18. Chelsea borrowed $3,200 for 180 days at simple interest of 4.15% p.a. Calculate the maturity value of the loan.
19. What is the periodic interest rate, rounded to 2 decimal places, if 5.25% p.a. is compounded
    a. annually?
    b. semi-annually?
    c. quarterly?
    d. monthly?
    e. daily?
20. What is the periodic interest rate if 8.50% p.a. is compounded rounded to 2 decimal places,
    a. annually?
    b. semi-annually?
    c. quarterly?
    d. monthly?
    e. daily?
21. What is the number of compounding periods per term if an investment earns 6.75% compounded quarterly and the term is 3.5 years?
22. What is the number of compounding periods per term if an investment earns 5.25% compounded annually and the term is 5 years?
23. Derek borrowed $12,000 at 4.60% compounded monthly to buy a boat. If the loan is 4 years, how much does he owe at the end of the term? How much interest is accrued?
24. If Ranjan lent his cousin $14,000 at 3.25% compounded semi-annually for 2.5 years, how much will he receive at the completion of the term? How much of it is interest?
25. If the compounding frequency per term of an investment is 56 and the term is 7 years, how often is the investment compounded?
26. If the compounding frequency per term of an investment is 35 and it's compounded quarterly, how long is the term?
27. Renata received a loan of $4,200 at 3.85% compounded daily. She pays it back in full in 1.5 years. How much interest does she pay at the end of the term?
28. Agnes invests a portion of her paycheque. If she invests $900 for 16 months at a rate of 3.50% compounded quarterly, how much interest will she have earned at the end of the 16 months?
29. What is the future value of $2,600 compounded monthly at 5.95% for 18 months?
30. What is the future value of $5 compounded quarterly at 3.15% for 35 years?
31. Amrita wants to have $75,000 saved by her 65th birthday in 11 years. If she invests at 5.50% compounded quarterly, how much does she need to invest today to reach her goal? How much interest does she make?
32. Ruby lent her brother money at a rate of 4.30% compounded monthly. 9 months later, Ruby received $4,500 from her brother when he paid back the loan in full. How much did Ruby lend her brother? How much interest did she make?

33. What is the principal value compounded quarterly at 8.40% that accumulates to $24,000 in 12 years?

34. What is the principal value compounded semi-annually at 4.25% that accumulates to $2,000,000 in 40 years?

CHAPTER 9

ANNUITIES, LOANS, AND MORTGAGES

LEARNING OBJECTIVES

Studying this chapter will provide you with the knowledge needed to:

- Calculate the future value and principal value of annuities.
- Calculate the payment amount of a loan.
- Construct loan amortization schedules.
- Calculate the payment amount of a mortgage.
- Understand mortgages and related calculations.

TOPICS

9.1 ANNUITIES

An annuity is an investment or loan product that has regular payments at regular intervals for a set period of time. Annuity payments are fixed, as is the payment frequency. The difference between compound interest calculations and annuity calculations is that compound interest uses a one-time lump sum amount (payment) for the loan or investment, while an annuity involves periodic payments made at regular intervals.

The value of an annuity depends on when the payments are made, the frequency of payments, and how the payment frequency compares to the compounding frequency.

If the annuity payments are made at the end of the period, the annuity is considered an **ordinary annuity**. When payments are made at the beginning of the period, the annuity is considered an **annuity due**.

These types of annuities can further be classified into simple and general annuities. When the payment frequency and the compounding frequency are the same, the annuity is considered a **simple annuity**, whereas when the payment frequency and the compounding frequency are different, the annuity is considered a **general annuity**.

Table 9.1: Types of Annuities

Ordinary	Payments are made at the *end* of the payment period. If the payment period is not indicate, we assume it is an ordinary annuity.
Due	Payments are made at the *beginning* of the payment period.
Simple	Payment frequency and compounding frequency are the *same* (e.g., payments are made monthly and interest rate is compounded monthly).
General	Payment frequency and compounding frequency are *different* (e.g., payments are made monthly and interest rate is compounded quarterly).

ORDINARY SIMPLE ANNUITY

Let's begin learning about annuities and how they function by looking at the equations used for an **ordinary simple annuity**. For annuities, *FV* and *PV* require their own equations as follows:

Ordinary Annuity Formulas

$$FV = PMT\left[\frac{(1+i)^n - 1}{i}\right] \qquad PV = PMT\left[\frac{1-(1+i)^{-n}}{i}\right]$$

- *PMT* is the payment made at the end of each period.
- *i* is the periodic interest rate.
- *n* is the number of compounding periods per term. For annuities, *n* also represents the number of payments over the term.

For annuities, we calculate n using the following formula:

Number of Payments per Term Formula

$$n = p \times t$$

- p is the payment frequency per year
- t is the interest period in years

*While for simple annuities the payments and compounding frequencies match and **m** and **p** are the same, for general annuities they are different; therefore, it is a good habit to always calculate **n = pt** instead of **n = mt** for annuities.*

The total interest paid over the time of the annuity is equal to the future value of the annuity less all of payments made.

Amount of Interest Earned

$$I = FV - n(PMT)$$

EXAMPLE 9.1 (A): Calculating the Future Value of an Ordinary Simple Annuity

Patricia makes month-end payments of $350 into her savings account that earns 4.50% compounded monthly. How much will Patricia have accumulated in her savings account after making payments for 5 years? What is the amount of interest earned from this annuity?

Solution:

This is an ordinary simple annuity since the payment frequency and the compounding frequency are the same, and payments are made at the end of each period. In this example, a payment of $350 is made **at the end** of every month for 5 years.

$PMT = \$350.00$ $\quad j = 4.50\% = 0.045$ $\quad p = m = 12$ (monthly) $\quad t = 5$ years

Calculating the periodic interest rate:

$$i = \frac{j}{m} = \frac{0.045}{12} = 0.00375$$

Calculating the number of payments:

$$n = p \times t = 12 \times 5 = 60$$

We can visualize the cash flow in this situation with a diagram:

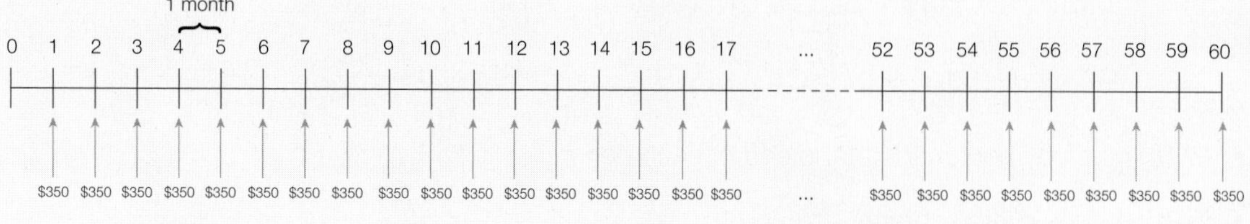

EXAMPLE 9.1 (A): Calculating the Future Value of an Ordinary Simple Annuity *continued*

Solution:

Therefore:

$$FV = PMT\left[\frac{(1+i)^n - 1}{i}\right]$$

$$= 350.00\left[\frac{(1+0.00375)^{60} - 1}{0.00375}\right]$$

$$= 23{,}500.94325... = \$23{,}500.94$$

Therefore, Patricia will have accumulated $23,500.94 in her savings account after 5 years.

To calculate the amount of interest earned, multiply the number of payments, n, by the payment amount, PMT, and subtract this value from the accumulated value of the investment, FV.

$$I = FV - (n \times PMT) = 23{,}500.94 - (60 \times 350.00) = \$2{,}500.94$$

Therefore, the amount of interest earned is $2,500.94.

EXAMPLE 9.1 (B): Calculating the Principal Value of an Ordinary Simple Annuity

Franco purchased an annuity that will provide him with end-of-quarter payments of $1,850 for the next 20 years. What was the purchase price of the annuity if the interest rate was 3.25% compounded quarterly? How much interest was accrued?

Solution:

This is an ordinary simple annuity since the payment frequency and the compounding frequency are the same, and payments are made at the end of each period.

$PMT = \$1{,}850.00$ $\quad j = 3.25\% = 0.0325$ $\quad p = m = 4$ (quarterly) $\quad t = 20$ years

Calculating the periodic interest rate:

$$i = \frac{j}{m} = \frac{0.0325}{4} = 0.008125$$

Calculating the number of payments:

$$n = p \times t = 4 \times 20 = 80$$

Therefore:

$$PV = PMT\left[\frac{1-(1+i)^{-n}}{i}\right]$$

$$= 1{,}850.00\left[\frac{1-(1+0.008125)^{-80}}{0.008125}\right]$$

'n' is negative in the PV formula because the payments include interest, and therefore, the '–' allows for the compounding to reverse and the interest to be removed to allow the 'pre-interest' amount to be calculated.

$$= 108{,}513.8996... = \$108{,}513.90$$

Therefore, the purchase price of the annuity was $108,513.90.

Calculating the amount of interest accrued:

$$I = (n \times PMT) - PV = (80 \times 1{,}850.00) - 108{,}513.90 = \$39{,}486.10$$

Therefore, the amount of interest accrued was $39,486.10.

SIMPLE ANNUITY DUE

Now that we understand ordinary simple annuities, let's look at a simple annuity where payments occur at the beginning of the payment period, or a **simple annuity due**.

Illustration 9.1: Comparison between Ordinary Annuity and Annuity Due

Consider an annuity that starts in January and makes 6 monthly payments.

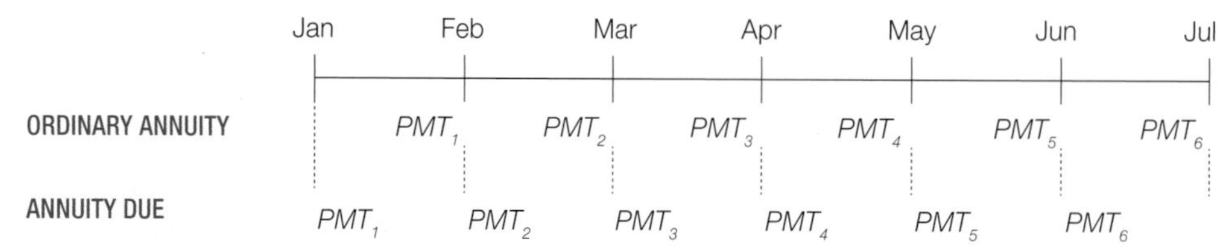

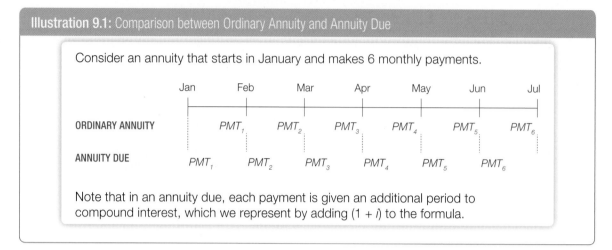

Note that in an annuity due, each payment is given an additional period to compound interest, which we represent by adding $(1 + i)$ to the formula.

Annuity Due Formulas

$$FV = PMT\left[\frac{(1+i)^n - 1}{i}\right] \times (1+i) \qquad PV = PMT\left[\frac{1-(1+i)^{-n}}{i}\right] \times (1+i)$$

EXAMPLE 9.1 (C): Calculating the Future Value of a Simple Annuity Due

Tabatha contributed $275 to her RRSP at the beginning of every month to save for her retirement. How much will she have accumulated after contributing for 25 years at a rate of 3.60% compounded monthly? How much interest will be accrued during this period?

Solution:

This is a simple annuity due since the payment frequency and the compounding frequency are the same, and payments are made at the beginning of each period. In this example, a $275 payment is made at **the beginning** of each month.

$PMT = \$275.00$ $\quad j = 3.60\% = 0.036$ $\quad p = m = 12$ (monthly) $\quad t = 25$ years

Calculating the periodic interest rate:

$$i = \frac{j}{m} = \frac{0.036}{12} = 0.003$$

Calculating the number of payments:

$$n = p \times t = 12 \times 25 = 300$$

EXAMPLE 9.1 (C): Calculating the Future Value of a Simple Annuity Due *continued*

Solution:

As seen in the calculations, there are 300 payments, each made at the beginning of the month. We can visualize the cash flow in this situation with a diagram:

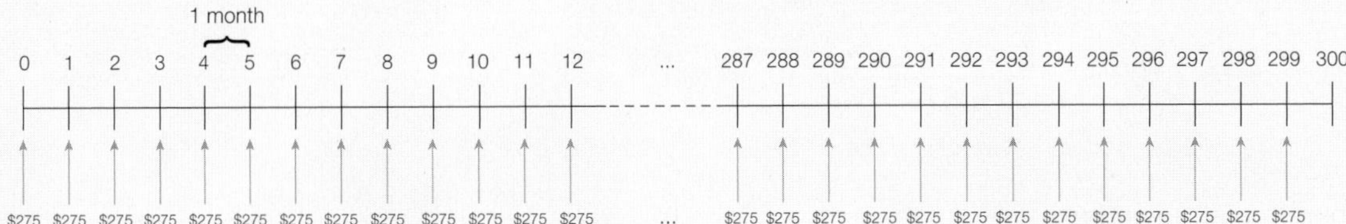

Therefore:

$$FV = PMT\left[\frac{(1+i)^n - 1}{i}\right] \times (1+i)$$

$$= 275.00\left[\frac{(1+0.003)^{300} - 1}{0.003}\right] \times (1+0.003)$$

$$= 133{,}893.8681... = \$133{,}893.87$$

Therefore, Tabatha will have accumulated $133,893.87 after 25 years.

Calculating the amount of interest earned:

$$I = FV - (n \times PMT) = 133{,}893.87 - (300 \times 275.00) = \$51{,}393.87$$

Therefore, the amount of interest accrued was $51,393.87.

EXAMPLE 9.1 (D): Calculating the Principal Value of a Simple Annuity Due

Charles purchased a car and signed a 4-year lease that required payments of $475 to be made at the beginning of every month. If the rate was 2.40% compounded monthly, what was the purchase price of the car? How much interest did he pay on the lease?

Solution:

This is a simple annuity due since the payment frequency and the compounding frequency are the same, and payments are made at the beginning of each period.

$PMT = \$475.00$ $j = 2.40\% = 0.024$ $p = m = 12$ (monthly) $t = 4$ years

Calculate the periodic interest rate:

$$i = \frac{j}{m} = \frac{0.024}{12} = 0.002$$

Calculate the compound frequency per term:

$$n = p \times t = 12 \times 4 = 48$$

EXAMPLE 9.1 (D): Calculating the Principal Value of a Simple Annuity Due *continued*

Solution:

Therefore:

$$PV = PMT\left[\frac{1-(1+i)^{-n}}{i}\right] \times (1+i)$$

$$= 475.00\left[\frac{1-(1+0.002)^{-48}}{0.002}\right] \times (1+0.002)$$

$$= 21{,}762.54801... = \$21{,}762.55$$

Therefore, the purchase price of the car was $21,762.55.

Calculating the amount of interest paid:

$$I = (n \times PMT) - PV = (48 \times 475.00) - 21{,}762.55 = \$1{,}037.45$$

Therefore, the amount of interest paid on the loan was $1,037.45.

GENERAL ANNUITY - ORDINARY AND DUE

When an annuity has a compounding frequency that is different than the payment frequency, it is called a **general annuity**. To solve a general annuity, we need to convert the periodic interest rate, i, to an interest rate which matches the payment frequency. This rate is denoted by i_2.

Converting the Periodic Interest Rate for General Annuities

$$i_2 = (1+i)^c - 1 \qquad \text{where, } c = \frac{m}{p}$$

Both the 'i' and 'i_2' are periodic interest rates, but the 'i' in a **simple annuity** is an interest rate where the **compounding frequency** and the **payment frequency** are **equal**. For example, if the interest rate is compounded **monthly** and the payment is **monthly**, then the interest rate is 'i' and we are dealing with a **simple annuity**. However, if the interest rate is compounded **semi-annually** and the payment is **monthly**, it is necessary to use 'i_2' and this occurs in a **general annuity**. The formula given in the yellow box shows the mathematics of changing the 'i' into the 'i_2'.

The main formulas for the future values and principal values of simple annuities and general annuities are the same, except that 'i' becomes 'i_2'.

EXAMPLE 9.1 (E): Calculating the Principal Value of an Ordinary General Annuity

Kelly purchased a house and pays $1,275 towards the mortgage at the end of every month. If the interest rate is 3.95% compounded semi-annually and the mortgage is amortized over 25 years, what is the purchase price of the house? How much interest will she pay over the course of the amortization?

Solution:

This is an ordinary general annuity since the payment frequency and the compounding frequency are different, and payments are made at the end of each period.

$PMT = \$1{,}275.00$ $\quad j = 3.95\% = 0.0395$ $\quad m = 2$ (semi-annually) $\quad p = 12$ (monthly) $\quad t = 25$ years

EXAMPLE 9.1 (E): Calculating the Principal Value of an Ordinary General Annuity *continued*

Solution:

Therefore,

$$i = \frac{j}{m} = \frac{0.0395}{2} = 0.01975 \qquad c = \frac{m}{p} = \frac{2}{12} = 0.166666...$$

Converting i to i_2:

$$i_2 = (1 + i)^c - 1 = (1 + 0.01975)^{0.166666...} - 1 = 0.003264...$$

Calculating the number of payments:

$$n = p \times t = 12 \times 25 = 300$$

Therefore,

$$PV = PMT\left[\frac{1-(1+i_2)^{-n}}{i_2}\right]$$

$$= 1{,}275.00\left[\frac{1-(1+0.003264...)^{-300}}{0.003264...}\right]$$

$$= 243{,}639.9413... = \$243{,}639.94$$

Therefore, the purchase price of the house is $243,639.94.

Calculating the amount of interest paid:

$$I = (n \times PMT) - PV = (300 \times 1{,}275.00) - 243{,}638.94 = \$138{,}860.06$$

Therefore, the amount of interest paid on the loan was $138,860.06.

EXAMPLE 9.1 (F): Calculating the Future Value of a General Annuity Due

Hamza set aside $650 from his pay-cheque at the beginning of every month to save for a car. If his investment earned 5.15% compounded annually, how much will he have saved after 3 years? How much interest will he earn from this investment?

Solution:

This is a general annuity due since the payment frequency and the compounding frequency are different, and payments are made at the beginning of each period.

$PMT = \$650.00$ $\quad j = 5.15\% = 0.0515$ $\quad m = 1$ (annually) $\quad p = 12$ (monthly) $\quad t = 3$ years

Therefore,

$$i = \frac{j}{m} = \frac{0.0515}{1} = 0.0515 \qquad c = \frac{m}{p} = \frac{1}{12} = 0.083333...$$

Converting i to i_2:

$$i_2 = (1 + i)^c - 1 = (1 + 0.0515)^{0.083333...} - 1 = 0.004193...$$

Calculating the number of payments per term, we get:

$$n = p \times t = 12 \times 3 = 36$$

Therefore,

$$FV = PMT\left[\frac{(1+i_2)^n - 1}{i_2}\right] \times (1 + i_2)$$

EXAMPLE 9.1 (F): Calculating the Future Value of a General Annuity Due *continued*

$$= 650.00\left[\frac{(1 + 0.004193...)^{36} - 1}{0.004193...}\right] \times (1 + 0.004193...)$$

$$= 25{,}307.47420... = \$25{,}307.47$$

Therefore, he would have earned $25,307.47 from this investment.

$$I = FV - (n \times PMT) = 25{,}307.47 - (36 \times 650.00) = \$1{,}907.47$$

Therefore, the amount of interest earned from this investment is $1,907.47.

9.1 EXERCISES

Answers to the odd numbered exercises are available at the end of the textbook.

1. Joanne bought a new hot tub and an above-ground swimming pool. She was able to pay $800 per month at the end of each month for 4 years. How much did she pay by the end of the 4 years if the interest rate was 3.4% compounded monthly?
2. Andre paid off his school debt in 6 years. He paid $150 at the end of every month at an interest rate of 2.3% compounded annually. How much was his loan?
3. Greg took out a loan to buy a car and paid $300 at the beginning of every month for 3 years. The interest rate was 1% compounded monthly. How much was the loan?
4. Coco has set up a new design studio. Her parents paid for it, but charged her $300 per quarter for extra items she wanted. If the interest rate was 3% quarterly, what was the total that Coco had to pay by the end of the 5 years?
5. Hugh bought a car and paid $350 at the beginning of every month for 5 years. The interest rate was 3.1% compounded semi-annually. How much was the price of the car?
6. Rachel deposited $2,000 at the beginning of every month for 5 years into her daughter's education account that pays 3.6% compounded quarterly. What will the balance in the account be after 5 years?
7. Tania deposited $2,000 at the beginning of every six months for 10 years into her daughter's education account that pays 3.8% compounded quarterly. What will the balance in the account be after 10 years?
8. Thalia deposited $4,000 at the beginning of every six months for 7 years for her design career account. The interest earned was 3.8% compounded quarterly. What will the balance in her account be after 7 years?
9. A college professor would like to receive $1,500 at the end of each month for 5 years after she retires. What amount should she invest if she retires today? Use the rate of return of 3.7% compounded quarterly.
10. Isaac bought a car for $23,000 and must pay interest at 4.75% compounded semi-annually. How much must he pay monthly to repay the loan in 3 years?
11. If Olivia is able to save $500 every month, how much will she accumulate by the end of 10 years if her money can earn 3.4% compounded semi-annually?
12. Chris has $8,000 in his account and deposited $3,000 at the beginning of every six months. It pays 3.5% compounded quarterly. What will the balance in the account be after 10 years?
13. A university graduate has saved $11,000 for a down payment on a home and plans to deposit another $2,000 at the end of each month for the next 6 years. He expects to earn 2.5% compounded annually on his savings. How much should he have at the end of the 6 years?

14. Jamal obtained a $20,000 loan to buy a car at 3% compounded quarterly. What is the size of the monthly payment (starting at the end of the month) that will repay the loan in 4 years?

15. Peter obtained a $25,000 loan to buy a car at 2.75% compounded semi-annually. What is the size of the monthly payment (starting at the beginning of the month) that will repay the loan in 5 years?

16. John and Michelle bought a boat for $2,000 down and monthly payments of $600 at the beginning of each month for 5 years including interest at 3.2% compounded monthly.
    a. What was the amount of the boat loan?
    b. What was the purchase price of the boat?

17. Mrs. Jones contributed $4,000 to her RRSP at the end of every year for 10 years. It earned 3.1% compounded semi-annually. Then, she didn't contribute for the next 6 years. How much did she have in her RRSP after the 16 years?

18. Sasha contributed $3,000 to her RRSP at the end of every year for 8 years. It earned 3.1% compounded annually. Then, she didn't contribute for the next 6 years. How much did she have in her RRSP after the 14 years?

9.2 LOANS

Loans are common in our daily life. Students often take out a loan so that they can go to college or university. There are a variety of reasons to take out loans, including to start or expand a business, to consolidate debts, to refinance smaller loans, to travel, to pay for medical or insurance expenses, damage to assets, funeral costs, veterinarian costs, weddings, to purchase items like a car or furniture, and many other expenditures.

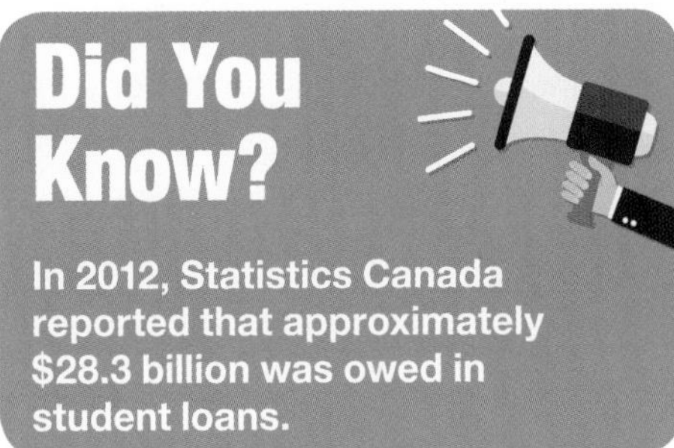

Did You Know?
In 2012, Statistics Canada reported that approximately $28.3 billion was owed in student loans.

Loans can be obtained in various ways. A small loan is often obtained at a **cash advance business**, where a high interest rate is often charged. **Wholesale and retail businesses** also offer loans, but again, it is important to be careful of high interest rates. Many use their home as equity to obtain a loan. This is referred to as a **home equity loan**. Often, this is used to consolidate a variety of pre-existing loans.

DISCUSSION

Think of different types of loans that you may take out during your life and discuss them in a group.

LOAN AMORTIZATION

A loan is paid off with equal payments over a set period of time. The periodic payments of the loan consist of two parts: the **interest** and the **principal**. The gradual reduction of the loan through these payments over the set period of time is called **loan amortization**.

The time period to pay off the entire loan, as decided by you or the financial lending institution, is called the **amortization period**. Financial institutions usually offer a variety of options; for example, you may wish to pay off a car loan in three, four, or five years, and it is even common to pay it off in six or seven years.

Common payment schedules for a loan include monthly, bi-weekly, or weekly payments. Payments can be set up to be at the end of the payment period (ordinary annuity) or at the beginning of the payment period (annuity due). The financial institution may insist on one specific payment schedule, or give several options.

Since loan amortization is simply a type of annuity, we can rearrange the formulas presented in section 9.1 to calculate payments. This will be illustrated in the following examples.

EXAMPLE 9.2 (A): Calculating Loan Payments for Simple Annuity Due

Sean took out a loan of $12,000 from his bank to help pay for school. He agreed to pay it back with beginning-of-month payments over 2 years, at an interest rate of 3.6%, compounded monthly. How much are his payments?

Solution:

This is a **simple annuity due** since the payment frequency and the compounding frequency are the same, and payments are made at the beginning of each period.

$PV = \$12{,}000.00$ $\quad j = 3.6\% = 0.036$ $\quad m = p = 12$ (monthly) $\quad t = 2$ years

Therefore,

$$i = \frac{j}{m} = \frac{0.036}{12} = 0.003$$

And the number of payments per term is

$$n = pt = 12(2) = 24$$

Therefore:

$$PV = PMT\left[\frac{1-(1+i)^{-n}}{i}\right] \times (1+i)$$

$$12{,}000.00 = \text{PMT}\left[\frac{1-(1+0.003)^{-24}}{0.003}\right] \times (1+0.003)$$

$$12{,}000.00 = \text{PMT}(23.122933...)(1.003)$$

$$12{,}000.00 = \text{PMT}(23.192302...) \qquad \text{Rearrange for PMT.}$$

$$\text{PMT} = \frac{12{,}000.00}{23.192302...}$$

$$\text{PMT} = 517.413044... = \$517.41$$

Therefore, Sean's monthly loan payments are $517.41.

EXAMPLE 9.2 (B): Calculating Loan Payments for Ordinary Simple Annuity

Taylor wants to take out a bank loan for $8,000 to start a fast food stand at a park beside a popular tourist lake. She wants to make her payments at the end of every month and would like to pay the loan off in five years. She is willing to pay the 4.2% compounded monthly interest rate that the bank requested. How much will her monthly payments be?

Solution:

This loan is an **ordinary simple annuity** since the payment frequency and the compounding frequency are the same and the payments are made at the end of each month.

EXAMPLE 9.2 (B): Calculating Loan Payments for Ordinary Simple Annuity *continued*

Solution:

We know the following information:

PV = \$8,000 (this is the loan amount) $j = 4.2\% = 0.042$ $m = p = 12$ (monthly) $t = 5$ years

Therefore,

$$i = \frac{j}{m} = \frac{0.042}{12} = 0.0035$$

and

$$n = pt = 12(5) = 60 \text{ (total number of payments in 5 years)}$$

We will use this formula and solve for PMT:

$$PV = PMT\left[\frac{1-(1+i)^{-n}}{i}\right]$$

$$\$8000 = PMT\left[\frac{1-(1+0.0035)^{-60}}{0.0035}\right]$$

$$\$8000 = PMT\,(54.03385802) \quad \text{Divide each side by 54.03385802.}$$

$$PMT = \$148.06$$

Therefore, Taylor's monthly loan payments are \$148.06.

EXAMPLE 9.2 (C): Calculating Loan Payments for General Annuity

Mitch and Barb want to buy office supplies for their company. They need these supplies as soon as possible and a credit union was quick to offer them a loan but at a high interest rate. They were offered a loan of \$30,000 at an interest rate of 15% compounded quarterly. If they need to repay the loan in eight years, what monthly payment would they need to pay at the end of every month?

Solution:

This loan is an **ordinary general annuity** since the payment frequency and the compounding frequency are **not** the same and the payments are made at the end of each month.

We know the following information:

PV = \$30,000 $j = 15\% = 0.15$ $m = 4$ (quarterly) $p = 12$ (monthly) $t = 8$ years

Therefore,

$$i = \frac{j}{m} = \frac{0.15}{4} = 0.0375 \qquad c = \frac{\text{\# compoundings per year}}{\text{\# payments per year}} = \frac{m}{p} = \frac{4}{12} = 0.33333\ldots$$

Converting i to i_2:

$$i_2 = (1+i)^c - 1 = (1+0.0375)^{0.33333\ldots} - 1 = 0.01234691$$

EXAMPLE 9.2 (C): Calculating Loan Payments for General Annuity *continued*

Solution:

Calculating the number of payments per term, we get:

$n = pt = 12(8) = 96$ payments in total

Now we put these numbers into the formula:

$$PV = PMT\left[\frac{1-(1+i_2)^{-n}}{i_2}\right]$$

$$\$30{,}000 = PMT\left[\frac{1-(1+0.01234691)^{-96}}{0.01234691}\right]$$

$\$30{,}000 = PMT\,(56.05614162)$ Divide each side by 56.05614162

$PMT = \$535.18$

Therefore, Mitch and Barb will have a monthly loan payment of $535.18.

EXAMPLE 9.2 (D): Calculating Loan Payments for Ordinary Simple Annuity Due

Anne wants to buy a condo in Halifax and her parents want to help her. They are willing to co-sign for $60,000 at an interest rate of 5.8% compounded monthly to help her. She wants to make payments at the beginning of every month. If they all agree to have this paid off in fifteen years, how much would Anne have to pay at the beginning of every month?

Solution:

This loan is a **simple annuity due** since the payment frequency and the compounding frequency are the **same** and the payments are made at the **beginning** of the time period.

We know the following information:

$PV = \$60{,}000$ $j = 5.8\% = 0.058$ $m = p = 12$ (monthly) $t = 15$ years

Therefore,

$$i = \frac{j}{m} = \frac{0.058}{12} = 0.0048333...$$

Calculating the number of payments per term, we get:

$n = pt = 12(15) = 180$ payments in total

Now we put these numbers into the formula for the PV (annuity due):

$$PV = PMT\left[\frac{1-(1+i)^{-n}}{i}\right] \times (1+i)$$

$$\$60{,}000 = \text{PMT}\left[\frac{1-(1+0.0048333333)^{-180}}{0.0048333333}\right] \times (1+0.0048333333)$$

$\$60{,}000 = \text{PMT}\,(120.615244)$ Divide each side by 120.615244

$\text{PMT} = \$497.45$

Therefore, Anne's beginning of month payment would be $497.45.

EXAMPLE 9.2 (E): Calculating Loan Amount for General Annuity Due

Sandra paid off her school loan in five years. She paid $300 at the beginning of every month at an interest rate of 3.9% compounded quarterly. How much was her loan?

Solution:

This loan is a **general annuity due** since the payment frequency and compounding frequency are **different** and the payment of $300 is at the **beginning** of the time period.

We know the following information:

$PMT = \$300 \quad j = 3.9\% = 0.039 \quad m = 4 \text{ (quarterly)} \quad p = 12 \text{ (monthly)} \quad t = 5 \text{ years}$

$$i = \frac{j}{m} = \frac{0.039}{4} = 0.00975 \qquad c = \frac{\#\text{ compoundings per year}}{\#\text{ payments per year}} = \frac{m}{p} = \frac{4}{12} = 0.33333...$$

Converting i to i_2:

$$i_2 = (1+i)^c - 1 = (1 + 0.00975)^{0.33333...} - 1 = 0.00323949$$

Calculating the number of payments per term, we get:

$$n = pt = 12(5) = 60 \text{ payments in total}$$

Now we put these numbers into the formula for an annuity due. In this case we will be solving for PV:

$$PV = PMT\left[\frac{1-(1+i_2)^{-n}}{i_2}\right] \times (1+i_2)$$

$$= \$300\left[\frac{1-(1+0.00323949)^{-60}}{0.00323949}\right] \times (1+0.00323949)$$

$$= \$16{,}387.67$$

Therefore, the loan amount was $16,387.67.

AMORTIZATION SCHEDULE

Customers need to know the remaining balance after each payment. As previously mentioned, each payment consists of two parts: **interest** and **principal**. Since the periodic payment is the same for each time period, the interest portion of the payment is greater at the beginning, and decreases over the amortization schedule. On the other hand, the principal portion of the payment is smaller at the beginning and increases over the amortization schedule.

DISCUSSION

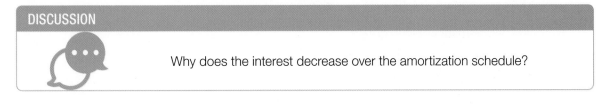

Why does the interest decrease over the amortization schedule?

The following is an amortization schedule that shows the calculations and each component of amortization.

Table 9.2: Amortization Schedule

Payment Number	Amount Paid (*PMT*)	Interest Portion	Principal Portion	Principal Balance
0	-	-	-	Total Loan Amount (*PV*)
1	*PMT*	$INT_1 = (PV \times i)$	$PRINC_1 = (PMT - INT_1)$	$BAL_1 = PV - PRINC_1$
2	*PMT*	$INT_2 = (BAL_1 \times i)$	$PRINC_2 = (PMT - INT_2)$	$BAL_2 = BAL_1 - PRINC_2$
3	*PMT*	$INT_3 = (BAL_2 \times i)$	$PRINC_3 = (PMT - INT_3)$	$BAL_3 = BAL_2 - PRINC_3$
...	continue for the total number of payments			
TOTAL	Total Amount Paid (*FV*)	Total Interest Paid (*FV* – *PV*)	Total Principal Paid (*PV*)	

EXAMPLE 9.2 (F): Constructing an Amortization Schedule

Zoe borrowed $4,000 from the bank at a rate of 3% compounded monthly. She agrees to pay back the loan in 6 equal payments, with each payment made at the end of each month. Set up an amortization schedule that shows the interest and principal portions of each payment, as well as the principal balance remaining at the end of each payment period.

Solution:

Zoe is making 6 equal payments, so we need to set up an amortization schedule with 6 payments. First, we can fill in the *PV* value of $4,000 in the Principal Balance column in the first row. This corresponds to the 0 entry in the Payment Number column.

Next, we need to calculate the amount of Zoe's payments. We will use the ordinary simple annuity formulas, since the payment frequency and the compounding frequency are the same, and payments are made at the end of each period.

$PV = \$4{,}000.00 \qquad j = 3.0\% = 0.03 \qquad n = 6 \qquad p = m = 12$ (monthly)

Calculating the periodic interest rate:

$$i = \frac{j}{m} = \frac{0.03}{12} = 0.0025$$

Calculating the payment amount, *PMT*:

$$PV = PMT\left[\frac{1-(1+i)^{-n}}{i}\right]$$

$$4{,}000.00 = PMT\left[\frac{1-(1+0.0025)^{-6}}{0.0025}\right]$$

$$4{,}000.00 = PMT(5.947848\ldots)$$

$$PMT = \frac{4{,}000.00}{5.947848\ldots} \qquad \text{Rearrange to solve for } PMT.$$

$$PMT = 672.512137\ldots = \$672.51$$

EXAMPLE 9.2 (F): Constructing an Amortization Schedule *continued*

Solution:

Fill in the Amount Paid (*PMT*) column in the row corresponding to the 1st payment. Calculate the interest and principal portions as well as the principal balance remaining after the 1st payment by following the formulas in Table 9.2.

Payment Number	Amount Paid (*PMT*)	Interest Portion	Principal Portion	Principal Balance
0	-	-	-	$4,000.00
1	$672.51	$INT_1 = (PV \times i)$ $= 4{,}000 \times 0.0025$ $= \$10.00$	$PRINC_1 = (PMT - INT_1)$ $= 672.51 - 10$ $= \$662.51$	$BAL_1 = PV - PRINC_1$ $= 4{,}000 - 662.51$ $= \$3{,}337.49$

By following the same process and the instructions from Table 9.2, complete the schedule for the remaining payments.

This is what the completed schedule looks like:

Payment Number	Amount Paid (*PMT*)	Interest Portion	Principal Portion	Principal Balance
0	-	-	-	$4,000.00
1	$672.51	$10.00	$662.51	$3,337.49
2	$672.51	$8.34	$664.17	$2,673.32
3	$672.51	$6.68	$665.83	$2,007.49
4	$672.51	$5.02	$667.49	$1,340.00
5	$672.51	$3.35	$669.16	$670.84
6	$672.52	$1.68	$670.84	$0.00
TOTAL	$4,035.07	$35.07	$4,000.00	

Notice that while the amount paid is constant, the interest portion decreases over the schedule and the principal portion increases over the schedule.

Note: The final payment is $0.01 more than the others. The final payment may be different from all the previous payments by a very small amount to make up for rounding which occurs when doing the calculations.

DISCUSSION

Think of another loan that you could potentially take out and prepare an amortization schedule for that loan.

9.2 EXERCISES

Answers to the odd numbered exercises are available at the end of the textbook.

1. Calculate the size of the payments of a $3,500 loan with a 7.5% interest rate compounded monthly that is paid off in 15 end-of-month installments.

2. Calculate the size of the payments of a $1,000 loan with a 4% interest rate compounded semi-annually that is paid off in 26 payments at the beginning of every month.

3. Calculate the size of the payments of a $4,000 loan with a 1.85% interest rate compounded annually that is paid off in 104 end-of-month installments.

4. Calculate the size of the payments of a $2,200 loan with a 7.5% interest rate compounded monthly that is paid off in 8 beginning-of-month installments.

For Exercises 5 to 8, calculate the size of the loan payments and construct an amortization schedule for the length of the term.

5. Yuen, a college graduate, borrowed $10,000 for one year to start his tea business. The interest rate was 8% compounded semi-annually and he settled the loan by making payments at the end of every six-month period for one year.

6. Jan, an interior designer, borrowed $15,000 to buy samples of material and design equipment. Her parents would gladly help her, but she would like to pay off the loan in one year by herself. The interest rate is 10% compounded semi-annually and the payments are made at the end of every six-month period.

7. Benjamin took out a loan for $6,000 which he plans to pay back in 6 equal end-of-month payments. He borrowed at a rate of 3% compounded monthly.

8. Alex took out a $1,500 loan at a rate of 5.6% compounded quarterly to help buy furniture for his new apartment. He agreed to pay it back in 6 beginning-of-month installments.

9.3 MORTGAGES

A **mortgage** is a special type of a loan that is used for buying real estate. When purchasing a house, it is common to have a twenty-five or thirty year mortgage, which means that the loan will be amortized over twenty-five or thirty years, respectively. The longer the amortization, the smaller the amount of each individual payment. Some countries allow a very long amortization term, while others place limits on how long the term can be.

DISCUSSION

What is the advantage of having a shorter amortization period?

DOWN PAYMENT

A down payment is the initial payment given upfront by the purchaser to the bank or financial institution at the time of finalizing the business transaction. The amount of the down payment varies. It might be as low as 5% or as high as 30% of the loan. Governments usually have laws indicating the amount necessary for a down payment. Clients with a poor credit rating may be required by the bank or another financial institution to have a higher down payment. The rest of the loan is in the form of a mortgage which is amortized.

EXAMPLE 9.3 (A): Calculating a Mortgage Down Payment

A purchaser wants to buy a house valued at $300,000 and needs to provide a 20% down payment. How much must she pay as a down payment, and what is the loan amount that will be amortized?

Solution:

Down payment = $300,000.00 × 0.2 = $60,000.00

The down payment is equal to $60,000.00. The mortgage value will be equal to the difference between the value of the house and her down payment.

$300,000.00 – $60,000.00 = $240,000.00

Therefore, the amount of the down payment is $60,000 and the amount of the loan is $240,000.

DISCUSSION

What are the advantages or disadvantages of a low down payment?

MORTGAGE TERM

A mortgage is split into smaller lengths of time called **mortgage terms**. For example, within a twenty-five year mortgage, you could have a six-month term, a one-year term, and a two-year term, all the way up to a ten-year term. The interest rate will vary with the term. Usually a shorter term has a lower interest rate because it is easier for a financial lending institution to predict the specific lending rate of the government. At the end of a mortgage term, a new term is negotiated. For example, a lending rate of 2.59% compounded semi-annually for two years may be renegotiated after the end of the two-year term for a lending rate of 3.15% compounded semi-annually fixed for five years. This renegotiation process continues until the total mortgage is paid off.

DISCUSSION

What are the advantages/disadvantages of a higher/lower mortgage term?

TYPES OF MORTGAGES AND INTEREST RATES

There are two types of mortgages that banks or other financial institutions offer: **fixed rate** and **variable rate** mortgages.

A **fixed rate** mortgage has an interest rate which does not change for the length of the mortgage term. The borrower may be able to start another fixed rate (or variable rate) term before the end of the mortgage term. Financial lending institutions have rules about this process. According to Canadian law, fixed rate mortgage payments are usually made at the end of every month and are compounded semi-annually. However, financial lending institutions may accept payments bi-weekly, semi-monthly, weekly, or on a specific day of the month.

A **variable rate** mortgage (or floating rate mortgage) has an interest rate that changes based on the economy of the country or market. For example, the Bank of Canada's prime lending rate at 0.5%. However, if the Government changes the prime lending rate, the variable interest rate will also change.

DISCUSSION

Discuss the advantages of the fixed rate versus the variable rate.

There are two types of fixed rate and variable rate mortgages: **closed** or **open**.

A **closed mortgage** is usually less expensive than an open mortgage because there are penalties if the borrower changes the agreed upon amount for each pay period or closes the loan during a mortgage term. A more expensive **open mortgage** allows the borrower to close the mortgage or transfer it to a different borrower without penalties. As well, it allows the borrower to pay a different amount at any time.

EXAMPLE 9.3 (B): Calculating Monthly Payments for Mortgage Term and Balance Owing

A couple in the north part of Toronto purchased a condominium for \$230,000. They paid 20% of the amount as a down payment and then the balance was negotiated with their bank for a 25-year mortgage with an interest rate of 3.2% compounded semi-annually with end-of-month payments for a 5-year fixed term.

i What was the size of the monthly payment for 5 years?

ii How much did they owe after the 5-year mortgage term?

Solution:

i First, we must calculate the amount of the mortgage by subtracting the down payment.

Total Purchase Price = \$230,000.00

Down Payment = \$230,000.00 × 0.2 = \$46,000.00

Mortgage Amount = \$230,000.00 – \$46,000.00 = \$184,000.00

Next, we calculate the monthly payments for the 25 year mortgage given the fixed interest rate of 3.2% compounded semi-annually for the next 5 years.

This is an ordinary general annuity since the payment frequency and the compounding frequency are different, and payments are made at the end of each period.

$PV = \$184{,}000.00$ $j = 3.2\% = 0.032$ $p = 12$ (monthly) $m = 2$ (semi-annually) $t = 25$ years

Calculating the periodic interest rate:

$$i = \frac{j}{m} = \frac{0.032}{2} = 0.016 \qquad c = \frac{m}{p} = \frac{2}{12} = 0.166666...$$

Convert i to i_2:

$$i_2 = (1 + i)^c - 1 = (1 + 0.016)^{0.166666...} - 1 = 0.002649...$$

Calculating the number of payments:

$$n = p \times t = 12 \times 25 = 300$$

EXAMPLE 9.3 (B): Calculating Monthly Payments for Mortgage Term and Balance Owing *continued*

Solution:

Therefore:

$$PV = PMT\left[\frac{1-(1+i_2)^{-n}}{i_2}\right]$$

$$184{,}000.00 = PMT\left[\frac{1-(1+0.002649...)^{-300}}{0.002649...}\right]$$

$$184{,}000.00 = PMT(206.796544...)$$

$$PMT = \frac{184{,}000.00}{206.796544...}$$ Rearrange for *PMT*.

$$PMT = 889.763417... = \$889.76$$

Therefore, the size of the monthly payments for the first 5 years is $889.76.

ii We must calculate the future value of the mortgage loan at the end of 5 years.

$PV = \$184{,}000.00$ $i_2 = 0.002649...$ $p = 12$ (monthly) $t = 5$ years

$n = p \times t = 12 \times 5 = 60$

Therefore:

$$FV = PV(1+i_2)^n$$
$$= 184{,}000.00\,(1+0.002649...)^{60}$$
$$= 215{,}652.7013... = \$215{,}652.70$$

Next, we will calculate the future value of the payments made, at the end of 5 years.

$PMT = \$889.76$ $i_2 = 0.002649...$ $n = 60$

$$FV = PMT\left[\frac{(1+i_2)^n-1}{i_2}\right]$$
$$= 889.76\left[\frac{(1+0.002649...)^{60}-1}{0.002649...}\right]$$
$$= 57{,}779.51772... = \$57{,}779.52$$

The amount owed after 5 years is equal to the difference between the future value of the total mortgage and the future value of the payments that have been made.

$215,652.70 – $57,779.52 = $157,873.18

Therefore, after the 5 year mortgage term, the couple will still owe $157,873.18.

QUALIFYING FOR A MORTGAGE

Most people would like to purchase a house or condominium. However, it is very important to investigate how much it would cost for the down payment and mortgage.

There are costs for the borrower to consider even after having an adequate down payment, such as mortgage payments, property taxes, utilities, cable, internet, and phone. It is generally accepted that these costs should not be more than 39% of the gross monthly income.

Total personal debt affects the borrower's ability to qualify for the desired mortgage. The housing costs mentioned above, car payments, personal loans, and credit card debt as well as other debts, should not exceed 44% of one's gross monthly income.

Other factors affecting qualification for a mortgage include:

- Credit history
- Annual income
- Employment history
- First time home buyers can take up to $25,000 from their Registered Retirement Savings Plan (RRSP) for their down payment (tax free but must be put back within 15 years)
- If the purchaser can only pay less than 20% of the house price, the mortgage must be insured (if in Canada) by the Canadian Mortgage and Housing Corporation (CMHC)

DISCUSSION

What could you do now to begin to qualify for a mortgage to buy a house or condominium?

PAYING OFF YOUR MORTGAGE FASTER

If you have the funds, there are many ways you can increase the speed at which you pay back your mortgage, which will save you money on interest payments. These strategies include:

- Make a lump-sum payment. Most banks and other financial institutions allow a lump-sum payment towards paying off a mortgage, once per year. Usually it is up to 15% per year.
- Reduce the amortization period.
- Increase the payment amount.
- Increase the payment frequency.

Did You Know?
Housing prices are usually lowest in winter and highest in summer.

9.3 EXERCISES

Answers to the odd numbered exercises are available at the end of the textbook.

1. A couple bought a business to rent apartments near a college in British Columbia. They purchased it for \$380,000. They made a down payment of 30% of the value of the rental business and received the rest of the purchase price in a 25-year amortized mortgage. The interest rate was 5.80% compounded semi-annually and the payments were at the end of each month. The interest rate was fixed for a three-year term.
   a. What is the dollar amount of the down payment?
   b. What was the amount left to be amortized over the 25 years?
   c. How many payments are there over the 25-year amortization?
   d. What would the monthly periodic interest rate be?
   e. Calculate the monthly payment amount.

2. A couple from Ottawa, Ontario purchased a condo in a resort in the Ottawa Valley for \$350,000. They made a down payment of 25% of the value of the condo. They received the rest of the purchase price in a 20-year amortized mortgage. The interest rate was 2.9% compounded semi-annually and the payments were at the end of each month. The interest rate was fixed for a two-year term.
   a. What is the dollar amount of the down payment?
   b. What was the amount left to be amortized over the 20 years?
   c. How many payments are there over the 20-year amortization?
   d. What would the monthly periodic interest rate be?
   e. Calculate the monthly payment amount.

3. Two sisters, Tanya and Matilda, purchased a townhouse for \$300,000. They made a down payment of 20% of the value of the townhouse, and received the rest of the purchase price in a 25-year amortized mortgage. The interest rate was 4.0% compounded semi-annually and the payments were at the end of each month. The interest rate was fixed for a two-year term.
   a. What is the dollar amount of the down payment?
   b. What was the amount left to be amortized over the 25 years?
   c. How many payments are there over the 25-year amortization?
   d. Calculate the monthly payment amount.
   e. How many payments are there over the two-year term?
   f. Calculate the balance at the end of the two-year term.

4. A couple bought real estate with ten small cabins on a remote island in northern Ontario to create a unique summer tourist resort. They purchased it for $500,000. They made a down payment of 30% of the value of the resort. They received the rest of the purchase price in a 20-year amortized mortgage. The interest rate was 3.80% compounded semi-annually and the payments were at the end of each month. The interest rate was fixed for a three-year term.
   a. What is the dollar amount of the down payment?
   b. What was the amount left to be amortized over the 20 years?
   c. How many payments are there over the 20-year amortization?
   d. Calculate the monthly payment amount.
   e. How many payments are there over the three-year term?
   f. Calculate the balance at the end of the three-year term.

REVIEW EXERCISES

Answers to the odd numbered exercises are available at the end of the textbook.

1. David has just finished university and wants to travel to Europe with some friends. For his vacation, train pass, food, taxes, and other expenses, he wants to borrow **$7,000** from a bank for his trip. If the bank charges an interest rate of **8.5% per month compounded monthly**, what would he have to **pay at the end every month for four years**?

2. Mariano wants to take out a bank loan for **$5,000** US to start a popcorn and candy apple stand at a soccer stadium in Mendoza, Argentina. He wants to make his **payments at the beginning** of every month and would like to pay the loan off in **five years**. He is willing to pay the **6.2%** interest rate that the bank requested. How much will his **monthly payments** be? (Taxes not included)

3. Calculate the size of the payments for a **$30,000** loan with a **6.5%** interest rate **compounded monthly** that is paid off in **15 beginning of month** installments.

4. Sergei and Beatriz want to buy a condo in Ottawa and their parents want to help them. They are willing to co-sign for **$120,000** at an interest rate of **6.8% payable monthly** to help them. Sergei and Beatriz want to **pay monthly** at the **end of every month**. If they all agree to have this **paid off in ten years**, how much would Sergei and Beatriz have to pay at the end of every month?

5. A couple own a chalet for tourists as well as locals in the ski hills of northern Quebec. They want to borrow **$45,000** (including taxes) to build an addition on their chalet, and the bank has offered an interest rate of **8% per year compounded monthly** for **5 years** at **fifteen years**. They want to **pay at the end of each month**. What will their payment be at the end of every month?

6. Vincent and Taylor want to start a catering business and want to borrow **$10,000** from a bank or credit union. A bank offered to loan them these funds for **5 years** at an interest rate of **7.5% compounded monthly**. If they need to **pay at the beginning of every month**, what would their monthly payment be?

7. Sudi paid off his school debt in **five years**. He paid **$250 at the end of every month** at an interest rate of **4.1% compounded annually**. How much was his loan?

8. Derya bought a car and paid **$400** at the **beginning of every month for four years**. The interest rate was **3.9% compounded quarterly**. How much was the price of the car?

9. If Dina is able to save **$800** by the **end of every month**, how much could she accumulate by the end of **seven years** if her money can earn **4.5% compounded semi-annually**?

10. Jorge wants to take culinary classes and wants to borrow **$8,000** from a bank to finance these classes. The bank wants him to **pay at the beginning of every month** at an interest rate of **6.7% compounded semi-annually**. How much will the monthly payments be?

CHAPTER 10

MATH APPLICATIONS FOR TOURISM

LEARNING OBJECTIVES

Studying this chapter will provide you with the knowledge needed to:

- Calculate cost and selling price of a service.
- Calculate commissions.
- Calculate taxes.
- Calculate discounts.
- Calculate occupancy rate.
- Calculate achievement factor.
- Calculate yield.

TOPICS

10.1 Tour Costing

10.2 Commissions, Taxes, and Discounts

10.3 Occupancy Rate and Yield Management

10.1 TOUR COSTING

In the tourism industry, mathematics is applied in various ways to provide tourists (clients) with accommodation, transportation, and other travel services. In this section, we will study how mathematics is applied to establish the selling price of a service (such as the price of flight tickets, hotel stays, etc.) so that all of the costs are covered with an acceptable profit margin.

Figure 10.1: Actual Photo of Nessie

Did You Know?
Loch Ness Monster tourism adds $40 million a year to Scotland's economy.

The **selling price** is the cost plus the amount of markup.

Selling Price Formula (A)

$$\text{Selling Price} = \text{Cost} + \text{Markup}$$

The **profit margin** (%) is the rate of markup on the selling price.

Profit Margin Formula

$$\text{Profit Margin (Rate of Markup on Selling Price)} = \frac{\text{Markup}}{\text{Selling Price}} \times 100\%$$

Substituting and rearranging the previous two formulas, we obtain the following formula for selling price:

Selling Price Formula (B)

$$\text{Selling Price} = \frac{\text{Cost}}{(1 - \text{Profit Margin})}$$

The following examples use these two assumptions:

- All costs are transferred to the client (tourist).
- The combined costs for Taxes, Gratuities (also called tips), and Service Charges (**TGSC**) are always quoted separately from the final price.

EXAMPLE 10.1 (A): Tour Costing

Safe Air Travel signed a contract with a tour company for 14 weeks over the winter. The aircraft has 130 seats and the tour company would have to pay Safe Air Travel C$1,400,000 for the 14 week season in addition to air taxes of C$325 per person. The tour company offers weekly tour packages that include return flights from Toronto to Puerto Vallarta once every week. The company also contracted a hotel in Puerto Vallarta at C$140 per room, per night, based on double occupancy. Clients would be required to pay an additional C$25 per person for baggage handling and transfer charges, and C$1.25 per person per night for gratuities at the hotel. Taxes are additional for all of the rates.

Calculate the following, before taxes:

i Cost per seat for the company
ii Hotel cost per person for the company
iii Total base cost per person for the company
iv Price per client, if the tour company has a profit margin of 20%
v Quoted price to clients (include TGSC separately)

Solution:

i Number of seats = 130

Number of weeks = 14

Cost to book the aircraft for 14 weeks = C$1,400,000.00

Cost to book the aircraft for 1 week = 1,400,000.00 ÷ 14 = C$100,000.00

Therefore, cost per seat = 100,000.00 ÷ 130 = C$769.23

ii C$140.00 for 1 room for 2 people (double occupancy)

Therefore, the cost per person per night = 140 ÷ 2 = C$70.00

For 7 nights, the cost per person would be 7 × 70 = C$490.00

iii Total base cost = C$769.23 (flight) + C$490.00 (hotel) = C$1,259.23 per person

iv $$\text{Selling price} = \frac{Cost}{(1 - Profit\ Margin)} = \frac{1{,}259.23}{(1 - 0.20)} = \text{C\$}1{,}574.04$$

v Air tax = $325.00 per person

Gratuity = $1.25 × 7 = $8.75 per person per week

Service charges = $25 per person

TGSC = 325.00 + 8.75 + 25.00 = $358.75 per person

Therefore, the price quoted to clients is C$1,574.04 plus TGSC of $358.75.

10.1 EXERCISES

Answers to the odd numbered exercises are available at the end of the textbook.

1. If the selling price of an all-inclusive trip for one is $1,200 (before taxes), what is the profit margin of a company if the markup is:

   a. $100? b. $175? c. $250?

2. If a company marks up the price of their trip to China by $300, what is their profit margin if the selling price before taxes is:

   a. $1,700? b. $2,000? c. $2,500?

3. What is the selling price of a tour package that costs $3,300 (before taxes) if the profit margin is:

   a. 12%? b. 18%? c. 24%?

4. What is the selling price of a tour package that costs $1,750 (before taxes) if the profit margin is:

   a. 22%? b. 26%? c. 30%?

5. A tour operating company in Greece organizes travel to Mykonos and other nearby islands by ferry on the way there, and flights for the return trip. The ferries take longer to go from the mainland to Mykonos but are cheaper than flying.

   The busiest time for the tour operating company is from May to September. These twenty weeks have twenty back to back hotel packages. During this time the tour company has five packages of one ferry crossing and one flight. Return flights to any of the islands are more expensive but take less time and can be a popular option so the company offers 15 return flight tours. Therefore, the company has a total of 20 tour packages.

   Last summer, a special deal was given to celebrate the anniversary of the tour company. In this anniversary deal, there were 130 seats on each flight and 130 seats on the ferry. The company's operating costs are C$2,000,000 per season for the twenty packages with five ferry crossings and flights, including the company's operating costs for the fifteen return flight packages.

   For the hotels, the company charges C$150.00 per person per night (based on double occupancy) plus C$3.00 gratuity per person per night. The taxes for all the packages are C$200.00. The airport/ferry/service charge/baggage handling is C$30. In addition, the bus fee to and from the airport and/or ferry dock is C$25.

   Calculate the following before taxes:

   a. Cost per seat for the company.

   b. Hotel cost for the company per person.

   c. Total base cost per person for the company.

   d. Price per client, if the company has a profit margin of 20%.

   e. Quoted price to clients including the tax, gratuity, service charges (TGSC) separately.

6. Ryan's tour company offers weekly tour packages that include return flights from Ottawa to Hawaii once every week. He contracted Phoenix Air Travel for $1,600,000 to use their 150-seater aircrafts for a period of 16 weeks.

   He also contracted a hotel in Hawaii at C$200 per room per night based on double occupancy. In addition to the price of the package, each client is required to pay C$450 for air taxes, C$20 for baggage handling and transfer charges, as well as C$3.25 per night for gratuities at the hotel. Taxes are additional for all the rates.

   Calculate the following before taxes:

   a. Cost per seat for the company.
   b. Hotel cost per person for the company.
   c. Total base cost per person for the company.
   d. Price per client, if the company has a profit margin of 30%.
   e. Quoted price to clients (include TGSC separately).

10.2 COMMISSIONS, TAXES, AND DISCOUNTS

TAXES

The Canadian federal and provincial governments charge a percent on the sales of various goods and services in the country. This amount is added to the price of the goods or services sold to bring revenue into the country, which helps maintain the infrastructure and operations throughout Canada. These charges are called **HST** (Harmonized Sales Tax) and **PST** (Provincial Sales Tax). The following table summarizes the HST and/or PST rates for common services in tourism:

Table 10.2 (A): Tax on Tourism Services

Service	Tax
Short-term domestic auto rentals	13%
Commercial parking	13%
Air travel originating in Ontario and terminating in the U.S[1]	5%
Air travel originating in Ontario and terminating outside of Canada and the U.S[2]	No HST
Rail, boat and bus travel originating in Ontario and terminating outside of Canada	No HST
Domestic air, rail, boat and bus travel originating in Ontario	13%
Travel service fees	13%

[1] *Includes air travel terminating in the French islands of St. Pierre and Miquelon but does not include air travel terminating in Hawaii.*

[2] *Includes air travel terminating in Hawaii but does not include air travel terminating in the French islands of St. Pierre and Miquelon.*

In Canada, there are 3 types of sales tax:

1. Provincial Sales Tax (PST) levied by provinces
2. Goods and Service Tax (GST) a value-added tax levied by the federal government
3. Combined Harmonized Sales Tax (PST + GST)

**The GST is always 5%

For tourism, the following table summarizes the GST, PST, and HST in Canada's provinces and territories. Notice that the three territories only have GST.

Table 10.2 (B): Tourism Taxes by Province

	PST	GST	Total Tax Rate (HST)
Alberta	0%	5%	5%
British Columbia	7%	5%	12%
Manitoba retail services	8%	5%	13%
New Brunswick	10%	5%	15%
Newfoundland & Labrador	10%	5%	15%
Ontario	8%	5%	13%
Prince Edward Island	10%	5%	15%
Nova Scotia	10%	5%	15%
Quebec	9.975%	5%	14.975%
Saskatchewan	6%	5%	11%
Yukon Territory	0%	5%	5%
Northwest Territories	0%	5%	5%
Nunavut	0%	5%	5%

**In Alberta there is a 4% tax for lodging and hotel room rates

**In Manitoba there is a 5% tax for lodging and hotel room rates

EXAMPLE 10.2 (A): Calculating Taxes on Domestic Car Rental

During his visit to Toronto, Henry rented a car for 10 days. If the rental company charged him $55 per day, excluding taxes, calculate the total cost, including taxes, for the entire period. The tax on car rentals is 13%.

Solution:

Rental cost = $55.00 per day × 10 days = $550.00

Tax amount = 13% of $550.00 = 0.13 × 550.00 = $71.50

Total cost, including taxes = $550.00 + $71.50 = $621.50

COMMISSIONS

Tour operators (or travel counsellors) receive commissions or charge fees for the services that they offer.

A few examples of common commissions as allocated for each booking are as follows:

Table 10.2 (C): Common Commission Percents

Service	Commission Percent
Car booking	6%
Prepaid hotels	10%
Hotels paid at checkout	7%
Activities	10%
Vacation packages (flight + hotel, flight + hotel + car rental for a minimum 3 hotel nights)	5%
Vacation packages (flight + hotel, flight + hotel + car rental for less than 3 hotel nights)	3%
GDS (Global Distribution System) hotel	2%

In situations where tour operators charge fees, it may be either a flat fee for a service or a fee per activity.

EXAMPLE 10.2 (B): Calculating Commission on Vacation Package Sale

Mountaineer Memories sold a vacation package to Henry and his wife for \$5,850 to travel to British Columbia's Rocky Mountains for 7 days. If the commission is 5% on this sale, calculate the amount of commission received.

Solution:

Selling price = \$5,850.00

Amount of commission = 0.05 × 5,850.00 = \$292.50

Therefore, the amount of commission received from this sale was \$292.50.

DISCOUNTS

Tour packages and services are often sold at a discount to entice customers to buy them. The percent of markdown is referred to as the discount rate. Since it is a markdown, we subtract the discount from the price of the good or service.

EXAMPLE 10.2 (C): Applying a Discount

Ron purchased a round-trip flight to San Francisco, California. The original selling price was C\$1,450, but he bought the tickets at a 30% discount. What is the dollar amount of his discount, and how much did he pay for his flights, including taxes (assuming a tax rate of 5%)?

Solution:

Discount amount = 1,450.00 × 0.3 = C\$435.00

Cost of flights, excluding taxes = 1,450.00 – 435.00 = C\$1,015.00

Tax amount = 1,015.00 × 0.05 = C\$50.75

Total cost, including taxes = 1,015.00 + 50.75 = C\$1,065.75

10.2 EXERCISES

Answers to the odd numbered exercises are available at the end of the textbook.

1. Polar Winter Tours sold a vacation package to Beth for \$2,000 to travel to Winnipeg for 3 days. If their commission on this sale is 3%, calculate the amount of commission received.

2. Aiden, a sales person at Arya Sunshine Tours, sold a vacation package to Oliver and his wife for \$10,000 to travel to the Bahamas for 10 days. If the commission on this sale is 5%, calculate the amount of commission received.

3. Natalia rented a car for 7 days during her visit to Toronto. If the rental company charged her $45 per day, excluding taxes, calculate the total cost, including taxes, for the entire period. The tax on car rentals is 13%.

4. Sofia purchased an air ticket from Toronto to New York. If she was charged $760 for the ticket, excluding taxes, calculate the total cost, including taxes. The tax on air travel originating in Ontario and terminating in the USA is 5%.

5. Fleur de Lis Tours offered a 45% discount on a four-star hotel package in Montreal that normally costs $300, excluding taxes. What is the discounted price, excluding taxes?

6. Lloyd's Legacy Tours in Moncton, New Brunswick offered 35% off a premium package that includes hotel and rail travel. The original cost was $3,500 excluding taxes. What was the sale package price, including taxes?

7. Tantalizing Tans offered a 65% discount to any of their Florida packages if they were booked within 7 days of departure. Karina and her husband took advantage of the deal. It would have cost $4,000 for the two of them, excluding taxes, without the discount. How much did it cost if they booked it 4 days prior to the departure (excluding taxes)?

8. SeaSights Touring Company offered a 15% discount on its excursion packages. A group of 15 from Halifax want to go on a 2 day excursion that would normally cost $335 each (excluding taxes). How much would each member pay for this excursion (excluding taxes) after the discount?

9. Susan rented a recreational vehicle for 7 days to visit a few cities in Ontario. The rental company usually charges $80 plus tax per day for the rental; however, they gave her a seasonal discount of 20%.
   a. How much did Susan receive as a 20% seasonal discount for the 7 days?
   b. What was the discounted price without commission or taxes?
   c. If she had to pay 6% commission, what was the final price without taxes?
   d. If the tax charged was 13% of the price above, how much was the final price with taxes?

10. The Woo family decided to go on a week-long vacation driving around Ontario. They rented a recreational vehicle from a rental company for $120 plus tax per day. They received a discount of 15% on this rental.
   a. How much did the Woo family receive as a 15% discount on this recreational vehicle?
   b. If the Woo family had to pay 6% commission to the rental company, what was the final price without taxes?
   c. If the tax charged was 13% of the above price, what was the final price with taxes?

10.3 OCCUPANCY RATE AND YIELD MANAGEMENT

Yield management is a variable pricing strategy used to maximize revenue and profits.

Consider a hotel room or an airline ticket. Often, the price a customer pays can vary significantly. The price of a flight booked 3 months in advance can typically be lower than the price of a ticket booked the day before a flight. Similarly, the price of a hotel room booked 3 months in advance could be significantly different from the price of the same room booked on the day.

Did You Know?
It would take a person about 200 years to spend a night in every hotel room in Las Vegas.
WELCOME
TO Fabulous
LAS VEGAS
NEVADA

REVENUE

Revenue is the amount of money that a company receives, in a specific period, from the sale of their products or services.

- Hotels receive revenue predominantly from the sale of (the use of) rooms.
- Restaurants receive revenue from the sale of food or beverages.
- Airlines receive revenue from the sale of seats on a flight.

PROFIT

Profit is the amount of money remaining after all costs have been covered by a company.

Profit Formula

$$\textit{Profit} = \textit{Revenue} - \textit{Expenses}$$

RACK RATE

Rack rate is the official or advertised price for a hotel room before any discount is applied. This is typically the highest rate charged for a room.

AVERAGE ROOM RATE

Hotels do not usually sell all of their rooms at the rack rate. The average room rate is the average of the rates that a hotel receives for a specific room over a specified period of time.

OCCUPANCY RATE

Occupancy rate is the percent of rooms a hotel sells compared to the total rooms a hotel has available. This rate is often used to compare a hotel's performance against other hotels and is used to forecast demand and proper levels of staffing. This is an important hotel statistic.

Occupancy Rate Formula

$$\textit{Occupancy Rate} = \frac{\textit{Rooms Sold}}{\textit{Total Rooms}}$$

EXAMPLE 10.3 (A): Calculating Occupancy Rate

The Grand Markham Suites sold 80 rooms on Monday, 80 on Tuesday, 90 each on Wednesday, Thursday, and Friday, 70 on Saturday and 20 on Sunday. The hotel has a total of 100 rooms. Calculate the occupancy rate for the week.

Solution:

$$\textit{Occupancy Rate} = \frac{\textit{Rooms Sold}}{\textit{Total Rooms}} = \frac{(80 + 80 + 90 + 90 + 90 + 70 + 20)}{(100 \times 7)} = 74.3\%$$

ACHIEVEMENT FACTOR

The achievement factor is the percent of the rack rate that a hotel typically receives.

Achievement Factor Formula

$$\textit{Achievement Factor} = \frac{\textit{Average Room Rate}}{\textit{Rack Rate}}$$

PERISHABILITY

Perishability of services implies that the service cannot be stored, saved, returned, or resold once provided to a customer, such as the transportation service that an airline ticket entitles a customer. Similarly, a product or service may also become perishable when it is not purchased within a given time frame. For example, a vacant seat on an airplane or an empty room in a hotel represents lost profit.

YIELD

Yield management is designed to measure the revenue achievement and is used to maximize a hotel's room revenues. Yield compares the actual room revenue to the potential room revenue.

Yield Formula (A)

$$\textit{Yield} = \textit{Occupancy Rate} \times \textit{Achievement Factor}$$

Substituting the formulas for Occupancy Rate and Achievement Factor, we get:

Yield Formula (B)

$$Yield = \frac{Rooms\ Sold}{Total\ Rooms} \times \frac{Average\ Room\ Rate}{Rack\ Rate}$$

A yield of 100% is the maximum revenue potential of a hotel. 100% means that a hotel sells all of its rooms every day, charging on average the rack rate. Similarly, a yield of 67.5% implies that a hotel is achieving 67.5% of its revenue potential.

EXAMPLE 10.3 (B): Calculating Yield

Wasaga Beach Party Suites has 200 rooms. On average, the hotel sells 128 rooms at an average room rate of $85 per night. The rack rate for the hotel is $100 per night. Calculate the yield.

Solution:

$$Occupancy\ Rate = \frac{Rooms\ Sold}{Total\ Rooms} = \frac{128}{200} = 0.64$$

$$Achievement\ Factor = \frac{Average\ Room\ Rate}{Rack\ Rate} = \frac{85}{100.00} = 0.85$$

$$Yield = Occupancy\ Rate \times Achievement\ Factor = 0.64 \times 0.85 = 0.544 = 54.40\%$$

Therefore, Wasaga Beach Party Suites is operating at 54.40% of its potential.

10.3 EXERCISES

Answers to the odd numbered exercises are available at the end of the textbook.

Calculate the missing values in the tables in Exercises 1 and 2.

		Total Rooms	Rooms Sold	Occupancy Rate	Rack Rate	Average Rate	Achievement Factor	Yield
1.	a.	300	270		$250	$200		
	b.	280	200		$300	$250		
	c.	250	210		$280	$250		
	d.	220	200		$200	$145		
	e.	200	150		$250	$200		
	f.	150	100		$170	$120		
	g.	100	80		$450	$380		

	Total Rooms	Rooms Sold	Occupancy Rate	Rack Rate	Average Rate	Achievement Factor	Yield
2. a.	300	270			$250		76%
b.	200			$280	$175		56%
c.	350			$320	$275		80%
d.	150	120		$220			57%
e.	275	200		$300			65%
f.	200	160		$120			67%
g.		147		$300	$178		53%

3. The Toronto Island Inn sold 50 rooms on Monday, 60 on Tuesday, 40 each on Wednesday, Thursday, and Friday, 55 on Saturday and 30 on Sunday. The inn has a total of 70 rooms. Calculate the occupancy rate.

4. A hotel that has 200 rooms sold 120 rooms on Monday, 180 rooms on Tuesday, 140 rooms on Wednesday, 160 rooms on Thursday, 100 rooms on Friday, 190 rooms on Saturday, and 200 rooms on Sunday. Calculate the occupancy rate.

5. Calculate the occupancy rate of the Beacon Hotel which has 150 rooms, but on average sells 102 rooms.

6. Calculate the occupancy rate of the Best Hotel and Suites which has 250 rooms, but on average sells 205 rooms.

7. If a 200 room hotel had an occupancy rate of 68% last week, calculate the average number of rooms sold per night during the week.

8. If Collingwood Ski Resort had an occupancy rate of 72% of their 180 rooms last night, calculate the number of rooms sold last night.

9. Calculate the achievement factor last weekend if a motel sold rooms for $75 while the rack rate was $90.

10. Calculate the achievement factor for Algonquin Backcountry Lodge if rooms sell for $90 while the rack rate is $100.

11. Calculate the yield of the 300 room Ballantrae Hotel on a golf course that averages 260 rooms sold. The rack rate is $180, but the average actual room rate is $150.

12. Calculate the yield during holiday season of the 350 room Sauble Beach Resort that averages 340 rooms sold during holiday season. The rack rate is $180, but the average actual room rate is $170.

13. Calculate the number of rooms in a hotel with a yield of 77% where the standard room rate is $140 but rooms are sold on average for $110. This hotel usually sells 160 rooms.

14. Calculate the number of rooms in a hotel with a yield of 56.5% where the standard room rate is $110 but rooms are sold on average for $80. This hotel usually sells 190 rooms.

15. Calculate the rack rate of the 180 room luxurious Tobermory Suites Hotel & Spa that usually sells 150 suites at an average rate of $160 and has a yield of 78%.

16. Calculate the rack rate of a 300 suite luxurious beach club hotel that usually sells 290 suites at an average rate of $190 and has a yield of 88%.

17. The 380 suite Hotel Killarney has a rack rate of $230 and an actual room rate of $180. If the yield last year was 75.3%, how many suites did the hotel sell?

18. Downhill Ski n' Board Resort, with 300 suites, has a rack rate of $250 and an actual room rate of $210. If the yield last year was 81.3%, how many suites did the hotel sell?

19. Calculate the achievement factor for the Golden Sands Hotel that has 250 rooms if its rooms usually sell for $190. The hotel has a yield of 86% and on an average they sell 230 rooms.

20. Calculate the achievement factor for the 200 suite Okanagan Mountain View Hotel and Spa if rooms usually sell for $180. The hotel has a yield of 80% and on an average they sell 180 rooms.

21. A restaurant stocks 200 cans a day of cold drinks and sells 160 cans a day at an average price of $1.34 and a yield of 60%. Calculate the rack rate of the cold drinks and write your final answer to 2 decimal places.

22. A chef plans to renew a contract with a wine supplier. After reviewing the records, he noticed that 530 bottles of wine were sold last month at the restaurant, while 600 bottles of wine (various brands and types) were purchased, with the most expensive bottle costing $69. If the yield of wine bottles was 73%, what was the average price of the wine bottles? Write your final answer to 2 decimal places.

REVIEW EXERCISES

Answers to the odd numbered exercises are available at the end of the textbook.

1. The Canadian Mini-Tour Company specializes in short tours of 3 to 5 days that are very popular in the summer and fall. The Collins family of 4 decide to go on a bus tour of northern Ontario to see the changing of the leaves. If the tour costs $390 per person for a 5-day tour and the tour company charges a commission of 5% per person, how much will the Collins family pay? (excluding taxes)

2. The Canadian Mini-Tour Company offers tours of the Thousand Islands leaving from Toronto, Ontario by bus. Jacque and Maria decide to go on a 3-day tour which includes 8 hours on a large tour boat with a capacity of 100 people as well as 2 meals each plus drinks. The cost of $390 per person includes the tour as well as their stay in Kingston, Ontario on the first and last night. The Tour company charges 5% commission and the HST is an additional 13%. What is the final cost of this tour for Jacque and Maria?

3. Fatima and her husband bought return tickets to fly to Calgary from Toronto. The price was C$2,100 (without tax) during the summer. The tax was 13%. How much was the final price they had to pay, including tax?

4. Hans and Selina wanted to buy a tour package to fly to Holland for 10 days in the winter. The $2,900 package had a discount of 25% during that season. How much would they have to pay if the tour company charged 10% commission on the discounted package and there was no tax?

5. Kevin and his brother bought round trip tickets to Orlando, Florida. The original selling price was C$1090 each but they bought the tickets with a special discount of 15%.
   a. How much did Kevin and his brother each have to pay for the tickets without tax?
   b. If they had to pay 5% tax on the tickets, how much was the final price they each had to pay, including the tax?
6. Wai-Chun and his wife bought round trip tickets to Sarasota, Florida. They wanted to pay less, so they took a "red-eye" flight. For that, they received a 15% discount off the regular price of $1,565. To keep the price as low as possible, they did not opt in to any meals, but only had coffee, tea, and biscuits. That gave them an additional 5% discount.
   a. How much did Wai-Chun and his wife have to pay for the tickets, excluding tax?
   b. If they had to pay 5% tax on the tickets, how much was the final price they had to pay including the tax?
7. Calculate the occupancy rate of a Holiday Inn and Suites on a beach in Florida that has 300 rooms, but on average sells 260 rooms.
8. If Hilton Head Island, South Carolina has a special beach hotel with 250 rooms, but on average sells 210 rooms, calculate the occupancy rate.
9. If a hotel in Orlando, Florida has 280 rooms and last week it had an occupancy rate of 75%, calculate the average number of rooms sold per night last week.
10. If a hotel in Hollywood, California has 300 rooms and last week it had an occupancy rate of 90%, calculate the average number of rooms sold per night last week.
11. A hotel in Old Quebec City had a special discount just after the Ice Performances. A room that usually costs C$320 had a 35% discount rate. How much did the room cost during the discount period?
12. A hotel in Vancouver has a special discount. Seniors receive a 10% discount for each room as well as an additional 15% discount for a tour around Vancouver and lunch in Stanley Park. How much does a room that usually costs C$480 for adults, cost for seniors, including the special tour and lunch in Stanley Park?
13. Calculate the achievement factor last month for a hotel in Niagara Falls that sold rooms for C$120 while the rack rate was C$140 for that month. The month had 30 days.
14. Calculate the achievement factor last month for a hotel in Toronto that sold rooms for C$300 while the rack rate was C$320 for that month. The month had 31 days.
15. Calculate the rack rate of the 250 suite Vancouver Island Resort that usually sells 200 suites at an average rate of C$300 and has a yield of 80%.
16. What is the rack rate for a hotel with 380 suites that usually sells 300 suites at an average rate of C$280 and has a yield of 72%?

17. Denise and her friend wanted a cheap trip across Canada. They started in Newfoundland and borrowed a friend's car to see most of that area. Then they went by ferry (cost $50 each including tax) to the Halifax area where her family lives and saw sights around that area. A relative was going to Vancouver by truck so Denise and her friend decided to go with him because it wouldn't cost much. They paid him $100 each including tax for gas, but slept in the back of the truck since it was warm in July. They had a great time touring various areas and each of them paid $250 including tax in total for mini tours and food. By the time they reached Vancouver, they each gave the truck owner a $200 cash tip for all of his help. If Denise and her friend had taken a flight from Newfoundland to Vancouver, they each would have had to pay C$650 plus 13% tax. How much did they each save by traveling the cheaper way?

18. Brian wanted to show his parents where he and his family live in Newfoundland. From the north coast, they went on a tour to see the icebergs. The tour cost C$100 each for 8 hours. A special lobster dinner buffet cost $35 each but Brian had coupons for 15% off the dinners. If the tax was 13%, how much did Brian have to pay for the three of them?

CHAPTER 11

MATH APPLICATIONS FOR HOSPITALITY

LEARNING OBJECTIVES

Studying this chapter will provide you with the knowledge needed to:

- Convert volumes and weights within the metric system.
- Calculate conversions between the metric and imperial systems.
- Calculate conversions between °C and °F.
- Calculate EP (edible portion), AP (as purchased), EPC (edible portion cost), and price factor.
- Calculate food cost percent, food cost, menu price, markup and % markup on food, and menu price yield.
- Write an income statement for a restaurant for 1 year.
- Write an income statement as a percent of sales.
- Calculate the break-even point of a business using break-even analysis.
- List at least 5 recommendations of menu pricing.
- Calculate contribution margin and menu mix %.

TOPICS

11.1 UNITS OF MEASUREMENT

MEASUREMENT OF VOLUME

In the measurement of volume, there are two measurement systems that are commonly used, metric and imperial.

METRIC SYSTEM

In most of the world, the litre is used as the basic metric unit for volume. Various prefixes are added to litre to signify different multiples of the base. In the hospitality industry, we usually work with **litres** (L) and **millilitres** (mL).

The following table lists common metric measurements of volume:

Table 11.1 (A): Common Metric Measurements of Volume

Measurement	Symbol	Multiple of Base Measurement (L)
kilolitre	kL	1,000
decilitre	dL	$\frac{1}{10}$
centilitre	cL	$\frac{1}{100}$
millilitre	mL	$\frac{1}{1,000}$

EXAMPLE 11.1 (A): Converting mL to L

Convert the following mL measurements to L measurements:

i 10 mL

ii 500 mL

iii 1,000 mL

Solution:

i $10\ \cancel{mL} \times \frac{1\ L}{1,000\ \cancel{mL}} = \frac{10\ L}{1,000} = \frac{1}{100}\ L$ or $0.01\ L$

ii $500\ \cancel{mL} \times \frac{1\ L}{1,000\ \cancel{mL}} = \frac{500\ L}{1,000} = \frac{1}{2}\ L$ or $0.5\ L$

iii $1,000\ \cancel{mL} \times \frac{1\ L}{1,000\ \cancel{mL}} = \frac{1,000\ L}{1,000} = 1\ L$

IMPERIAL SYSTEM

Instead of using prefixes like the metric system, the imperial system uses entirely different names to denote different measurements. The **fluid ounce** (fl oz) is the base imperial unit for volume.

The following table lists common imperial measurements of volume:

Table 11.1 (B): Common Imperial Measurements of Volume

Measurement	Symbol	Multiple of Base Measurement (fl oz)
Gallon	gal	160
Quart	qt	40
Pint	pt	20

EXAMPLE 11.1 (B): Converting Volumes Within Imperial Units

i Convert 3.5 gal to fluid ounces (fl oz).

ii Convert 1,000 fl oz to pints (pt).

Solution:

i 1 gal = 160 fl oz

Therefore,

$$3.5 \text{ gal} = 3.5 \cancel{\text{gal}} \times \frac{160 \text{ fl oz}}{1 \cancel{\text{gal}}} = 560 \text{ fl oz}$$

ii 1 pt = 20 fl oz, or 1 fl oz = $\frac{1}{20}$ pt

Therefore,

$$1{,}000 \text{ fl oz} = 1{,}000 \text{ fl } \cancel{\text{oz}} \times \frac{1 \text{ pt}}{20 \text{ fl } \cancel{\text{oz}}} = 50 \text{ pt}$$

CONVERTING BETWEEN THE METRIC AND IMPERIAL SYSTEMS

It is important for hospitality professionals to be able to convert between the metric and imperial systems. We may buy in one system and sell in another. For example, a restaurant often buys wine in 750 mL bottles, but serves it in 6 fl oz glasses. Accuracy is needed in converting the cost per unit in which a food or beverage was purchased to the cost per unit in which it will be served.

Below is a table of the common volume conversions between the metric and imperial systems. Typical container sizes (e.g. 750 mL bottles of wine from France) are denoted in their imperial volumes.

Table 11.1 (C): Common Metric to Imperial Conversions of Volume

Metric	Imperial
750 mL (or 0.75 L)	26.4 fl oz
1 L (or 1,000 mL)	35.2 fl oz
1.14 L (or 1,140 mL)	40.1 fl oz
1.75 L (or 1,750 mL)	61.6 fl oz

Although the chart above denotes accurate conversions, the reality is that in the hospitality industry, common sizes and portions are rounded to the nearest whole number.

For example: 750 ml = 26 fl oz, 1.14 L = 40 fl oz, and 1.75 L = 62 fl oz.

MEASUREMENT OF WEIGHT

In the measurement of weight, there are two measurement systems that are commonly used, metric and imperial.

METRIC SYSTEM

The **gram** (g) is the base measurement of the metric system for weight. The **kilogram** (kg), which is equal to 1,000 g, is more commonly used.

EXAMPLE 11.1 (C): Converting Masses Within Metric Units

i Convert 960 g into kilograms.

ii Convert 5 kg 730 g into grams.

Solution:

i $1 \text{ kg} = 1{,}000 \text{ g, or } 1 \text{ g} = \frac{1}{1{,}000} \text{ kg}$

Therefore,

$$960 \text{ g} = 960 \cancel{\text{g}} \times \frac{1 \text{ kg}}{1{,}000 \cancel{\text{g}}} = 0.96 \text{ kg}$$

ii $1 \text{ kg} = 1{,}000 \text{ g}$

Therefore,

$$5 \text{ kg } 730 \text{ g} = 5 \cancel{\text{kg}} \times \frac{1000 \text{ g}}{1 \cancel{\text{kg}}} + 730 \text{ g} = 5{,}730 \text{ g}$$

Did You Know?

In a lifetime, the average person consumes 60,000 lbs of food....how many kg is that?

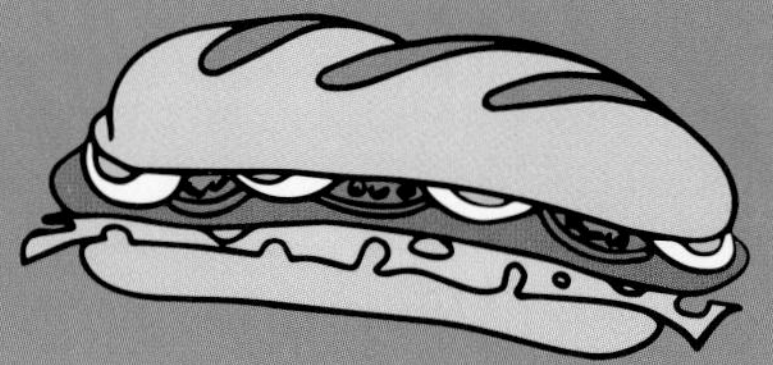

IMPERIAL SYSTEM

The **ounce** (oz) is the base measurement of the imperial system for weight. The **pound** (lb), which is equal to 16 oz, is more commonly used.

EXAMPLE 11.1 (D): Converting Masses Within Imperial Units

i Convert 3 lb 6 oz into ounces.

ii Convert 100 oz into pounds and ounces.

Solution:

i $1 \text{ lb} = 16 \text{ oz}$

Therefore,

$$3 \text{ lb } 6 \text{ oz} = 3 \cancel{\text{lb}} \times \frac{16 \text{ oz}}{1 \cancel{\text{lb}}} + 6 \text{ oz} = 54 \text{ oz}$$

ii $1 \text{ lb} = 16 \text{ oz, or } 1 \text{ oz} = \frac{1}{16} \text{ lb}$

Therefore,

$$\begin{aligned} 100 \text{ oz} &= 100 \cancel{\text{oz}} \times \frac{\frac{1}{16} \text{ lb}}{1 \cancel{\text{oz}}} \\ &= 6.25 \text{ lb} \\ &= 6 \text{ lb} + 0.25 \text{ lb} \\ &= 6 \text{ lb} + (0.25 \cancel{\text{lb}} \times \frac{16 \text{ oz}}{1 \cancel{\text{lb}}}) \\ &= 6 \text{ lb } 4 \text{ oz} \end{aligned}$$

CONVERTING BETWEEN THE METRIC AND IMPERIAL SYSTEMS

The conversion factor between the metric and imperial systems is:

1 lb = 454 g

EXAMPLE 11.1 (E): Converting Masses Between Imperial and Metric Units

Convert 3 lb into kilograms.

Solution:

1 lb = 454 g

Since,

$$3 \text{ lb} = 3 \cancel{\text{lb}} \times \frac{454 \text{ g}}{1 \cancel{\text{lb}}} = 1{,}362 \text{ g} \quad \text{and} \quad 1 \text{ kg} = 1{,}000 \text{ g, or } 1 \text{ g} = \frac{1}{1{,}000} \text{ kg}$$

We get: $1{,}362 \text{ g} = 1{,}362 \cancel{\text{g}} \times \frac{1 \text{ kg}}{1{,}000 \cancel{\text{g}}} = 1.362 \text{ kg}$

Below is a handy reference table of some common conversions that are helpful in setting up calculations.

Table 11.1(D): Conversion Reference Table

1 lb	16 oz	454 g	
1 g	$\frac{1}{454}$ lb	$\frac{1}{1000}$ kg	
1 oz	$\frac{1}{16}$ lb	$\frac{454}{16}$ g	
1 kg	1000 g	2.2 lb	
1 pt	20 fl oz		
1 qt	40 fl oz		
1 gal	160 fl oz		
1 fl oz	$\frac{1}{40}$ qt	$\frac{1}{20}$ pt	$\frac{1}{160}$ gal
1 mL	$\frac{26.4}{750}$ fl oz		
1 L	35.2 fl oz	1000 mL	

MEASUREMENT OF TEMPERATURE

In the measurement of temperature, there are two measurement systems used:

- **Celsius (°C) system:** used in Canada and most of Europe
- **Fahrenheit (°F) system:** used in the United States

The formulas used to convert from one system to the other are outlined as follows:

Conversions Between °C and °F

$$°F = \left(°C \times \frac{9}{5}\right) + 32 \qquad °C = \left(°F - 32\right) \times \frac{5}{9}$$

EXAMPLE 11.1 (F): Converting from Celsius to Fahrenheit

Convert 20°C to Fahrenheit.

Solution:

$$\left(20°C \times \frac{9}{5}\right) + 32 = 36 + 32 = 68°F$$

EXAMPLE 11.1 (G): Converting from Fahrenheit to Celsius

Convert 50°F to Celsius.

Solution:

$$(50°F - 32) \times \frac{5}{9} = 18 \times \frac{5}{9} = 10°C$$

11.1 EXERCISES

Answers to the odd numbered exercises are available at the end of the textbook.

In Exercises 1 to 4, fill in the missing values. Round to two decimal places wherever applicable.

1.

	MEASUREMENT OF VOLUME
a.	8.9 L = ______ mL
b.	750 mL = ______ L
c.	3 pt = ______ fl oz
d.	4 qt = ______ fl oz
e.	3 gal = ______ fl oz
f.	3,000 fl oz = ______ qt
g.	4,000 fl oz = ______ gal
h.	500 fl oz = ______ pt
i.	2 kg = ______ g
j.	1,550 g = ______ kg
k.	8 kg 500 g = ______ g
l.	8 lb = ______ oz
m.	12 oz = ______ lb
n.	5 lb 8 oz = ______ oz
o.	18°C = ______ °F
p.	64°F = ______ °C

2.

	MEASUREMENT OF VOLUME
a.	10.8 L = ______ mL
b.	2,000 mL = ______ L
c.	5 pt = ______ fl oz
d.	2 qt = ______ fl oz
e.	2.5 gal = ______ fl oz
f.	800 fl oz = ______ qt
g.	6,400 fl oz = ______ gal
h.	1,500 fl oz = ______ pt
i.	4.5 kg = ______ g
j.	800 g = ______ kg
k.	5 kg 200 g = ______ g
l.	3 lb = ______ oz
m.	6 oz = ______ lb
n.	2 lb 5 oz = ______ oz
o.	30°C = ______ °F
p.	85°F = ______ °C

3.

	MEASUREMENT OF VOLUME
a.	600 mL = _______ fl oz
b.	3.8 L = _______ fl oz
c.	5 qt = _______ mL
d.	6 gal = _______ mL
e.	6.4 pt = _______ mL
f.	1.5 L = _______ qt
g.	4 L = _______ gal
h.	0.75 L = _______ pt

	MEASUREMENT OF WEIGHT
i.	2 lb = _______ g
j.	8 oz = _______ g
k.	2 lb 6 oz = _______ g
l.	600 g = _______ lb
m.	850 g = _______ oz
n.	4 kg = _______ lb
o.	1.8 kg = _______ oz

4.

	MEASUREMENT OF VOLUME
a.	350 mL = _______ fl oz
b.	6.2 L = _______ fl oz
c.	8 qt = _______ mL
d.	2.5 gal = _______ mL
e.	12 pt = _______ mL
f.	2.8 L = _______ qt
g.	7 L = _______ gal
h.	0.5 L = _______ pt

	MEASUREMENT OF WEIGHT
i.	6 lb = _______ g
j.	10 oz = _______ g
k.	4 lb 5 oz = _______ g
l.	1,500 g = _______ lb
m.	400 g = _______ oz
n.	8 kg = _______ lb
o.	3.2 kg = _______ oz

5. A restaurant orders 30 kg of chicken for their chicken curry dish. Every serving of the curry needs 4 oz of chicken. How many servings can they make from their order?

6. The beef portion of Hungarian goulash is 3 oz per serving. The Hungarian chef wants as many servings as possible from 10 kg of beef. How many servings are there?

7. James purchased 50 pounds of top sirloin steak and sold 18 kg. How many ounces were left?

8. A bag of flour weighs 11 pounds. A bakery owner used 3 kg of flour to make wedding cakes. How many ounces of flour were left?

9. Thirty-six 750 mL bottles of wine are needed for a party. How many 6 oz glasses can be served?

10. Sunny bought twenty-four bottles of beer for a BBQ. If one bottle is 440 mL, how many pint glasses can be served?

11. One hundred fifty 6 oz glasses of wine are needed for a reception. How many 750 mL bottles of wine are needed?

12. Two hundred guests have been invited to a wedding. The couple wants to be able to offer two 6 oz glasses of wine to each guest. How many 750 mL bottles of wine will be needed?

13. The average low temperatures in December were 28°F in New York and –4°C in Toronto. Which city is colder during the month and by how much? Provide your answer in °C and °F.

14. Roberto and his friends went to Cancun, Mexico for a week and the average temperature was 32°C. Janeesha and her friends went to southern Spain for a week and the average temperature was 88°F. Which group had the hotter weather and by how much? Provide your answer in °C and °F.

11.2 YIELD

YIELD

In restaurants and hotels, during the food preparation process (peeling, chopping, trimming, and cooking), foods often shrink and lose weight (fluid evaporation or the breaking down of tissues). The amount of usable food that is left behind after the preparation process is called **yield**.

AS PURCHASED (AP)

The raw, unprocessed food that is used in the preparation process is called the **as purchased** or AP quantity.

EDIBLE PORTION (EP)

The portion of food ready to be served is the **edible portion** or EP. In other words, the EP is the AP minus the waste amount.

YIELD PERCENT

The food **yield percent** is the approximate percent of usable yield after cooking. For example, after cooking a 10-pound leg of lamb (AP), only 5 to 8 pounds of usable meat remains (EP). We can use the following formula to calculate the yield percent:

Yield Percent Formula

$$\textit{Yield Percent} = \frac{EP}{AP} \times 100\%$$

The yield is always less than 100% as EP is always less than AP.

When the yield percent is expressed in its decimal form, it is commonly known as the **yield factor**.

EXAMPLE 11.2 (A): Calculating Yield Percent

i 40 oz of canned lima beans were purchased. After the lima beans were drained, 28 oz remained. Calculate the yield percent.

ii The chef at the King Chinese Restaurant bought a 22 lb king salmon. The trimming, boning, and cooking process resulted in a loss of 3 lb 8 oz. Determine the yield percent.

Solution:

i $\textit{Yield Percent} = \frac{EP}{AP} \times 100\% = \frac{28}{40} \times 100\% = 70\%$

ii $AP = 22 \text{ lb} = (22 \times 16) \text{ oz} = 352 \text{ oz}$

$\text{Waste Amount} = 3 \text{ lb } 8 \text{ oz} = (3 \times 16 + 8) \text{ oz} = 56 \text{ oz}$

$EP = AP - \text{Waste Amount} = 352 - 56 = 296 \text{ oz}$

$\textit{Yield Percent} = \frac{EP}{AP} \times 100\% = \frac{296}{352} \times 100\% = 0.840909... \times 100\% = 84.09\%$

EXAMPLE 11.2 (B): Calculating the Edible Portion (EP)

i Sirloin steak has a yield factor of 0.90. Calculate the Edible Portion (EP) of 40 lb of steak.

ii Halibut has a yield factor of 0.84. Calculate the Edible Portion (EP) of 5 lb 3 oz of halibut.

Solution:

i $\text{Yield Factor} = \frac{EP}{AP}$

$EP = AP \times \text{Yield Factor}$

$= 40 \text{ lb} \times 0.90$

$= 36 \text{ lb}$

ii $AP = 5 \text{ lb } 3 \text{ oz} = (5 \times 16 + 3) \text{ oz} = 83 \text{ oz}$

$\text{Yield Factor} = \frac{EP}{AP}$

$EP = AP \times \text{Yield Factor}$

$= 83 \text{ oz} \times 0.84$

$= 69.72 \text{ oz}$

AS PURCHASED COST (APC) AND EDIBLE PORTION COST (EPC)

To make a profit on each plate served, it is necessary to know the exact cost of the food on each plate (food cost per portion).

The **as purchased cost** (APC) is the total cost of a unit of raw product. The **edible portion cost** (EPC) is the cost of a cooked product per a unit of weight. The APC and EPC are both important factors to calculate the food cost per portion. The EPC is always more expensive than the APC because the weight is less after peeling and/or cooking.

Edible Portion Cost (EPC) Formula

$$EPC = \frac{APC}{EP}$$

EXAMPLE 11.2 (C): Calculating the Edible Portion Cost (EPC)

i Three pounds of chicken cost $2.29 per pound. The EP after cooking was 2 lb. Calculate the EPC.

ii 16 kg of apples cost $22.85. The EP after coring and peeling the apples was 10.5 kg. Calculate the EPC.

Solution:

i $APC = 2.29 \times 3 = \$6.87$

$EPC = \frac{APC}{EP} = \frac{6.87}{2} = 3.435 = \$3.44 \text{ per lb}$

ii $EPC = \frac{APC}{EP} = \frac{22.85}{10.5} = 2.176190... = \$2.18 \text{ per kg}$

PRICE FACTOR

The **price factor** is the ratio of the **EPC** to the **APC** per unit. It is also the inverse of the yield factor. Since the EPC is always larger than the APC (and yield is always less than 100%), the price factor is always greater than 1.

Price Factor Formulas

$$Price\ Factor = \frac{EPC}{APC/unit} \quad \textbf{or} \quad Price\ Factor = \frac{1}{Yield}$$

EXAMPLE 11.2 (D): Calculating Price Factor

i Calculate the price factor if the EPC for chicken is $22 and the APC is $16.

ii Calculate the price factor if the yield factor is 0.7.

Solution:

i $Price\ Factor = \frac{EPC}{APC/unit} = \frac{22.00}{16.00} = 1.375$

ii $Price\ Factor = \frac{1}{Yield} = \frac{1}{0.7} = 1.428571... = 1.429$

11.2 EXERCISES

Answers to the odd numbered exercises are available at the end of the textbook.

1. 80 lb of apples were purchased to make applesauce. After peeling and taking out the cores, their weight was reduced to 60 lb. Calculate the yield percent.

2. 30 lb of bananas were purchased to be used in a fruit salad for a reception. After peeling, their weight was reduced to 22 lb. Calculate the yield percent.

3. 25 lb of pears were obtained to use in a fruit salad. After they were peeled, cored, and diced for the salad, 18 lb 2 oz remained. Calculate the yield percent.

4. 5 lb of raw garlic was peeled and crushed to prepare a stir-fry. 3 lb 5 oz was left. Calculate the yield percent.

5. 20 kg of potatoes were obtained to make a potato salad. After they were peeled and boiled, 17 kg 200 g remained for the salad. Calculate the yield percent.

6. 15 kg of lemons were to be used to make lemonade. After cutting and peeling, 7 kg 750 g of lemons were left. Determine the yield percent.

7. A turkey dinner was prepared using a 24 lb turkey. After the turkey was cooked, it had lost 9 lb 3 oz in weight. Determine the yield percent.

8. 10 lb of frozen cranberries were thawed, cleaned, and boiled to prepare them for a turkey dinner. They lost 3 lb 4 oz in weight during preparation. Determine the yield percent.

9. Calculate the EP for:
   a. Broiled chicken with an AP of 25 lb and a yield factor of 0.78.
   b. Salmon with an AP of 6 lb 6 oz and a yield factor of 0.82.
   c. Turnips with an AP of 10 kg 50 g and a yield factor of 0.72.

10. Calculate the EP for:
    a. Stewing beef with an AP of 16 lb and a yield factor of 0.74.
    b. Tilapia with an AP of 8 lb 3 oz and a yield factor of 0.88.
    c. Onions with an AP of 14 kg 230 g and a yield factor of 0.84.
11. Calculate the AP for:
    a. Carrots with an EP of 7 lb and a yield factor of 0.87.
    b. Tomatoes with an EP of 8 lb 2 oz and a yield factor of 0.54.
    c. Haddock with an EP of 5 kg 120 g and a yield factor of 0.75.
12. Calculate the AP for:
    a. Ground beef with an EP of 12 lb and a yield factor of 0.70.
    b. Spinach with an EP of 4 lb 1 oz and a yield factor of 0.63.
    c. Potatoes with an EP of 8 kg 730 g and a yield factor of 0.85.
13. Nectarines have a yield percent of 72%. If 30 lb of nectarines were ordered by a store, calculate the EP.
14. Raspberries have a yield percent of 34%. How many pounds will have to be ordered for a market that serves 4 oz to each of its 100 customers?
15. For a wedding dinner, each guest will have an 8 oz filet steak. There will be 200 guests. The yield percent of filet steak is 85%. What is the AP in lbs?
16. For a wedding dinner where stuffed trout is to be served, what is the AP for the trout if each of the 100 guests are served a 6 oz portion? The yield percent of the trout is 55%.
17. The Mapleview Nursing Home was trying to conserve the cost of food served to the residents. The chef purchased 300 lb of vegetables for $1.50/lb. After peeling and cooking, 220 lb were left to serve the residents. Calculate the EPC.
18. A restaurant was facing increased rent and was trying to cut back the cost of raw materials. The chef purchased 20 lb of chicken for $3.20/lb. After cooking, 16 lb were left to serve the customers. Calculate the EPC.
19. A chef purchased 30 lb of fish (various types). The fish lost 4.3 lb during deboning and cooking. If the total APC was $50.56, calculate the EPC/lb.
20. When preparing a beef stew, 10 lb of beef were used. The cost was $24.87. Only 0.5 lb were lost when cooking. Calculate the EPC/lb.
21. Calculate the price factor if the yield factor is 0.8.
22. Calculate the price factor if the EPC for lamb is $26 and the APC is $18.

11.3 MENU PRICING

Menu pricing is done to establish a new menu or to revise an existing menu. In this process, it may be necessary to compare the price with other restaurants' menus. This process is called benchmarking. However, with benchmarking, it is not possible to identify the costs incurred, which may vary significantly between restaurants, especially if they are in different countries.

FOOD COST PERCENT

Food cost is often expressed as a percent of the menu price.

Food Cost Percent Formula

$$\textit{Food Cost}\ (\%) = \frac{\textit{Food Cost}\ (\$)}{\textit{Menu Price}}$$

EXAMPLE 11.3 (A): Calculating Menu Price

The food cost for an appetizer is $6 and your desired food cost percent is 35%. What should the menu price of the appetizer be?

Solution:

$$\textit{Food Cost}\ (\%) = \frac{\textit{Food Cost}\ (\$)}{\textit{Menu Price}}$$

$$\textit{Menu Price} = \frac{\textit{Food Cost}\ (\$)}{\textit{Food Cost}\ (\%)}$$

$$= \frac{6.00}{0.35}$$

$$= 17.142857... = \$17.14$$

Therefore, the menu price should be $17.14.

EXAMPLE 11.3 (B): Calculating Food Cost

The owner of a restaurant specializing in homemade burgers would like to sell his burger platter at the same price as his competitor. The competitor charges $8.95. What should the food cost be to maintain a 35% food cost percent?

Solution:

$$\textit{Food Cost}\ (\%) = \frac{\textit{Food Cost}\ (\$)}{\textit{Menu Price}}$$

$$\textit{Food Cost}\ (\$) = \textit{Menu Price} \times \textit{Food Cost}\ (\%)$$

$$= 8.95 \times 0.35$$

$$= 3.1325 = \$3.13$$

Therefore, the food cost should be $3.13.

MARKUP ON FOOD PRICING

Another way to describe food pricing is by calculating the markup.

$$\textit{Menu Price} = \textit{Food Cost} + \textit{Markup}\ (\$)$$

We can rerarrange this formula to solve for Markup ($):

Markup Value Formula

$$\textit{Markup}\ (\$) = \textit{Menu Price} - \textit{Food Cost}$$

It is also possible to express markup as a percent of the menu price.

Markup Percent Formula

$$\textit{Markup}\ (\%) = \frac{\textit{Markup}\ (\$)}{\textit{Menu Price}} \times 100\%$$

EXAMPLE 11.3 (C): Calculating Markup Value and Percent

i If the food cost is $4.23 and the menu price is $11.59, calculate the markup.

ii Calculate the markup percent if the markup is $6.20 and the menu price is $8.99.

iii Calculate the markup value and the markup percent if the menu price is $12.99 and the food cost percent is 35%.

Solution:

i $\textit{Markup}\ (\$) = \textit{Menu Price} - \textit{Food Cost} = 11.59 - 4.23 = \$7.36$

ii $\textit{Markup}\ (\%) = \dfrac{\textit{Markup}\ (\$)}{\textit{Menu Price}} \times 100\% = \dfrac{6.20}{8.99} \times 100\% = 0.689655... \times 100\% = 68.97\%$

iii $\textit{Food Cost}\ (\$) = \textit{Menu Price} \times \textit{Food Cost}\ (\%) = 12.99 \times 0.35 = 4.5465 = \$4.55$

$\textit{Markup}\ (\$) = \textit{Menu Price} - \textit{Food Cost} = 12.99 - 4.55 = \$8.44$

$\textit{Markup}\ (\%) = \dfrac{\textit{Markup}\ (\$)}{\textit{Menu Price}} \times 100\% = \dfrac{8.44}{12.99} \times 100\% = 0.649730... \times 100\% = 64.97\%$

MENU PRICE AND YIELD

Menu prices are set based on the EPC (edible portion cost), not the APC. An example of using the EPC to calculate the menu price is shown in the following example.

EXAMPLE 11.3 (D): Setting Menu Price

The top chef at a resort is setting up a new menu with new pricing. One of the specialties is duck. He can buy 30 lb of duck at $4.50 per pound. He expects the trimming waste and cooking to reduce the weight by 34%. His portion size for the menu is 5 oz and he wants to have a 30% food cost. Help him set the menu price.

Solution:

First, calculate the EP:

$$EP = AP \times Yield\ Factor = 30 \text{ lb} \times (100\% - 34\%) = 30 \times 0.66 = 19.8 \text{ lb}$$

Next, calculate the EPC (the cost of cooked duck per pound):

$$EPC \text{ per pound} = \frac{APC}{EP} = \frac{4.50 \times 30 \text{ lb}}{19.8 \text{ lb}} = 6.818181... = \$6.82$$

Next, calculate the cost of one portion:

$$\begin{aligned} 5 \text{ oz portion cost} &= EPC \text{ per ounce} \times 5 \\ &= \frac{EPC \text{ per pound}}{16} \times 5 \\ &= \frac{6.82}{16} \times 5 \\ &= 2.13125 = \$2.13 \end{aligned}$$

Finally, use the food cost to calculate the menu price:

$$Menu\ Price = \frac{Food\ Cost\ (\$)}{Food\ Cost\ (\%)} = \frac{2.13}{0.3} = \$7.10$$

Therefore, the menu price for the 5 oz portion of duck is $7.10.

11.3 EXERCISES

Answers to the odd numbered exercises are available at the end of the textbook.

1. Complete the chart below.

	FOOD COST (%)	FOOD COST ($)	MENU PRICE ($)
a.	35%	$4.45	
b.	28%	$5.65	
c.	25%		$15.79
d.	30%		$13.49
e.		$6.56	$18.49
f.		$3.12	$9.99

2. Complete the chart below.

	FOOD COST (%)	FOOD COST ($)	MENU PRICE ($)
a.	25%	$5.78	
b.	40%	$8.20	
c.	28%		$18.99
d.	32%		$12.49
e.		$5.45	$15.49
f.		$4.05	$8.99

3. Calculate the cost of ingredients of chicken noodle soup priced at $4.49 with a 38% food cost percent.

4. Calculate the cost of ingredients of a turkey sandwich priced at $3.99 with a 25% food cost percent.

5. Calculate the food cost percent of a beef taco with a food cost of $2.56 and a menu price of $4.99.

6. Calculate the food cost percent of a falafel wrap with a food cost of $1.95 and a menu price of $5.50.

7. If the food cost of a serving of chocolate fudge cake and ice cream is $2.90, and a 30% food cost percent is desired, what should the selling price on the menu be?

8. If the food cost of a serving of pasta is $4.50, and a 40% food cost percent is desired, what should the selling price on the menu be?

9. Last month, King Dragon Restaurant spent $62,000 on food. The monthly sales were $145,000. What was the food cost percent for the month?

10. In January, Creamy Frozen Yogurt spent $22,000 on yogurt and other food items. The monthly sales were $42,000. What was the food cost percent for the month?

11. If the menu price for a burger at Lakefront Grill is $15.99 and the food cost is $4.54, what is the markup and the markup percent?

12. The menu price for a steak at Molly's Steakhouse is $28.99 and the food cost is $8.75. Calculate the markup and the markup percent.

13. A bistro had three specials on the menu. Calculate the markup and percent markup on each:
    a. $9.99 for calamari (with a food cost of $5.00)
    b. $11.99 for a lobster Kaiser (with a food cost of $5.00)
    c. $12.00 for a vegetarian quiche and salad (with a food cost of $4.00)

14. A pastry shop had three specials on the menu. Calculate the markup and percent markup on each:
    a. $10.99 for apple pie (with a food cost of $4.20)
    b. $6.99 for a serving of cheese cake (with a food cost of $2.35)
    c. $8.99 for a serving of carrot cake (with a food cost of $3.00)

15. Calculate the markup on a gourmet chicken salad if the food cost is $3.24 and the food cost percent is 36%.

16. Calculate the markup on a Cornish pasty if the food cost is $4.75 and the food cost percent is 40%.

17. A golf club is hosting a dinner for its members and their families. One of the menu options is an 8 oz beef filet (after cooking). The chef is told that there will be 100 guests and he needs to be ready for 80 servings of filet, as it is a popular choice. The trimming and cooking waste is usually 25%. The raw filet costs $5.68 per pound. Calculate:

    a. edible portion quantity (EP)
    b. as purchased quantity (AP)
    c. EPC
    d. APC
    e. price factor
    f. cost of one serving

18. Another option for the golf club in Exercise 17 is a 6 oz chicken dinner. The chef is told that he needs to be ready for 50 servings of chicken. The yield is 70%. This chicken costs $4.97 per pound raw. Calculate:

    a. edible portion quantity (EP)
    b. as purchased quantity (AP)
    c. EPC
    d. APC
    e. price factor
    f. cost of one serving

19. Fantasy Inc. has agreed to plan an event to celebrate the Raptors winning the 2019 NBA Championship. The planning manager estimated the cost to serve 400 guests to be $248,200, and the cost percentage is 85%.

    a. What is the total price offered by Fantasy Inc. for this event? How much will each guest have to pay to attend this event?
    b. What is the markup that the planning manager included in the offered price?

20. A catering company signed a contract to cater for a golf tournament and offered the service at a price of $230 per person. The event manager estimated the cost percentage of the service to be 28%.

    a. What is the cost of the catering service in dollars?
    b. What is the markup in this offered price?

11.4 BUSINESS MANAGEMENT

PROFIT AND LOSS ANALYSIS

In a restaurant, it is necessary to record the **sales** of food and beverages (also called revenue), the cost of the food and beverages sold (also called **cost of goods sold** or cost of sales), and all the **expenses** such as rent, maintenance, wages, salaries, etc., to know if the business is making a profit or incurring a loss. These values are periodically (monthly, quarterly, yearly) tracked on an **income statement.**

The **gross profit** (also called gross margin) is the result of subtracting the costs of goods sold from the sales.

Gross Profit Formula

$$\textit{Gross Profit} = \textit{Sales} - \textit{Cost of Goods Sold}$$

The **net profit** (also called net income) is the result of subtracting the expenses from the gross profit.

Net Profit Formula

$$\textit{Net Profit} = \textit{Gross Profit} - \textit{Operating Expenses}$$

The following exhibit illustrates a sample **income statement**.

Exhibit 11.4: Sample Income Statement

Income Statement The Burger Haven *for the period ending December 31, 2018*			*Percent of Total Sales*
Sales			
	Food	$120,000	63.16%
	Beverages	$70,000	36.84%
Total Sales		**$190,000**	**100.00%**
Cost of Goods Sold			
	Food	$30,000	15.79%
	Beverages	$16,000	8.42%
Total Cost of Goods Sold		**$46,000**	**24.21%**
Gross Profit (Margin)		**$144,000**	**75.79%**
Expenses			
	Rent	$15,000	7.89%
	Wages (labour expenses)	$70,000	36.84%
	Utilities and Maintenance	$25,000	13.16%
Total Expenses		**$110,000**	**57.89%**
Net Profit		**$34,000**	**17.89%**

The above income statement also includes a column showing the **percent of total sales** which expresses the values as a percent of the total sales ($190,000).

For example:

$$\text{Expenses as a percent of total sales} = \frac{\textit{Expenses}}{\textit{Total Sales}} = \frac{110{,}000}{190{,}000} \times 100\% = 57.89\%$$

$$\text{Net profit as a percent of total sales} = \frac{\textit{Net Profit}}{\textit{Total Sales}} = \frac{34{,}000}{190{,}000} \times 100\% = 17.89\%$$

BREAK-EVEN ANALYSIS

Break-even occurs when a business makes no profit and incurs no loss. At this point, the sales are equal to the costs and expenses. This point is called the **break-even point**.

To determine the break-even point, we must first define the following terms:

- **Fixed Costs:** represent the costs that do not change, regardless of the quantity sold (e.g. rent, utilities, insurance, etc.) These costs are not dependent on the sales.
- **Variable Costs:** represent the costs that vary with the quantity sold (e.g. the cost of food, beverages, and labour are variable costs at a restaurant). These costs are dependent on the sales.

- **Contribution Margin:** represents the amount that remains after the variable costs are subtracted from the sales.

Contribution Margin Formula

$$\text{Contribution Margin} = \text{Sales} - \text{Variable Costs}$$

- **Contribution Margin Percent:** represents the ratio of the contribution margin to the sales expressed as a percent.

Contribution Margin Percent Formula

$$\text{Contribution Margin Percent} = \frac{\text{Contribution Margin}}{\text{Sales}} \times 100\%$$

- **Break-Even Point:** represents the point when the sales cover the costs and expenses. It is the point at which the business makes no profit but incurs no loss.

Break-Even Point Formula

$$\text{Break-Even Point} = \frac{\text{Fixed Costs}}{\text{Contribution Margin Percent}}$$

EXAMPLE 11.4: Performing Break-Even Analysis

Using the Income Statement for "The Burger Haven" in Exhibit 11.4, calculate the following:

i Variable Costs
ii Fixed Costs
iii Contribution Margin
iv Contribution Margin Percent
v Break-Even Point

Solution:

i *Variable Costs = Total Cost of Goods Sold + Wages*

= 46,000.00 + 70,000.00 = $116,000.00

EXAMPLE 11.4: Performing Break-Even Analysis *continued* 

Solution:

ii $\quad Fixed\ Costs = Rent + Utilities\ and\ Maintenance$

$$= 15{,}000.00 + 25{,}000.00 = \$40{,}000.00$$

iii $\quad Contribution\ Margin = Sales - Variable\ Costs$

$$= 190{,}000.00 - 116{,}000.00 = \$74{,}000.00$$

iv $\quad Contribution\ Margin\ Percent = \dfrac{Contribution\ Margin}{Sales} \times 100\%$

$$= \frac{74{,}000.00}{190{,}000.00} \times 100\%$$

$$= 0.389473... \times 100\ \% = 38.95\%$$

v $\quad Break\text{-}Even\ Point = \dfrac{Fixed\ Costs}{Contribution\ Margin\ Percent}$

$$= \frac{40{,}000.00}{0.3895} = \$102{,}695.76$$

If sales are above the break-even point of \$102,695.76, there will be a profit, and if sales fall below this point, there will be a loss.

11.4 EXERCISES

Answers to the odd numbered exercises are available at the end of the textbook.

For Exercises 1 and 2, all percents given are a percent of total sales.

1. Southern Comfort Restaurant's food sales for a year are \$171,240 and are 65% of the total sales. The food cost percent is 35%, beverage cost percent is 30%, labour expenses are 28%, of total sales and other expenses are 20% of total sales.
   a. Calculate the total sales.
   b. Calculate the beverage sales.
   c. Calculate the cost of beverage sales.
   d. Calculate the cost of food sales.
   e. Calculate the gross profit.
   f. Calculate gross profit as a percent of total sales.
   g. Calculate the labour cost.
   h. Calculate the other costs.
   i. Calculate the total expenses.
   j. Calculate the net profit.
   k. Calculate the net profit as a percent of total sales.

2. Food sales for a restaurant for a month are \$80,000 and are 70% of the total sales. The food cost percent is 36% and the beverage cost percent is 28%. Labour expenses are 30% and other expenses are 21%.
   a. Calculate the total sales.
   b. Calculate the beverage sales.
   c. Calculate the cost of beverage sales.
   d. Calculate the cost of food sales.
   e. Calculate the gross profit.
   f. Calculate gross profit as a percent of total sales.
   g. Calculate the labour cost.
   h. Calculate the other costs.
   i. Calculate the total expenses.
   j. Calculate the net profit.
   k. Calculate the net profit as a percent of total sales.

3. For the month of July, Firgin Bar and Restaurant had sales of $30,000, variable costs of $8,000, and fixed costs of $2,000.
    a. Calculate the break-even point.
    b. If the sales had been $25,000 in July, calculate the profit or loss.

4. Last year The Golden Pot restaurant had sales of $350,000, variable costs of $100,000, and fixed costs of $80,000.
    a. Calculate the break-even point.
    b. If the sales were $250,000 last year, calculate the profit or loss.

5. An ocean side cafe and bar is a popular place for seafood, steak, and drinks. What is the break-even point per month for the cafe and bar if we have the following information?
    - Cost of sales = 40% of total sales
    - Wages = 35% of total sales
    - Rent = $12,000 per month
    - Utilities = $4,000 per month
    - Insurance cost = $4,000 per month

6. Rhonda's Pie in the Sky cafe is a popular dessert, pastry, and drinks destination. What is the break-even point per month for the cafe if we have the following information?
    - Cost of sales = 25% of total sales
    - Wages = 40% of total sales
    - Rent = $8,000 per month
    - Utilities = $3,200 per month
    - Insurance cost = $2,000 per month

11.5 MENU ENGINEERING AND PROFITABILITY

Menu engineering is an approach to maximize the profitability of a menu. It often includes appearance and functionality. Often, restaurant owners hire specialists in menu engineering to make a greater profit. It is also common for restaurant owners to put their best products in "eye catching" positions on the menu.

Illustration 11.5 (A): Menu Engineering Recommendations

1. Use current trends on the menu. For example, some gluten-free products may be highlighted.
2. Seasonal products are often successful in terms of popularity and profitability.
3. "House Specials" and "Holiday Specials" are often popular.
4. "Happy Hours" extend serving hours and profit, as well as popularity.
5. Often, à la carte items should be priced so that customers will be encouraged to buy them.
6. There are special ways to list items on a menu:
    - In each section of the menu, customers focus on the first few items.
    - Lists should be short (in each section).
    - Don't print the dollar signs.
    - Don't put the prices in a column.
    - Use visual appeal for dishes that are the most profitable.
    - Write a description of a dish to create a "mouth-watering" appetite or desire.
    - Limited time offers or daily specials can help boost revenue.

One recommendation of the menu engineering approach is to classify menu items based on their **contribution margin** (CM). Recall from the previous section that the contribution margin is the amount that remains after the variable costs (e.g. cost of food, beverages, labour, etc.) are subtracted from the sales.

In the previous section, we calculated the total contribution margin based on the total sales and total variable costs incurred by the business. We can also calculate the contribution margin for each item on the menu and compare each item's contribution margin to the **average contribution margin**, as defined below:

Average Contribution Margin Formula

$$\text{Average CM} = \frac{\text{Total CM of Each Item Sold}}{\text{Total Number of Items Sold}}$$

A high or low contribution margin is an important part of menu item classification.

For example: If the average CM of all menu items is \$2.50 but a pasta crab alfredo dish has a CM of \$5.00, the crab alfredo dish would be classified as having a **high (H)** CM. However, if the crab alfredo dish were to have a CM of \$2.00, it would be classified as having a **low (L)** CM.

In addition to contribution margin, the **menu mix** is used in menu engineering to determine the popularity of an item. It expresses the popularity of an item as a percent of the total number of items sold.

Menu Mix Formula

$$\text{Menu Mix} = \frac{\text{Number of One Item Sold}}{\text{Total Number of Items Sold}} \times 100\%$$

When considering the popularity of an item, we compare the menu mix of the item with the **average menu mix** of all the items on the menu.

Those developing this concept have decided that the minimum popularity of each item should be approximately 70% of the average popularity number.

Average Menu Mix Formula

$$\text{Average Menu Mix} = \frac{1}{\text{Total Number of Menu Items}} \times 70\%$$

For example: If a menu has 20 items, the average menu mix would be $\frac{1}{20} \times 0.70 = 0.035 = 3.5\%$.

Therefore, if a chicken fajita dish has a menu mix of 6%, it would be classified as having a **high (H)** menu mix. However, if the chicken fajita dish has a menu mix of 2.5%, it would be classified as having a **low (L)** menu mix.

EXAMPLE 11.5 (A): Comparing Menu Mix with Average Menu Mix

Determine whether the following dishes have a high or low menu mix.

i A spicy stir-fry dish that represents 12% of all menu items sold on an 8 item menu.

ii A taco bowl dish that represents 3% of all menu items sold on a 20 item menu.

Solution:

i $\textit{Average Menu Mix} = \frac{1}{\textit{Total Number of Menu Items}} \times 70\% = \frac{1}{8} \times 0.70 = 0.0875 = 8.75\%$

The spicy stir-fry dish has a *high* (H) menu mix because its menu mix of 12% is greater than the average menu mix of 8.75%.

ii $\textit{Average Menu Mix} = \frac{1}{\textit{Total Number of Menu Items}} \times 70\% = \frac{1}{20} \times 0.70 = 0.035 = 3.5\%$

The taco bowl dish has a *low* (L) menu mix because its menu mix of 3% is lower than the average menu mix of 3.5%.

COMMON MENU ITEM CLASSIFICATIONS

Although there are a few variations of the following classification, the four following classifications are common.

Illustration 11.5 (B): Common Menu Item Classifications

1. "Stars" (HH): Star menu items have a high CM and high popularity.
2. "Plow Horses" (LH): Plow horse menu items have a low CM but high popularity.
3. "Challenges" (HL): Challenge menu items have high CM and low popularity.
4. "Dogs" (LL): Dog menu items have low CM and low popularity.

Restaurant owners want to get rid of the dog items, try to increase the popularity of the challenge items, keep the star items for certain, and maybe keep the plow horse items.

EXAMPLE 11.5 (B): Menu Engineering

Given the following table,

i Determine the missing values for each menu item.

ii Calculate the average contribution margin and the average menu mix.

Menu Item	Number Sold	Menu Mix (%)	Menu Price ($)	Variable Costs ($)	Item CM	Item CM × Number Sold	CM Category	Menu Mix Category	Classification
Salmon	250		15.95	5.67					
Goulash	100		10.49	2.65					
Lamb	300		18.95	5.34					
Lobster	350		20.99	8.00					
Steak	332		19.99	5.65					
Pork	165		12.69	4.00					
Prime Rib	360		17.99	6.56					
Chicken	210		10.99	4.12					
KFC	287		9.99	3.45					
Crab	156		14.95	6.00					
Total									

EXAMPLE 11.5 (B): Menu Engineering *continued*

Solution:

i

Menu Item	Number Sold	Menu Mix (%)	Menu Price ($)	Variable Costs ($)	Item CM	Item CM × Number Sold	CM Category	Menu Mix Category	Classification
Salmon	250	9.96	15.95	5.67	10.28	2,570	L	H	Plow Horse
Goulash	100	3.98	10.49	2.65	7.84	784	L	L	Dog
Lamb	300	11.95	18.95	5.34	13.61	4,083	H	H	Star
Lobster	350	13.94	20.99	8.00	12.99	4,547	H	H	Star
Steak	332	13.23	19.99	5.65	14.34	4,761	H	H	Star
Pork	165	6.57	12.69	4.00	8.69	1,434	L	L	Dog
Prime Rib	360	14.34	17.99	6.56	11.43	4,115	H	H	Star
Chicken	210	8.37	10.99	4.12	6.87	1,443	L	H	Plow Horse
KFC	287	11.43	9.99	3.45	6.54	1,877	L	H	Plow Horse
Crab	156	6.22	14.95	6.00	8.95	1,396	L	L	Dog
Total	2,510					27,010			

The calculations for the menu item "Salmon" are as follows:

$$\textit{Menu Mix} = \frac{250}{2,510} \times 100\% = 0.099601... \times 100\% = 9.96\%$$

$\textit{Item CM} = 15.95 - 5.67 = \$10.28$

$\textit{Item CM} \times \textit{Number Sold} = 10.28 \times 250 = \$2,750.00$

CM Category: Since the item CM of $10.28 is less than the average CM of $10.76, the menu item salmon has a low (L) CM.

Menu Mix Category: Since the item menu mix of 9.96% is greater than the average menu mix of 7%, salmon has a high (H) menu mix.

Classification: With a low (L) CM and high (H) popularity, the salmon is a "plow horse".

The calculations for each of the other menu items are calculated in a similar way.

ii $$\textit{Average CM} = \frac{\textit{Total CM of Each Item Sold}}{\textit{Total Number of Items Sold}} = \frac{27,010}{2,510} = 10.760956... = \$10.76$$

$$\textit{Average Menu Mix (\%)} = \frac{1}{\textit{Total Number of Menu Items}} \times 70\% = \frac{1}{10} \times 0.7 = 0.07 = 7\%$$

11.5 EXERCISES

Answers to the odd numbered exercises are available at the end of the textbook.

For Exercises 1 and 2, complete the table and calculate the average contribution margin and the average menu mix.

1.

Menu Item	Number Sold	Menu Mix (%)	Menu Price ($)	Variable Costs ($)	Item CM	Item CM × Number Sold	CM Category	Menu Mix Category	Classification
Pulled Pork	350		10.95	5.67					
Ribs	300		14.49	3.65					
Fish & Chips	320		12.95	5.34					
Hamburger	350		10.99	3.00					
Taco	150		4.99	1.65					
Pizza	165		5.69	2.00					
Mushrooms & Chicken	260		14.99	3.56					
Spaghetti	240		10.99	3.12					
Nachos	200		3.99	1.45					
Steak Filet	320		19.95	6.00					
Total									

2.

Menu Item	Number Sold	Menu Mix (%)	Menu Price ($)	Variable Costs ($)	Item CM	Item CM × Number Sold	CM Category	Menu Mix Category	Classification
Pesto	185		7.95	2.67					
Calamari	220		16.49	5.35					
Mussels	250		13.95	4.50					
Salmon Linguine	380		22.99	8.25					
Goulash	110		8.99	3.65					
Pizza	145		11.29	4.00					
Lasagne	260		12.99	3.85					
Chicken Parmigiano	280		16.99	5.25					
Fettucine Alfredo	200		14.99	4.35					
Chicken Ravioli	360		18.95	5.25					
Total									

REVIEW EXERCISES

Answers to the odd numbered exercises are available at the end of the textbook.

1. The manager of a steak and seafood restaurant ordered 40 pounds of various types of steak and sold 16 kg of them. How many ounces were left?
2. A bag of mixed vegetables weighing 15 pounds is used as pizza toppings. The pizza chef only used 5 kg for the pizzas. How many ounces of vegetables were left?
3. Twenty-five 750 mL bottles of wine are needed for John's birthday party. How many 6 oz glasses can be served?
4. One hundred 6 oz glasses of wine are needed for a reception. How many 750 mL bottles of wine are needed?
5. Julia and her friends went to Los Cabos, Mexico for a week and the average temperature was 30 °C. Julia's brother Chris and his friends went to Bermuda for the same week and the average temperature was 23°F. Which group had the coolest weather and by how much? Provide your answer in °C and °F.
6. The average July temperature in Vancouver was 30°C last year whereas in Miami, the average temperature in July last year was 96°F. Which city was hotter and by how much? Provide your answer in °C and °F.
7. Salmon has a yield factor of 0.88. Calculate the EP of 8 lb 4 oz of salmon.
8. Chicken legs have a yield factor of 0.68. Calculate the EP of 20 pounds of chicken legs.
9. Three pounds of stewing beef cost $2.29 per pound (as purchased cost). The edible portion (EP) after cooking was 2.5 pounds. Calculate the edible portion cost (EPC).
10. In northern Ontario, 20 kg of apples cost $25. The EP after getting rid of the peel and cores is 14 kg. Calculate the edible portion cost (EPC).
11. 20 lb of pears were used in a fruit salad. After being peeled, cored, and diced for the salad, 15.5 lb remained. Calculate the yield percent.
12. 38 oz of canned fruit salad were to be used in a cake. After the fruit salad was drained, 27 oz remained. Calculate the yield percent.
13. Calculate the price factor if the yield factor is 0.87.
14. Calculate the price factor if the edible portion cost (EPC) for Cornish hen is $32 and the as purchased cost (APC) is $25.
15. Mangos have a yield percent of 68%. If 50 pounds of mangos were ordered by a Mexican store, calculate the EP.
16. Blueberries have a yield percent of 42%. How many pounds will have to be ordered each day for a fruit boutique that sells fruit shakes that include 3 oz of blueberries in each shake? In the summer, 200 customers buy these fruit shakes each day.
17. The food cost for a beef stew is $7 and your desired food cost is 30%. What should your menu price be?
18. Neelam is competing for first prize in a cherry pie baking contest. The food cost for the pie is $3.95 per slice. To maintain a 35% food cost percent, how much should she charge per slice?
19. If the food cost of a burger is $4.58 and the menu price is $12.50, calculate the markup.

20. Calculate the amount of markup and percent of markup if the menu price is $13.99 and the food cost is 35%.

21. Calculate the cost of the ingredients of won ton soup if it is priced at $4.50 with a 30% food cost percent.

22. If the food cost of a serving of apple pie with ice cream is $3, and a 35% food cost percent is desired, what should the selling price be on the menu?

23. Calculate the markup of a gourmet steak goulash if the food cost is $4.56 and the food cost percent is 40%.

24. Calculate the markup of a chocolate pastry if the food cost is $2.50 and the food cost percent is 35%.

25. Calculate the markup percent if the markup of a pork dinner is $7.20 and the menu price is $9.49.

26. Calculate the markup percent if the markup of chicken stew is $3.80 and the menu price is $8.49.

27. For the month of December, 2018, a casino hotel in Niagara Falls, Ontario, had sales of $50,000, variable costs of $14,000, and fixed costs of $3,000. Calculate the break-even point.

28. For the year of 2018, the Castilla Restaurant had sales of $400,000, variable costs of $150,000, and fixed costs of $90,000. Calculate the break-even point.

29. Determine whether the fish & chips at a restaurant in Halifax has a high or low menu mix. The fish & chips represents 50% of all menu items on a 16-item menu.

30. Determine whether a seafood salad has a high or low menu mix if it represents 5% of all menu items sold on a 25-item menu.

31. If a menu has 20 items and a beef/cheese taco has a menu mix of 8%, does it have a high or low menu mix?

32. If a menu has 10 items and a crab and rice dish has a menu mix of 9%, does it have a high or low menu mix?

ANSWER KEY

CHAPTER 1

1.1 Place Value of Whole Numbers

1. a. 20,000 + 3,000 + 700 + 40 + 8
   b. 600,000 + 5,000 + 300 + 1
   c. 10,000,000 + 2,000,000 + 400,000 + 50,000 + 3,000 + 800 + 80 + 9
   d. 5,000,000,000,000 + 20,000,000,000 + 9,000,000,000 + 600,000,000 + 80,000,000 + 4,000,000 + 100,000 + 70,000 + 3,000 + 200 + 70

3. a. hundred millions b. hundred thousands c. ones d. billions
   e. millions f. tens g. ten thousands h. hundreds
   i. ten millions j. thousands

5. a. 3 b. 1 c. 9 d. 0 e. 5
   f. 8 g. 9 h. 6 i. 8 j. 3

1.2 Reading and Writing Whole Numbers

1. a. nine hundred fifty-six dollars
   b. one thousand, two hundred thirty-nine dollars
   c. thirty-four thousand, two hundred twenty-one
   d. seventy-five thousand, eight hundred eighty-four
   e. eight hundred eighteen thousand, thirty-four dollars
   f. three billion, nine hundred ninety-nine million, sixty-five thousand, one hundred dollars

3. a. one thousand, two hundred thirty-four
   b. twenty-three thousand, three hundred forty-five
   c. two hundred ninety-eight thousand, four hundred forty-two
   d. four million, six hundred seventy-five thousand, nine hundred eighty-seven dollars
   e. ninety-eight million, three hundred forty-five thousand, two hundred twenty-four
   f. five hundred sixty-seven million, four hundred forty-eight thousand, nine hundred eighty-two dollars

5. a. $384 b. 12,932 c. $32,500,023 d. $16,295,001,654 e. 17,427,045

7. a. $3,425 b. 19,084 c. $1,002,222 d. 230,043 e. $5,131,000,089

1.3 Rounding Whole Numbers

1. a. 820 b. 8,000 c. 43,600 d. 19,000,000

3. a. $23,608,540 b. $23,609,000 c. $24,000,000 d. $23,608,500
   e. $23,610,000 f. $20,000,000 g. $23,600,000

5. a. $32,700 b. $9,270 c. $100,000
   d. $7,840,000 e. $4,360,000 f. $630

7. 14,000,000; 5,000,000

9. 3,600 km

1.4 Addition of Whole Numbers

1. a. 670 b. 8,003 c. 1,127 d. 7,143
   e. 649 f. 9,218 g. 1,312 h. 1,115

3. $305

5. $1,411

7. 141

9. 691

1.5 Subtraction of Whole Numbers

1. a. 78 b. 1,996 c. 2,541 d. 10,480
   e. 510 f. 5,860 g. 22,122 h. 484

3. $8

5. 477

7. $676

1.6 Multiplication of Whole Numbers

1. a. 2,550 b. 1,932 c. 3,045 d. 720
   e. 47,456 f. 26,880 g. 13,760 h. 433,998
   i. 5,661 j. 80,487 k. 30,342 l. 8,869

3. $5,658

5. 6,264

7. $7,920

1.7 Division of Whole Numbers

1. a. 93 b. 65 c. 118 d. 982
   e. 3,022 f. 2,750 g. 1,358 h. 768

3. a. quotient 12, remainder 2 b. quotient 15, remainder 5
   c. quotient 5, remainder 10 d. quotient 8, remainder 7

5. $1,463

7. 42

9. $27

Review Exercises

1. Sixty-one billion, fifty-seven million, six hundred eighty-nine thousand, four hundred nine dollars

3. 2,332,709

5. $3,000,000,000 + $800,000,000 + $90,000,000 + $7,000,000 + $100,000 + $400 + $50 + $3

7. a. 9 b. 0 c. 7 d. 6 e. 4

9. a. ten billions; hundred thousands b. none c. ten millions
   d. hundred millions; tens e. billions f. hundreds
   g. millions h. ten thousands i. none
   j. thousands; ones

11. a. 310 b. $57,000

13. a. $714 b. 3 boxes c. $2,154 d. 950,000 parcels e. $4,964

15.

Bank name
Date May 1, 2019
№
Pay to the order of Duka Property Management
$ 782.00
The sum of seven hundred eighty-two
Dollars
Memo maintenance
Authorized signature
123894593 123893 38923467843

17. 110

CHAPTER 2

2.2 Place Value of Decimal Numbers

1. a. 50 + 3 + 0.8 + 0.03
   b. 100 + 20 + 3 + 0.4 + 0.05 + 0.006
   c. 200 + 40 + 5 + 0.9 + 0.01 + 0.008 + 0.0003
   d. 7,000 + 800 + 20 + 1 + 0.01 + 0.003 + 0.0002 + 0.00005

3. a. tenths b. hundred thousandths c. ten thousands d. hundreds e. ten thousandths
   f. ones g. thousandths h. tens i. hundredths j. thousands

5. a. 2 b. 9 c. 6 d. 7 e. 1
   f. 0 g. 3 h. 5 i. 8

2.3 Reading and Writing Decimal Numbers

1. a. eight hundred sixty-four thousand, four hundred ten and eight tenths
   b. thirty-two thousand, nine hundred eighty-five dollars and two cents
   c. sixty thousand, two hundred fifty-seven dollars and forty-nine cents
   d. thirty-two and nine hundred fifty-eight thousandths
   e. four hundred ten thousand, six hundred sixty-four and eight hundred seventy-two thousandths
   f. three thousand, eight hundred fifty-five ten thousandths
   g. ninety-five thousand, two hundred thirty-one and four hundred seventy-six ten thousandths
   h. five hundred thirty-seven thousand, thirty-two and sixty-one thousand, nine hundred forty-one hundred thousandths

3. a. 500.69 b. 4.8362 c. 0.00345
   d. 26,597.305 e. $68,954.36 f. $1,070,928,005.03

2.4 Rounding Decimal Numbers

1. a. 15 b. 902 c. 6 d. $11 e. $13

3. a. 74.9 b. 6.7 c. 985.5 d. 1 e. $58.40

5. a. 4.66 b. 76.31 c. 65.74 d. $948.03 e. $15.00

7. a. 0.471 b. 647.927 c. $1.565 d. $105.000 e. $6,470.319

9. a. 3,440,930 b. 3,440,929.634925 c. 3,441,000 d. 3,440,929.6349252
e. 3,440,929.6 f. 3,440,929.63 g. 3,400,000 h. 3,440,929.6349
i. 3,000,000 j. 3,440,929.635 k. 3,440,900 l. 3,440,929.63493

2.5 Addition of Decimal Numbers

1. a. 123.54 b. 97.355 c. 641.671 d. 75.991
e. 90.2948 f. 118.671 g. 177.898 h. 935.873

3. $241.73 5. 45.87 km 7. $1,820.54

2.6 Subtraction of Decimal Numbers

1. a. 262.55 b. 63.84 c. 407.79 d. 323.65
e. 19.64 f. 355.463 g. 12.953 h. 1.5252

3. $3,220.37 5. 32.79 inches 7. $100.43

2.7 Multiplication of Decimal Numbers

1. a. 12,659.3 b. 148.143 c. 289.3212 d. 1,339.95
e. 150.8616 f. 15.9168 g. 591.30864 h. 42.895996

3. $463.75; $927.50 5. $357.50

2.8 Division of Decimal Numbers

1. a. 790 b. 97.875 c. 17.086 d. 4,581.5
e. 6.50833... f. 5,397.5 g. 264.8 h. 1,538.4

3. $33.2175 (approximately $33.22) 5. $11.47

2.9 Estimating Decimal Numbers

		Nearest Whole Number	Nearest Tenth	Actual
1.	a.	38	38.9	38.88
	b.	17	16.4	16.35
	c.	12	11.9	11.87
	d.	13	12.7	12.6

		Nearest Whole Number	Nearest Tenth	Actual
3.	a.	6	5.7	5.72
	b.	8	8.3	8.29
	c.	15	14.4	14.47
	d.	48	47.9	47.98

		Nearest Tenth	Actual
5.	a.	915.92	914.4205
	b.	879.45	878.04306
	c.	5.1	5.10020040...
	d.	5.02	5.01178397...

		Nearest Hundredth	Actual
7.	a.	182.41	182.4124
	b.	202.15	202.144
	c.	1,171.317	1,171.38519675
	d.	10.63125	10.62617137...

9. 106.7 L

11. $1.50

13. $250.80

15. $63.825 (approximately $63.83)

Review Exercises

1. a. tenths
   b. ten thousandths
   c. ones
   d. hundreds
   e. thousandths
   f. hundredths
   g. tens
   h. hundred thousandths
   i. millionths

3. 60 + 8 + 0.01 + 0.002 + 0.0003 + 0.00009

5. a. 3 b. 2 c. 0 d. 8
   e. 3 f. 4 g. 1

7. a. Twenty-three and sixteen hundredths
   b. Five hundred sixty and one hundred seventy-eight thousandths
   c. Six and three hundred twenty-four thousandths
   d. Seven hundred eighty-nine dollars and fifty-six cents
   e. Five hundred thirty-eight dollars and nine cents
   f. Three thousand dollars and five cents

9. a. $7,000.69 b. 46.8 c. 100.024
   d. $56.75 e. $1,000,745.23 f. $650.89

11. a. 2,642.394 b. 2,600 c. 2,642.4 d. 2,642.39402

13. a. 141.2 km
    b. $157.50; Samuel earns $17.50 more each week
    c. $3,034.90
    d. $850

CHAPTER 3

3.1 Exponents

1. a. $9^3 \times 6^4$ b. $2^2 \times 3^2 \times 4^2$ c. $4^2 \times 2^5$
   d. $2^2 \times 3^2 \times 4^2 \times 5^2$ e. $1^2 \times 5^2 \times 2^3$ f. $4^3 \times 2^3 \times 1^2$

3. a. $2 \times 2 \times 2 \times 2 \times 2 \times 2 \times 2$ b. $3 \times 3 \times 3$
   c. $10 \times 10 \times 10 \times 10 \times 10 \times 10$ d. $2 \times 2 \times 2 \times 2$
   e. $3 \times 3 \times 3 \times 3$ f. $4 \times 4 \times 4 \times 4$
   g. 3×3 h. 5

5. $20^2 = 400$ metres^2
7. $5^3 = 125$ metres^3
9. $64 = 8^2$; 8 centimetres
11. $27 = 3^3$; 3 metres

3.2 Arithmetic Operations with Exponents

1. a. 27 b. 8 c. 109
   d. 82 e. 729 f. 32

3. a. 243 b. 100 c. 27
   d. 32 e. 6 f. 5
   g. 5 h. 4 i. 8

5. a. 64 b. 1 c. 729
   d. 1 e. 6 f. 7

7. a. $2 \times 2 \times 2 \times 2 \times 2 \times 2$ b. $3 \times 3 \times 3 \times 3 \times 3 \times 3 \times 3 \times 3$
   c. $6 \times 6 \times 6 \times 6$ d. $4 \times 4 \times 4 \times 4 \times 4$
   e. $3 \times 3 \times 3$ f. 7×7
   g. $8 \times 8 \times 8$ h. $2 \times 2 \times 2 \times 2 \times 2 \times 2 \times 2 \times 2$

9. a. $3 \times 3 \times 3 \times 3 \times 3 \times 3$ b. $6 \times 6 \times 6 \times 6 \times 6$
   c. $5 \times 5 \times 5 + 5 \times 5$ d. $4 \times 4 + 4 - 1$
   e. 10×10 f. 3×3
   g. $4 \times 4 + 2 \times 2$ h. $5 \times 5 \times 5 - 3 \times 3 \times 3 \times 3$

11. a. 3.69×10^8 b. 4.21×10^6 c. 4.5×10^{10} d. 1.0×10^{-4}

13. a. 26,200 b. 130,000,000 c. 6,990,000 d. 50,200

3.3 Signed Numbers

1. a. 20 b. 4 c. –3 d. 4
   e. –6 f. –26 g. 172 h. –79

3. a. 7 b. –3 c. 22 d. –31
   e. 3 f. –24 g. 262 h. –336

5. a. 15 b. 6 c. –56 d. –24 e. 5
   f. 3 g. –8 h. –4 i. –1,470 j. –51

7. a. 4 b. 0 c. –19 d. 58

9. $140
11. –9°C
13. 200 hours
15. $13

3.4 Order of Operations (BEDMAS)

1. a. 1 b. 0 c. 23 d. 9

3. a. 6 b. 65 c. 22 d. 187

5. a. 20 b. –1 c. 6 d. 141

7. a. 2 b. 160 c. 23 d. 64

9. a. 1 b. –8 c. –4 d. 167

11. a. –10.2 b. 0.11 c. –5.89 d. –48

13. a. 18,225 b. 4 c. 23.4 d. –36

15. a. 0.75 b. 445 c. 2,963.46 d. 269.33

Review Exercises

1. a. $3^3 \times 5^5$ b. $7^2 \times 4^4$ c. $2^3 \times 6^2 \times 9^3$ d. $1^2 \times 5^2 \times 7^3$

3. a. $4 \times 4 \times 4 \times 4 \times 4$ b. $8 \times 8 \times 8 \times 8$ c. $3 \times 3 \times 3 \times 3 \times 3 \times 3 \times 3$ d. $7 \times 7 \times 7 \times 7$

5. a. 476 b. 23 c. 2,409 d. 52

7. a. 65,536 b. 13,060,694,016 c. 2,401 d. 729

9. a. 1.82 b. 11.18 c. 1 d. 36

11. a. $3 \times 3 \times 3 \times 3 \times 3 \times 3 \times 3$ b. $6 \times 6 \times 6 \times 6 \times 6 \times 6 \times 6$ c. 4×4
    d. $7 \times 7 \times 7 \times 7 \times 7$ e. $5 \times 5 + 8 \times 8$ f. $7 \times 7 \times 7 - 4 \times 4 \times 4$

13. a. 4.25×10^8 b. 6×10^6 c. 1.2×10^{10} d. 4.57×10

15. a. 345,000 b. 5,700,000 c. 415,000 d. 921,000

17. a. 21 b. 3 c. –20 d. 13 e. 20 f. –7

19. a. 42 b. –18 c. 25 d. 3 e. –5 f. 3

21. a. 36 b. 3 c. –26 d. –7

23. $700 25. $1,512 27. 10 degrees Celsius

29. a. 56 b. 0 c. 53 d. 91

CHAPTER 4

4.1 Introduction to Fractions

1. a. $4\frac{2}{4}$ b. $1\frac{2}{5}$ c. $2\frac{1}{4}$ d. $1\frac{1}{3}$
   e. $5\frac{3}{8}$ f. $2\frac{1}{2}$ g. $2\frac{1}{11}$ h. $3\frac{3}{4}$

3. a. $\frac{7}{2}$ b. $\frac{25}{4}$ c. $\frac{17}{3}$ d. $\frac{22}{5}$
   e. $\frac{5}{4}$ f. $\frac{15}{2}$ g. $\frac{26}{5}$ h. $\frac{9}{4}$

5. $\frac{165}{2}$

7. $6\frac{3}{4}$

9. a. $\frac{4}{3}$ b. $\frac{2}{9}$ c. $-\frac{5}{1}$, or –5 d. $-\frac{6}{19}$

11. a. $\frac{1}{2}$ b. $\frac{1}{5}$ c. $\frac{1}{6}$
d. $\frac{3}{4}$ e. $\frac{1}{10}$ f. $\frac{1}{3}$
g. $8\frac{1}{2}$ h. $11\frac{1}{3}$ i. $2\frac{1}{4}$

13. a. $\frac{2}{14}, \frac{3}{21}, \frac{4}{28}$, etc.
b. $5, \frac{15}{3}, \frac{20}{4}$, etc.
c. $4\frac{6}{10}, \frac{23}{5}, \frac{46}{10}$, etc.

15. a. 0.2 b. 0.43 c. 1.67 d. 7.33
e. 2.5 f. –0.38 g. –2.4 h. –3.75

17. 35.75 hours

19. $228.33

4.2 Addition and Subtraction of Fractions

1. 21

3. 12

5. 36

7. 24

9. 20

11. 24

13. a. 2 b. 6 c. $\frac{21}{2}$, or $10\frac{1}{2}$
d. $\frac{37}{18}$, or $2\frac{1}{18}$ e. $\frac{25}{4}$, or $6\frac{1}{4}$ f. $\frac{32}{3}$, or $10\frac{2}{3}$
g. $\frac{29}{8}$, or $3\frac{5}{8}$ h. $\frac{28}{3}$, or $9\frac{1}{3}$ i. $\frac{379}{24}$, or $15\frac{19}{24}$

15. a. 3 b. $\frac{7}{2}$, or $3\frac{1}{2}$ c. $\frac{20}{3}$, or $6\frac{2}{3}$
d. $\frac{2}{9}$ e. $-\frac{11}{3}$, or $-3\frac{2}{3}$ f. $\frac{153}{14}$, or $10\frac{13}{14}$
g. $\frac{19}{14}$, or $1\frac{5}{14}$ h. $\frac{101}{42}$, or $2\frac{17}{42}$ i. $\frac{19}{3}$, or $6\frac{1}{3}$

17. $32\frac{3}{4}$ hours

19. $5\frac{11}{12}$ km

4.3 Multiplication and Division of Fractions

1. a. $\frac{1}{3}$ b. $\frac{11}{3}$, or $3\frac{2}{3}$ c. $\frac{1}{4}$
d. $\frac{1}{3}$ e. $\frac{9}{4}$, or $2\frac{1}{4}$ f. 6
g. $\frac{3}{5}$ h. $\frac{11}{10}$, or $1\frac{1}{10}$ i. $\frac{4}{15}$

3. a. $\frac{2}{3}$ b. $\frac{11}{2}$, or $5\frac{1}{2}$ c. 7
d. $\frac{11}{3}$, or $3\frac{2}{3}$ e. $\frac{1}{3}$ f. $\frac{5}{4}$, or $1\frac{1}{4}$
g. $\frac{7}{9}$ h. $\frac{10}{3}$, or $3\frac{1}{3}$ i. $\frac{30}{11}$, or $2\frac{8}{11}$

5. a. 0.69 b. 0.09 c. 0.06 d. 4.11

7. $127\frac{1}{2}$ km 9. $\$357\frac{1}{2}$ 11. $\$20\frac{1}{8}$ 13. $5\frac{1}{2}$ 15. $6\frac{2}{5}$ km

17. a. $\$224\frac{2}{3}$ b. $\$112\frac{1}{3}$

Review Exercises

1. a. $3\frac{3}{4}$ b. $1\frac{4}{5}$ c. $3\frac{3}{5}$ d. $1\frac{1}{4}$ e. $4\frac{1}{3}$

3. a. $\frac{9}{2}$ b. $\frac{20}{3}$ c. $\frac{21}{4}$ d. $\frac{48}{7}$

5. $\frac{169}{2}$ 7. $7\frac{3}{4}$

9. a. $\frac{2}{1}$ or 2 b. $\frac{4}{3}$ c. $\frac{7}{5}$ d. $\frac{5}{4}$ e. $-\frac{6}{1}$ or -6

11. a. $\frac{1}{2}$ b. $\frac{1}{4}$ c. $\frac{1}{5}$ d. $\frac{1}{2}$ e. $7\frac{1}{2}$ f. $12\frac{1}{4}$

13. a. $\frac{6}{8}, \frac{30}{40}$ etc. b. $\frac{12}{14}, \frac{18}{21}$ etc. c. $\frac{4}{10}, \frac{6}{15}$ etc. d. $2\frac{8}{10}, \frac{14}{5}$ etc.

15. 33.75 hours 17. $428.33

19. a. 28 b. 15 c. 20 d. 6 e. 18 f. 20

21. a. $\frac{5}{2}$ b. 6 c. $\frac{33}{20}$ d. $15\frac{4}{15}$

23. a. $\frac{5}{3}$ b. $4\frac{1}{5}$ c. $2\frac{1}{12}$ d. $2\frac{3}{4}$

25. $5\frac{11}{12}$ km

27. a. $\frac{12}{25}$ b. 4 c. $\frac{9}{4}$ or $2\frac{1}{4}$ d. $\frac{1}{6}$

29. a. $\frac{33}{4}$ or $8\frac{1}{4}$ b. $\frac{4}{3}$ or $1\frac{1}{3}$ c. $\frac{25}{3}$ or $8\frac{1}{3}$ d. 9

31. $48\frac{3}{4}$ km 33. $600 35. $3\frac{3}{16}$ bags

37. a. $64 b. $32

CHAPTER 5

5.1 Algebraic Expressions

1. a. x b. x, y
3. a. y b. a, b
5. a. $14r + 10db$ b. $9z$
7. a. $5w - 3t + 4m$ b. $22t - 4w - k$
9. a. $5B + s + 9z$ b. $-2j + 3n + F$
11. a. $-6hr + 10k - 3sd$ b. $-7fx + 14r + 13e$
13. a. $5ab + 5p$ b. $-6A - 4B + 4AB + C$
15. a. $2r = -4g$ b. $4a = -b$
17. a. $11m = 7n$ b. $14o = 15p$
19. a. $5p = 2h$ b. $-4b = 5c + 4a$
21. a. $o = -2pq + 11n$ b. $-9v = x + 3l$
23. a. $11A = 7B - 3C$ b. $-2M = -7N + 6P$

5.2 Simple Algebraic Equations

1. 52
3. –6
5. 20 = 20
7. 15 = 15
9. a. $s = 4$ b. $t = 4$ c. $A = 3$ d. $Q = -5$
11. a. $k = 15$ b. $g = 13$ c. $S = 16$ d. $T = 12$
13. a. $q = 4$ b. $k = 3$ c. $k = 6$ d. $m = 4$
15. a. $u = 36$ b. $m = 63$ c. $g = 36$ d. $X = 72$
17. a. $M = 5$ b. $A = 6$ c. $k = 6$ d. $n = 4$
19. a. $x = 6$ b. $b = 13$ c. $n = 9$ d. $k = 7.5$
21. a. $y = 2$ b. $z = 3$ c. $m = 7$ d. $u = 10$
23. a. $p = 96$ b. $v = 15$ c. $n = 49$ d. $r = 6$
25. a. $x = 24$ b. $z = 12$ c. $u = 180$ d. $r = 128$
27. a. $Q = 4$ b. $b = 24$ c. $m = 21$ d. $w = 9$
29. a. $H = P - 3$ b. $K = L - 6$ c. $W = 7 + T$ d. $V = H + 9$
31. a. $R = 9H$ b. $S = \frac{T}{3}$ c. $M = \frac{8}{U}$ d. $K = \frac{6}{L}$
33. a. $M = P - WD$ b. $W = \frac{P + M}{D}$ c. $S = B(18 + P)$ d. $B = \frac{S}{18 + P}$
35. $B = 11$
37. $K = 2$
39. $Q = 72$

5.3 Solving Word Problems using Algebraic Equations

1. $x + 2$
3. $x - 2$
5. $\frac{2}{4}x$
7. $x + \$59$
9. $x - 3°C$
11. $3x$
13. $\frac{x}{9}$
15. $x + 67 = 126; x = 59$
17. $x - 49 = 82; x = 131$
19. $x = 23°C + 4°C; x = 27°C$
21. $x + \$49.50 = \$120; x = \$70.50$
23. $x = \frac{240}{6}; x = 40$ students

Review Exercises

1. a. x b. x, k c. p, r d. n, b e. z, w, s f. G, H, F
3. a. $5k + 9tp + 2r$ b. $-2bn + 6w$
5. a. $9H + 2E + 4C$ b. $8S + 4X - 7LP$
7. a. $2t = -4w$ b. $-5a = f$
9. a. $9y = -5s$ b. $-3c = 7a$
11. a. $-e = -22j + 19g$ b. $2a = 11k - 10p$
13. 14
15. 24
17. $9 = 9$
19. $20 = 20$
21. a. $j = 2$ b. $m = 12$ c. $K = 5$ d. $b = 11$
23. a. $f = 3$ b. $k = 8$ c. $g = 8$ d. $m = 4$
25. a. $r = 32$ b. $j = 35$ c. $v = 40$ d. $C = 42$
27. a. $K = 6$ b. $g = 9$ c. $p = 7$ d. $k = 7$
29. a. $y = 3$ b. $t = 3$ c. $k = 49$ d. $h = 9$
31. a. $t = 55$ b. $k = 27$ c. $f = 9$ d. $z = 6$
33. a. $J = P - 7$ b. $K = Q + 4$ c. $G = 6Z$ d. $H = \frac{5}{L}$
35. a. $M = K - JY$ b. $R = \frac{P + N}{D}$ c. $A = \frac{12 + O}{H}$ d. $B = \frac{9 + R}{U}$
37. $x + 4$
39. $x - 8$
41. $\frac{7}{5}x$
43. $2x$
45. $\frac{x}{3}$
47. $18 + 41 + x = 92; x = 33$
49. $x - 28 = 56; x = 84$
51. $\$246 + 2x = \$650; x = \$202$

CHAPTER 6

6.1 Averages

1. a. 17 b. 6 c. 12 d. 15

3. 5

5. 32

7. $3.12

9. $17.23

11. $86

13. $115

6.2 Percents

1. a. 0.03 b. 0.3 c. 3 d. 0.95 e. 0.13
   f. 0.055 g. 2.503 h. 0.366 i. 0.152 j. 0.755

3. a. 13% b. 90% c. 63% d. 50% e. 600%
   f. 33.333% g. 255% h. 3,600% i. 15% j. 0.75%

5. a. 13% b. 0.33 c. 25.55%
   d. 0.252 e. 108.5% f. 1.037

7. $21.32

9. $0.98; $14.98

11. $11.76; $90.18

13. $81.55

15. 806; 494

6.3 Percent Changes

1. a. 19.38 b. 200 c. 271.30
   d. 30.89 e. 130.30 f. 454.55

3. 14,944 students

5. 29.55°C

7. –26.25%

9.

	Final Value	*Original Value*	*Final Value – Original Value*	*% Change*
a.	11	10	1	10%
b.	9	10	–1	–10%
c.	10	8	2	25%
d.	4	7	–3	–42.86%
e.	25	30	–5	–16.67%
f.	100	90	10	11.11%
g.	24	20	4	20%
h.	74.75	115	–40.25	–35%

11. 20.83%

13. –1.67%

15. 13,508; 1.91%

17. $221.40

19. $28.50

21. $45.50; 14%

23. $3.04

25.

FRACTION	PERCENTAGE	DECIMAL
$\frac{1}{2}$	50%	0.5
$\frac{13}{20}$	65%	0.65
$\frac{2}{25}$	8%	0.08
$\frac{1}{4}$	25%	0.25
$\frac{3}{8}$	37.5%	0.375
$\frac{27}{20}$	135%	1.35
$\frac{2}{5}$	40%	0.4
$\frac{1}{3}$	33.3333...%	0.333333...

6.4 Payroll

1. $2,115
3. $185.58
5. Option 2 has a higher pay per period of $492
7. 174.36 hours
9. a. $4,125 b. $2,062.50 c. $1,903.85 d. $951.92
11. $3,500
13. Company A has a higher weekly earning of $134.62
15. $1,504.63
17. $1,438.82
19. $8,050
21. $840
23. $970

Review Exercises

1. a. 20 b. 6 c. 14 d. 13.25
3. 5.25
5. 32.2; 33 students
7. $2.23
9. $20.10
11. a. 0.05 b. 0.28 c. 4.20 d. 0.73 e. 0.61 f. 0.078
13. a. 21% b. 70% c. 41% d. 30% e. 800% f. 41.4141%

15.

Fraction	Percent	Decimal
$\frac{1}{2}$	50%	0.5
$\frac{12}{25}$	48%	0.48
$\frac{7}{100}$	7%	0.07
$\frac{1}{4}$	25%	0.25

17. $15.86

19. $1.44 ; $17.44

21. $14.21; $108.93

23. $2,299.50

25. 23,568 students

27. 26.09°C

29. –34.17%

31. $3,250

33. $194.53

35. a. $4,375 b. $2,187.50 c. $2,019.23 d. $1,009.62

37. $3,439.58

39. $1,342.53

41. $17,250

43. $1,107

45. $1,081.50

CHAPTER 7

7.1 Ratios

1. a. 1 : 2 b. 1 : 3 c. 6 : 11
   d. 2 : 3 e. 7 : 8 f. 8 : 5
   g. 2 : 3 h. 1 : 2 : 4 i. 10 : 6 : 5

3. a. 20 : 600; 1 : 30 b. 6 : 4; 3 : 2 c. 3 : 1
   d. 2 : 1 e. 40 : 35 : 30; 8 : 7 : 6 f. 15 : 12 : 8

5. $9,600, $14,400

7. $1,875, $3,125

9. $1,200, $2,800

11. $7,500, $10,000, $12,500

13. $16.67

7.2 Proportions

1. a. 11.25 b. 6

3. a. 10 b. 24

5. a. 6 b. 6

7. 27

9. 22.94 minutes

11. $55.25

13. €1,377.80

15. €406.16

17. US$334.78

19. a. $x = 8, y = 12$ b. $x = 9, y = 12$

21. a. $x = \frac{130}{3}, y = \frac{208}{3}$ b. $x = 18, y = 24$

23. a. $3,750, $5,000

25. $4,000, $2,666.67, $5,333.33

Review Exercises

1. a. 2 : 3 b. 1 : 6 c. 7 : 12 d. 30 : 37
   e. 5 : 8 f. 1 : 2 : 4 g. 14 : 8 : 11
3. 18 : 540; 1 : 30
5. 35 : 30 : 40; 7 : 6 : 8
7. $12,000, $16,000
9. $7,500, $12,500, $10,000
11. a. $x = 10$ b. $x = 24$ c. $x = 1$ d. $x = 6$
13. 26.67 minutes
15. $50.05
17. €862.35
19. US$611.83
21. a. $a = 8, b = 12$ b. $z = 12, b = 15$ c. $w = 9, y = 21$
23. $4,666.67, $5,833.33
25. $6,250, $3,750, $5,000

CHAPTER 8

8.1 Simple Interest

1. $1,001.25
3. $43.15
5. $47.95
7. $810
9. $13,468.70
11. 3.43% p.a.
13. 5.38% p.a.
15. 33 days
17. 5 years
19. 6.21% p.a.
21. $5,722.74
23. $11,713.87

8.2 Compound Interest

1. a. 6% b. 3% c. 1.5% d. 0.5% e. 0.02%
3. $n = 30$
5. $n = 3$
7. $FV = \$17,010.49$; $I = \$2,010.49$
9. monthly
11. $280.36
13. $1,945.09
15. $PV = \$39,545.95$; $I = \$20,454.05$
17. $4,545.41
19. $6,712.57

Review Exercises

1. $870
3. $31.07
5. $10,509.39
7. 4.38%
9. 2.46%
11. 21.03 days
13. 1 year 6 months
15. 3.67%
17. $5,016.66
19. a. 5.25% b. 2.63% c. 1.31% d. 0.44% e. 0.01%
21. 14
23. $14,419.12, $2,419.12
25. Every 1.5 months
27. $249.68
29. $2,842.09
31. $41,124.73, $33,875.27
33. $8,850.66

CHAPTER 9

9.1 Annuities

1. $41,071.51
3. $10,644.11
5. $19,489.66
7. $49,076.28
9. $82,073.28
11. $71,253.38
13. $167,811.11
15. $445.26
17. $55,466.71

9.2 Loans

1. \$245.17
3. \$41.63
5. PMT = \$5,301.96

Payment Number	Amount Paid (PMT)	Interest Portion	Principal Portion	Principal Balance
0	-	-	-	\$10,000.00
1	\$5,301.96	\$400.00	\$4,901.96	\$5,098.04
2	\$5,301.96	\$203.92	\$5,098.04	\$0.00
TOTAL	\$10,603.92	\$603.92	\$10,000	

7. PMT = \$1,008.77

Payment Number	Amount Paid (PMT)	Interest Portion	Principal Portion	Principal Balance
0	-	-	-	\$6,000.00
1	\$1,008.77	\$15.00	\$993.77	\$5,006.23
2	\$1,008.77	\$12.52	\$996.25	\$4,009.98
3	\$1,008.77	\$10.02	\$998.75	\$3,011.23
4	\$1,008.77	\$7.53	\$1,001.24	\$2,009.99
5	\$1,008.77	\$5.02	\$1,003.75	\$1,006.24
6	\$1,008.76	\$2.52	\$1,006.24	\$0.00
TOTAL	\$6,052.61	\$52.61	\$6,000.00	

9.3 Mortgages

1. a. \$114,000.00 b. \$266,000.00 c. $n = 300$
   d. $i_2 = 0.00477594...$ e. PMT = \$1,670.39
3. a. \$60,000.00 b. \$240,000.00 c. $n = 300$
   d. PMT = \$1,262.45 e. 24 f. \$228,304.61

Review Exercises

1. \$172.54
3. \$2,076.51
5. \$430.04
7. \$13,566.48
9. \$78,697.60

CHAPTER 10

10.1 Tour Costing

1. a. 8.33% b. 14.58% c. 20.83%

3. a. $3,750.00 b. $4,024.39 c. $4,342.11

5. a. $769.23
   b. $525.00
   c. $1,294.23
   d. $1,617.79
   e. $1,617.79 plus $276.00 TGSC

10.2 Commissions, Taxes, and Discounts

1. $60.00
3. $355.95
5. $165.00
7. $1,400.00
9. a. $112.00 b. $448.00
   c. $474.88 d. $536.61

10.3 Occupancy Rate and Yield Management

	Total Rooms	Rooms Sold	Occupancy Rate	Rack Rate	Average Rate	Achievement Factor	Yield
1. a.	300	270	90.00%	$250	$200	80.00%	72.00%
b.	280	200	71.43%	$300	$250	83.33%	59.52%
c.	250	210	84.00%	$280	$250	89.29%	75.00%
d.	220	200	90.91%	$200	$145	72.50%	65.91%
e.	200	150	75.00%	$250	$200	80.00%	60.00%
f.	150	100	66.67%	$170	$120	70.59%	47.06%
g.	100	80	80.00%	$450	$380	84.44%	67.55%

3. 64.29%
5. 68%
7. 136
9. 83.33%
11. 72.22%
13. 164
15. $170.94
17. 366
19. 93.48%
21. $1.79

Review Exercises

1. $1,638
3. $2,373
5. a. $926.50 b. $972.83
7. 86.67%
9. 210
11. $208
13. 85.71%
15. $300
17. $134.50

CHAPTER 11

11.1 Units of Measurement

1. a. 8,900 mL b. 0.75 L c. 60 fl oz d. 160 fl oz
   e. 480 fl oz f. 75 qt g. 25 gal h. 25 pt
   i. 2,000 g j. 1.55 kg k. 8,500 g l. 128 oz
   m. 0.75 lb n. 88 oz o. 64.4 °F p. 17.78 °C

3. a. 21.12 fl oz b. 133.76 fl oz c. 5,681.82 mL d. 27,272.73 mL
   e. 3,636.36 mL f. 1.32 qt g. 0.88 gal h. 1.32 pt
   i. 908 g j. 227 g k. 1,078.25 g l. 1.32 lb
   m. 29.96 oz n. 8.81 lb o. 63.44 oz

5. 264 servings 7. 165.64 oz 9. 158 glasses

11. 35 bottles 13. Toronto is colder by 1.78°C or 3.2°F.

11.2 Yield

1. 75% 3. 72.5% 5. 86% 7. 61.72%

9. a. 19.5 lb b. 83.64 oz c. 7,236 g

11. a. 8.05 lb b. 240.74 oz c. 6,826.67 g

13. 21.6 lb 15. 117.65 lb 17. $2.05 per lb.

19. $1.97 per lb. 21. 1.25

11.3 Menu Pricing

1. a. $12.71 b. $20.18 c. $3.95
   d. $4.05 e. 35.48% f. 31.23%

3. $1.71 5. 51.30% 7. $9.67

9. 42.76% 11. $11.45, 71.61%

13. a. $4.99, 49.95% b. $6.99, 58.30% c. $8.00, 66.67%

15. $5.76

17. a. 40 lb b. 53.33 lb c. $7.57 per lb
    d. $302.92 e. 1.33 f. $3.79

19. a. $292,000; $730 b. $43,800

11.4 Business Management

1. a. $263,446.15 b. $92,206.15 c. $27,661.85 d. $59,934.00
   e. $175,850.30 f. 66.75% g. $73,764.92 h. $52,689.23
   i. $126,454.15 j. $49,396.15 k. 18.75%

3. a. $2727.27 b. Profit = $15,000

5. a. $80,000

11.5 Menu Engineering and Profitability

1. Average CM = 8.01%, Average Menu Mix = 7%

Menu Item	Number Sold	Menu Mix (%)	Menu Price ($)	Variable Costs ($)	Item CM	Item CM x Number Sold	CM Category	Menu Mix Category	Classification
Pulled Pork	350	13.18	10.95	5.67	5.28	1,848	L	H	Plow Horse
Ribs	300	11.30	14.49	3.65	10.84	3,252	H	H	Star
Fish & chips	320	12.05	12.95	5.34	7.61	2,435.2	L	H	Plow Horse
Hamburger	350	13.18	10.99	3.00	7.99	2,796.5	L	H	Plow Horse
Taco	150	5.65	4.99	1.65	3.34	501	L	L	Dog
Pizza	165	6.21	5.69	2.00	3.69	608.85	L	L	Dog
Mushrooms & chicken	260	9.79	14.99	3.56	11.43	2,971.8	H	H	Star
Spaghetti	240	9.04	10.99	3.12	7.87	1,888.8	L	H	Plow Horse
Nachos	200	7.53	3.99	1.45	2.54	508	L	H	Plow Horse
Steak Filet	320	12.05	19.95	6.00	13.95	4464	H	H	Star
Totals	2,655					21,274.15			

Review Exercises

1. 76.80 oz
3. 110
5. Chris; 35°C, 63°F
7. 116.16 oz
9. $2.75 per lb
11. 77.5%
13. 1.15
15. 34 lb
17. $23.33
19. $7.92
21. $1.35
23. $6.84
25. 75.87%
27. $4,166.67
29. High
31. High

Glossary

Achievement Factor is the percent of the rack rate that a hotel typically receives.

Addition is the operation that determines the total number of objects within a collection, or from different groups.

Algebraic Equation expresses the equality between two algebraic expressions.

Algebraic Expression is an expression that contains constants, variables, and algebraic operations.

Amortization Period is the time period to pay off the entire loan, as decided by you or the financial lending institution.

Amortization Schedule is a table used to outline the interest and principal portions of each loan payment, as well as the principal balance remaining.

Annual Interest Rate (j) is the interest rate earned on the investment or charged on the loan, per annum (p.a.).

Annual Salary is amount paid out to full time employees at a set frequency that allows the employees to organize their funds throughout the year.

Annuity is an investment or loan product that has regular payments at regular intervals for a set period of time.

Annuity Due is an annuity where payments are made at the beginning of the payment period.

Arithmetic Average is calculated by adding up all the numbers and dividing the result by the number of items.

Average Room Rate is the average of the rates that a hotel receives for a specific room over a specific period of time.

Base + Commission allows an employee to receive a base pay plus the ability to earn more money based on the sales made for the payment period.

Closed Mortgage is usually less expensive than an open mortgage because there are penalties if the borrower changes the agreed upon amount for each pay period or closes the loan during a mortgage term.

Commission is meant to reward employees for the total sales they make for a given period, based on the percent of commission that is offered.

Compounding Frequency per Year (m) is the number of times interest accrues per year.

Compound Interest is interest that accrues on itself in addition to the principal, depending on the compounding frequency.

Decimal Number consists of a whole number portion and a decimal portion, which represents a value greater than 0 but less than 1.

Denominator is the number on the bottom of a fraction.

Discount is a markdown to entice customers to buy a product or service.

Division is the opposite operation of multiplication. It can be thought of as splitting a number into smaller parts, or finding out how many times a number is contained in another number.

Down Payment is the initial payment given upfront by the purchaser upfront to the bank or financial institution at the time of finalizing the business transaction.

Exponent is used in exponential notation to represent the number of times a number (base) is multiplied by itself.

Fixed Rate Mortgage has an interest rate which does not change for the length of the mortgage term.

Fraction is a number that is expressed by a numerator divided by a denominator.

Future Value (FV) is the amount of the investment/loan including the interest that has accrued.

General Annuity is an annuity where the payment frequency and compounding frequency are *different.*

Hourly Rate employees are paid on an hour-by-hour basis.

Improper Fraction is a fraction in which the numerator is greater than the denominator.

Interest (I) is the amount of money earned on an investment or charged on a loan.

Loan is a sum of money borrowed from a lender which must be paid back in full with interest.

Loan Amortization is the gradual reduction of a loan through equal payments over a set period of time.

Lowest Common Multiple is the smallest multiple in common of a group of numbers.

Maturity Value (S) is the sum of the principal and interest.

Mixed Number is a number that is made up of a whole number and a proper fraction.

Mortgage is a special type of loan used for buying real estate.

Mortgage Term is a smaller length of time within a mortgage.

Multiplication can be thought of as repeated additions.

Negative Number has a value less than 0.

Number of Compounding Periods (*n*) is the number of compounding periods over the entire term of an investment or loan.

Numerator is the number on the top of a fraction.

Numerical Expression consists of a single number, or two or more numbers joined by an operational symbol.

Occupancy Rate is the percent of rooms a hotel sells compared to the total rooms a hotel has available.

Open Mortgage allows the borrower to close the mortgage or transfer it to a different borrower without penalties.

Order of Operations (BEDMAS) is the order which must be followed when performing arithmetic operations: Brackets, Exponents, Division and Multiplication, Addition and Subtraction.

Ordinary Annuity is an annuity where payments are made at the end of the payment period.

Payment (*PMT*) is the regular dollar amount paid each period in an annuity.

Payment Frequency per Year (*p*) is the number of payments made each year in an annuity.

Payroll represents the number of employees, their payment periods, and the amount of payment.

Percent is the relationship of a number to 100, or ratio of a number to 100.

Periodic Interest Rate (*i*) is the interest rate earned on the investment or charged on the loan per compounding period.

Perishability of services implies that the services cannot be stored, saved, returned, or resold once provided to a customer.

Place Value is the position of each digit in a number.

Positive Number has a value greater than 0.

Principal Value (*PV*) is the amount of investment/loan before any interest has accrued.

Profit Margin is the rate of markup on the selling price.

Profit is the amount of money remaining after all costs have been covered by a company.

Proper Fraction is a fraction in which the numerator is less than the denominator.

Proportion is used to represent two sets of ratios that are equal.

Rack Rate is the official or advertised price of a hotel room before a discount is applied.

Rate (*r*) is the interest rate earned on an investment or charged on a loan.

Ratio is the relationship between two or more quantities.

Reciprocal of a Fraction is the fraction that results from interchanging the numerator and denominator.

Revenue is the amount of money a company receives in a specific period from the sale of products or services.

Rounding is the process through which we express numbers to an approximate value.

Selling Price is the cost plus the amount of markup.

Simple Annuity is an annuity where the payment frequency and compounding frequency are the same.

Simple Interest is interest based solely on the original loan amount.

Subtraction is the reverse operation of addition. It can be thought of as removing objects from a group.

Taxes are a percent on the sale of goods and services, added to the price of the good or service.

Tiered Commission means that there is an increase in the percent of commission earned depending on the amount of sales made.

Time (*t*) is the interest period, usually expressed in years.

Unit Rate is the ratio of the first term to a single unit of the second term.

Variable is a symbol that holds the place of an unknown number.

Variable Rate Mortgage has an interest rate that changes due to the economy of the country or market.

Weighted Average is calculated by adding up all the numbers times their weighting factor and dividing the result by the number of items.

Whole Numbers represent all of the numbers starting at zero and increasing by a value of 1 (0, 1, 2, 3, 4, ...).

Yield measures the revenue achievement and is used to maximize a hotel's room revenues.

Index

O

P

Q

R

S

T

U

V

W

Y

Appendix

Table 8.1: Days Table

DAY OF MONTH	Jan	Feb	Mar	Apr	May	Jun	Jul	Aug	Sep	Oct	Nov	Dec	DAY OF MONTH
	DAY OF THE YEAR												
1	1	32	60	91	121	152	182	213	244	274	305	335	**1**
2	2	33	61	92	122	153	183	214	245	275	306	336	**2**
3	3	34	62	93	123	154	184	215	246	276	307	337	**3**
4	4	35	63	94	124	155	185	216	247	277	308	338	**4**
5	5	36	64	95	125	156	186	217	248	278	309	339	**5**
6	6	37	65	96	126	157	187	218	249	279	310	340	**6**
7	7	38	66	97	127	158	188	219	250	280	311	341	**7**
8	8	39	67	98	128	159	189	220	251	281	312	342	**8**
9	9	40	68	99	129	160	190	221	252	282	313	343	**9**
10	10	41	69	100	130	161	191	222	253	283	314	344	**10**
11	11	42	70	101	131	162	192	223	254	284	315	345	**11**
12	12	43	71	102	132	163	193	224	255	285	316	346	**12**
13	13	44	72	103	133	164	194	225	256	286	317	347	**13**
14	14	45	73	104	134	165	195	226	257	287	318	348	**14**
15	15	46	74	105	135	166	196	227	258	288	319	349	**15**
16	16	47	75	106	136	167	197	228	259	289	320	350	**16**
17	17	48	76	107	137	168	198	229	260	290	321	351	**17**
18	18	49	77	108	138	169	199	230	261	291	322	352	**18**
19	19	50	78	109	139	170	200	231	262	292	323	353	**19**
20	20	51	79	110	140	171	201	232	263	293	324	354	**20**
21	21	52	80	111	141	172	202	233	264	294	325	355	**21**
22	22	53	81	112	142	173	203	234	265	295	326	356	**22**
23	23	54	82	113	143	174	204	235	266	296	327	357	**23**
24	24	55	83	114	144	175	205	236	267	297	328	358	**24**
25	25	56	84	115	145	176	206	237	268	298	329	359	**25**
26	26	57	85	116	146	177	207	238	269	299	330	360	**26**
27	27	58	86	117	147	178	208	239	270	300	331	361	**27**
28	28	59	87	118	148	179	209	240	271	301	332	362	**28**
29	29		88	119	149	180	210	241	272	302	333	363	**29**
30	30		89	120	150	181	211	242	273	303	334	364	**30**
31	31		90		151		212	243		304		365	**31**

Note: For leap years, February 29 becomes day number 60. Therefore, you will need to add one day to any date that comes after February 29.